IMAGE UNDERSTANDING
IN
UNSTRUCTURED
ENVIRONMENT

World Scientific Series in Automation
Editor-in-chief: Su-shing Chen

Series in Automation — Volume 2

IMAGE UNDERSTANDING IN UNSTRUCTURED ENVIRONMENT

Editor

Su-shing Chen

Department of Computer Science
University of North Carolina-Charlotte

World Scientific
Singapore • New Jersey • London • Hong Kong

Published by

World Scientific Publishing Co. Pte. Ltd.
P O Box 128, Farrer Road, Singapore 9128

USA office: World Scientific Publishing Co., Inc.
687 Hartwell Street, Teaneck, NJ 07666, USA

UK office: World Scientific Publishing Co. Pte. Ltd.
P O Box 379, London N12 7JS, England

Library of Congress Cataloging-in-Publication Data

Image understanding in unstructured environment /
    edited by Su-shing Chen.
        p.   cm.   –– (Series in automation, ISSN 0218-0197; vol. 2)
    Contents: A knowledge-based information manager for autonomous
    vehicles / Thomas M. Strat and Grahame B. Smith –– Plausible
    reasoning in classification problem solving / Lashon B. Booker –– A
    region correspondence approach to the recovery of 3-dimensional
    motion and structure in dynamic scenes / Seetharaman Gunasekaran and
    Tzay Y. Young –– Spherical analysis in computer vision and image
    understanding / Michael A. Penna and Su-shing Chen –– Spatial
    information processing-understanding remote sensing images /
    Mingchuan Zhang and Su-shing Chen.
        ISBN 9971504774.   ISBN 9971504782 (pbk.)
        1. Image processing –– Digital techniques. 2. Computer vision.
    I. Chen, Su-shing.   II. Series.
    TA1632.I489 1988
    629.8'92––dc19   88-5466

Printed in Singapore by JBW Printers & Binders Pte. Ltd.

PREFACE

In the development of autonomous sensory controlled systems, image understanding of sensory data is a difficult but important topic. Due to the unpredictable and uncertain nature of environment, current image processing and computer vision approaches are not adequate to provide the capabilities needed by the systems. Thus, new approaches are required in the overall system design, including sophisticated reasoning processes, uncertainty management and adaptable architectures. This general issue is addressed by Thomas M. Strat and Grahame B. Smith in the first chapter, "A knowledge-based information manager for autonomous vehicles". In the remaining chapters, several specific areas are presented. Although it is impossible to survey an emerging and growing field, these papers represent some important ideas and approaches. In Chapter 2 ("Plausible reasoning in classification problem solving"), Lashon B. Booker discusses the Bayesian approach in plausible reasoning for classification of complex ship images based on incomplete and uncertain evidence. Dynamic scene analysis is treated by Seetharaman Gunasekaran and Tzay Y. Young in Chapter 3, entitled "A region correspondence approach to the recovery of 3-dimensional motion and structure in dynamic scenes". In Chapter 4, a spherical perspective approach ("Spherical analysis in computer vision and image understanding") is introduced to overcome some limitations of the current vision systems by Michael Penna and Su-shing Chen. Finally, Markov image models and their pixel-level approaches are extended to global approaches through Dempster-Shafer and other techniques, by Mingchuan Zhang and Su-shing Chen in "Spatial information processing: understanding remote sensing imagery".

Su-shing Chen

CONTENTS

vii

IMAGE UNDERSTANDING
IN UNSTRUCTURED ENVIRONMENT

1

A KNOWLEDGE-BASED INFORMATION
MANAGER FOR AUTONOMOUS VEHICLES

Thomas M. Strat and Grahame B. Smith

Artificial Intelligence Center
SRI International
333 Ravenswood Avenue
Menlo Park, CA 94025, USA

1. INTRODUCTION

Much current work in image understanding is motivated by the desire
to provide autonomous systems with a means for perceiving their environment. These goals have forced researchers to expand the set of techniques
that traditionally have been used in image interpretation. While present-
day successes have relied on image feature recognition and model-based approaches, the next generation will require sophisticated reasoning processes
and adaptable architectures to achieve the competence that autonomous
systems must have.

As an example of the type of system we envision, consider designing
a robot to guard a farmer's storage shed in a sparsely populated area.
Such a system would be expected to detect intruders (and perhaps im-
pede them), to discriminate between humans and deer, to function in all
seasons and under varying lighting conditions, to discover fires in the vicinity, and so on. It may or may not be mobile, and it may or may not be
working alone. Such a system is clearly beyond the state of the art although some ongoing work is directed towards achieving similar goals[1,2].
There is substantial interest in the research community in developing autonomous land vehicles, and some impressive results have already been
demonstrated. However, the adaptability and range of competence of these
systems must be substantially improved to meet the goals of these projects.
The designers of autonomous underwater vehicles and aircraft face similar
challenges. While the focus of effort, the level of difficulty, and range of
capabilities varies among these projects, they are inherently similar to the
storage shed surveillance system.

What are the common requirements of these autonomous systems that
force the development of new approaches to their design?

First, all have a fundamental need to perceive their environment and
image understanding is likely to be the primary sensory modality. The
medium may not necessarily be visual — underwater vehicles may rely
primarily on sonar data while air vehicles may make best use of radar
images of various sorts. Whatever the source of data, all these systems need
to perform image understanding, to match data with stored expectations,
and to incrementally build a model of their surroundings.

Second, each system is expected to operate in the natural world, unmod-
ified by artificial guides to navigation, recognition, or interpretation. These
environments are largely unstructured, and consequently, highly complex.
Traditional model-based approaches to image understanding are simply not

applicable. Highly adaptable procedures making use of novel representations of natural form are called for.

Third, the environment each system operates in is dynamic, and is so in many ways. The mobility of the robot itself is only one source of change. Other objects will be moving as well — aircraft, deer, clouds, leaves on trees, etc. Still other types of change will be present, such as leaves changing color, trees growing, sands on the ocean bottom shifting, and fires burning.

Fourth, the processing that must be carried out for perception, for planning, and for execution must be knowledge intensive. The tasks that face autonomous systems in natural environments are too unpredictable for the use of modules with limited reasoning capabilities. Domain specific knowledge must be encoded and available for use in nearly all stages of computational processing.

Fifth, information will be available from a variety of sources. An autonomous system will almost certainly have access to a suite of sensors that can provide information of the surroundings with various characteristics. Further information will be available from premission briefings, from the experience of its own operation, and perhaps from other robots. This wealth of data must be integrated to achieve competence. Information integration is crucial for successful operation in natural environments. Available information will be imperfect, and superior information integration techniques can mitigate adverse effects of the imperfections. The insensitivity to noise of model-based recognition techniques can be achieved by integrating newly acquired information with stored models. Fusion of redundant information from multiple sources can help reduce uncertainty about the state of the world. Information integration also fills in gaps that would be present if available information were not combined. All these factors contribute to improved perception based upon imperfect information.

In this paper we describe an architecture that has been designed to support the requirements outlined above. It incorporates many diverse facilities to provide a substantial foundation for constructing autonomous systems. It includes features from many technologies including blackboard architectures, relational and spatial databases, uncertain reasoning, epistemic logic, computer graphics and knowledge bases. While the system we describe is not a complete cognitive model for an autonomous system, it is an open-ended architecture that can be used as the basis to build incrementally an autonomous system that displays competent performance in a natural environment.

The approach stands at an intermediate position between the model-driven techniques employed in present-day industrial vision systems, and the weak, general-purpose techniques that have been developed for attempting to interpret relatively unstructured, unpredictable imagery. It is built around the notion of being a system that exists in the world and persists over time, thereby raising the possibility for reasoning within a dynamic world and for learning from its experience. Its design as a community of intelligent processes allows for incremental increases in functionality and for modular development of islands of expertise. Its support of uncertain reasoning and the maintenance of multiple opinions allows information integration to be carried out in a sensible fashion.

In short, its goal is to serve as the central information manager within a community of specialized experts. With this view, the availability of a successful information manager should encourage the development of new algorithms for image understanding that make use of centrally available, stored knowledge and the opinions of other algorithms with relevant expertise.

2. OVERVIEW OF THE DESIGN

In this paper, we describe a knowledge system that integrates data from a variety of sensors, as well as from other sources of stored knowledge, to form a world model that is ultimately used by an autonomous system to plan and execute its tasks. The overall architecture of our Core Knowledge System (CKS) can be viewed as a *community* of interacting *processes*, each of which has its own limited goals and expertise, but all of which cooperate to achieve the higher goals of the system. The various processes may represent sensors, interpreters, controllers, user-interface drivers, planners, or any other information processor that can be imagined. Each process can be both a producer of information and a consumer. Information is shared among processes by allowing them to read data stored by other processes and to update that information. Each process continually and asynchronously updates information based on sensor readings, deductions, renderings, or other interpretations that it makes. Figure 1 portrays the interrelationships between the CKS and the various processes that can be expected to be present in an autonomous vehicle.

A simple example of object recognition may help to show the CKS approach. During cross-country navigation an autonomous land vehicle must be able to detect small gullies in its path. Suppose that the vehicle has a range sensor and analyzer that can segment the world into surface

SRI CORE KNOWLEDGE SYSTEM

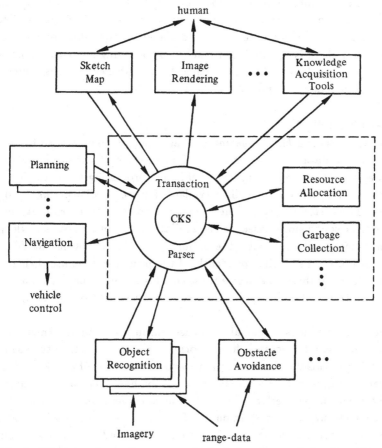

Fig.1. Architecture of an autonomous vehicle designed around the Core Knowledge System.

terrain and objects on that terrain, a drainage expert that can derive run-off patterns from surface topography, a multispectral analyzer that can classify objects on the basis of their spectral signature, a gully detector that determines the likelihood of a gully in the vehicle's path on the basis of the surface drainage pattern and vegetation cover, and a pilot that makes navigational decisions. Each process contributes expert knowledge about aspects of the world. The determination that there is a gully is not made by a single process that calculates a drainage pattern, vegetation type, and the like, but rather, by each expert looking at the objects that have been placed in the database and deciding if it can contribute further information. When there is sufficient information from which to conclude that a gully is present, the gully expert will annotate the database to this effect. This annotation will then influence steerage decisions of the pilot process. The decision that there is a gully is not reached by applying a fixed sequence of operations to the data, but is made when the available evidence is sufficient to support such a conclusion.

2.1. Representation

Each process is a *knowledge source* that brings its expertise to the processing of the data that represent the known state of the world. These processes span the range from low-level image processing to symbolic manipulation, and their output will be available for use by all other knowledge sources. The system design is one of expert knowledge sources that know how to draw conclusions based on the available data, but whose knowledge does not necessarily prescribe the actions required to obtain that data. Such procedures are run independently of the processes that use their conclusions. The database that stores these conclusions must be able to accept a vast assortment of data types and make them available to requesting processes.

The CKS includes a global database through which information is shared. Because all processes share information, the communication bandwidth between this database and the various processes is of concern. If the granularity of the information to be shared is too fine, then the communication channels will be overloaded with an enormous number of transactions, each of which involves small amounts of data, while a granularity that is too coarse requires complex processes that are beyond our ability to construct. We view the knowledge sources as substantial entities that attempt to share data objects that are composite in nature. For example, we do not expect that an image-processing routine would write intensity-edge information into the database, but rather that it would share conclusions about the physical objects that are in the world. Of course, these objects may not be identified, nor need they be the final partitioning of the scene into world objects, but they will be entities with which other processes can associate parameters and semantics. This does not mean that the database contains only symbolic objects, but rather that it contains objects that have some semantic character, such as horizontal planar surface with approximately constant albedo. This minimizes the volume of transactions within the system by associating a significant amount of data with each transaction.

Some knowledge sources may need to communicate with others at a level that is not provided by the global database. Such communication is private to those sources, and implementation is the responsibility of the designers of those processes. This level of information sharing often entails a certain computational speed requirement and usually a processing sequence that can be prespecified. Although any pair of processes may use this form of close coupling, we have focused on expediting the sharing of information that is of a higher level and is substantially unstructured.

If processes are to communicate through the database, the language of communication must be rich enough to allow items to be shared. Relevant information extracted from the database is of little use if the receiving process cannot understand or use it. With the diversity of information that is available, we choose to share that information through *semantic labels* that classify the information in the database. These labels must reflect the multiple levels of specificity inherent in the information itself. The labels form a *vocabulary* describing the information that is stored in the database. Accessing information by means of the semantic label allows processes to be unconcerned with the particular data syntax used to stored the information. We allow database access through logical combinations of the semantic labels, as well as through procedural definitions passed to the databse so that a user may supplement the vocabulary with additional terms. Passing procedural definitions to the database also reduces the communication bandwidth otherwise needed to return the results.

A system that views processes as individual experts that may make conflicting interpretations of the data must have a policy to determine what is stored in the database. For example, if two processes determine that the height of a particular tree is substantially different, which opinion should be stored: the last one given, that of the process with more expertise, or the average of the two? There is no "correct" way to determine a single value. Traditionally, information integration is accomplished as the data are inserted into the database, and the data that are then retained are expected to be free of conflict. In our system, all processes are considered equal, and only their *opinions* are stored. This approach reflects the view that conclusions are not only a function of the data used, but also of the knowledge sources that provide that data, and of the anticipated use of the conclusion. The user of the information should have the opportunity to filter that information with knowledge of both its content and its source. Information in the data store can be modified only by the process that created it, although other processes can cast their opinions.

2.2. Control

Any system that consists of a collection of independent, asynchronous processes must have a control mechanism that coordinates these processes to achieve the system's goals. In our design, each process is continually active, going about its task of processing the data that define the current state of the world and placing its opinions in the database. When certain combinations of data occur, we must be able to interrupt particular processes and have them deal with this new information. In our previous example of cross-country navigation, we needed to detect gullies. A clump of snowberry bushes is often an indication of a gully. Consequently, we should activate the gully detector whenever snowberries are detected. A daemon mechanism is used to implement this strategy. Daemons are placed in the database by the processes that should be informed when particular events occur, and the processes are responsible for determining how to proceed when they are interrupted by these daemons. Control by means of the database is, therefore, data-driven. Alternatively, any process is free to call procedures that are embedded within another process, thus allowing control to be passed by procedure call.

Data-driven control is unlikely to be coordinated to achieve the goals of the system if those goals are not available to the various processes that are performing the data transformations. An important part of sensory integration is planning which activities will contribute to the more general goals of the larger system in which the sensory system is embedded. In our case, we interface with the goals of a *planning system* that controls the activities of an autonomous vehicle. A planning system is viewed simply as another process or set of processes that may have access to the database. The list of tasks that the vision system is attempting to achieve are data that individual processes must use to establish priorities for their own activities. Conclusions and data transformations, no matter how correct or clever, are irrelevant if they are unrelated to fulfilling the mission of the highest-level system.

3. THE CKS DATABASE

The database that we have designed to store the domain data has many of the usual database features. It stores a collection of *data tokens* that contain the domain information and has a set of indexing structures overlaid on these tokens so that data retrieval based on domain requirements may be implemented efficiently. Unlike many vision-system databases, the database has a continuity of life that exceeds a single execution of the system. In this respect it is much more like a conventional database, whose integrity and usefulness must persist over an extended period. Data acquired during execution of the system become information stored in the database for future use.

3.1. Data Storage and Retrieval

To ensure that the internal integrity of the database is maintained, processes do not have direct access to the data tokens; instead copies of the data are transferred between the database and the process. Clearly, data copying is computationally expensive, which is incompatible with real-time performance. For this reason, a mechanism is provided in the data access language that allows a process to pass a trustworthy procedure to the database so that internal processing can be used to minimize the volume of data transferred and the amount of copying that is necessary. This approach for controlling integrity is dictated by a development environment in which the system is not built by a single person or group but rather is a set of processes provided by disparate implementors. Protecting the data from corruption by an errant process is necessary if we are to avoid rolling back the database to a previous version or editing it between actual uses. However the mechanism used to reduce data copying, sometimes at the expense of jeopardizing integrity, is desirable for certain time-critical processes so that they may achieve real-time performance.

Because the opinions of all processes are stored, the database will contain conflicting and incompatible views of the state of the world. Some processes may exist solely for the purpose of resolving such data inconsistencies. Of course, even these processes will only be allowed to cast an opinion. User processes may choose to take more notice of the opinions of these conflict-resolution processes than of the opinions of processes whose conclusions are drawn from less data. The conflict-resolution processes will continually process data in the database (as spare computational resources allow), but they are conservative in nature, preferring not to cast an opinion unless they have compelling evidence to support their conclusion. However, a user process may call one of these conflict resolvers to cast an opinion even if it would not have otherwise intervened. Our approach then is to allow inconsistencies to be resolved whenever the data are sufficient to support the resolution, or whenever a user process requires that resolution, i.e. at access time. This approach differs from the more usual practice of maintaining a consistent data set in which resolution must occur at insertion time. The approach we adopt is to resolve when necessary, rather than to resolve always. Often a decision-making process can take action without the need to expend resources in resolving data discrepancies. For example, the navigation module of an autonomous land vehicle may be faced with the conflicting data that the object ahead is either a tree or a telephone pole. If the task is to move forward avoiding obstacles, the vision system does not need to resolve whether the object ahead is a tree or telephone pole. The resolution requirement is a function of the task, not simply the data.

A database that stores opinions will rapidly consume resources unless a mechanism is provided that will allow data to be deleted (or at least archived). A process that is the supplier of data may have little ability to evaluate the usefulness of that data, yet it is the useful data that we want available in the database. The approach adopted is to have processes sponsor data; that is, a process (probably a process that uses a particular data token) will allow that data token to be "charged" against its resource allocation. Many processes can sponsor a single data token, and they are charged proportionately. When a process nears its resource limit (or at any time) it can withdraw its sponsorship from any data that it has sponsored. Data that are unsponsored are available for garbage collection (these data may be archived or deleted). In this manner each process is responsible for deciding what data it finds useful, and this collection of data forms the base of current available information. Clearly, this procedure is not fail safe. Critical data may be removed before their criticality is realized. However, the criticality of data is measured in terms of a process's willingness to pay for them and presumably in terms of the current usefulness of those data.

An unsponsored data token will not necessarily be removed immediately. An information producer may not wish to sponsor data for which it has little use, so it may be some time before a sponsor for this information is found. To avoid deleting potentially useful data, the process whose job is to remove data tokens evaluates additional information, such as length of time the token has been in the database, as well as sponsorship information, before it is removed. Data removal is a continuous process (primarily using spare computational resources), so that the database can be assured of having adequate storage when time-critical tasks demand that computational resources for garbage collection be suspended.

Each process in the system does not have the same resource allocation. At particular times some processes may be more valuable than others. For example, the gully detector used by an autonomous vehicle is a vital process during cross-country navigation but is rarely used while travelling along roads. One process has the task of allocating database resources to the processes performing useful tasks. The allocation is based on the relative importance of the task and on the frequency with which data tokens are consumed by the process performing that task. Such a frequency measure is a moving statistic that allows the allocation to adapt to the current situation. Data tokens are time stamped to indicate the last time they were modified — that is, the last time a new opinion was added to one of the data slots — and they are time stamped for last use. The time stamps provide data for the resource allocator and the garbage collector.

3.2. Data Tokens

Data tokens are produced by individual processes and are passed to the database for storage and subsequent retrieval. For the database to access information from within the token, or for a requesting process to be able to extract information from a token, each must either know the form of that information or have some procedure for recovering it. In the design of a system, we can use a standard structure for a data token, such as a record structure in which the position of parameter slots are known, or we can adopt a standard syntax for the token, such as a list of attribute-value pairs, or we can add functions that retrieve values from the internal data structure of the token, i.e. through procedural attachment.

With standard structures, position, rather than name, gives access to the data, but all processes are required to use some predetermined set of structures. In a system in which different processes do entirely different tasks, it is unlikely that we could find, no matter how clever, a small number of data structures that would be natural representations of all the data for all the processes that use those data.

With both fixed syntax and procedural attachement to a data structure, a vocabulary of terms is needed to access the data slots. This is the approach we take. A vocabulary of terms is used that spans the entities and relationships of interest in the application domain. For an autonomous land vehicle, the vocabulary consists of words or labels that describe the outdoor environment, e.g. TREE and HEIGHT, so a process could ask a data token that represents a tree for that tree's height. The actual structure used to hold the data can be invisible to the process that gains access to the information through the labels. The labels must be known by all processes that wish to have access to this information in the database. This semantic level does seem to be the appropriate level on which to share information.

Should we use a fixed syntax like attribute-value pairs to hold the information in the database and provide a simple routine to retrieve the value given the attribute, or should we use the more complex approach of attaching to a data structure a set of functions that can retrieve the value of a data slot given the slot name? We take the latter approach to increase the functionality that is available when a value is retrieved based on slot name. From the point of view of systems building, in which parts of the system are built by independent groups, this approach places the decisions for the form of the data structure and the mechanism for data access within a single group. This approach provides a clean interface with the database. Each process can select its own internal representations for the data it produces, and those data can be shared through access functions that are based on terms or labels in the vocabulary that describe the underlying domain. A common vocabulary requires each process to know how to translate from its internal representation to information in vocabulary form. This avoids the need for each process to know how to translate into the individual representations used by other processes. Additionally, new processes can be added to the system without retrofitting the new representations to the older processes.

A collection of data tokens is not a database unless there is a means of gaining access to the information in the collection in a manner that does not require a search through the entire set. A set of indexing structures that allows access in a more direct manner must be based on the subsets of the data that need to be retrieved. These structures are, therefore, based on the domain requirements and relate to the semantics of the actual data stored. Our architecture for sensory integration is implemented in the task domain of mobile robot navigation. The indexing structures that we use are associated with the need to retrieve information that is appropriately grouped for the task of navigation in the three-dimensional world. A *spatial directory* that forms subsets of the data based on spatial location, and a *semantic directory* that forms subsets of the data based on object class are the principal indexing schemes that we use to organize storage and retrieval of data tokens. Figure 2 gives an overview of transaction processing by means of directories in the database designed to support autonomous vehicle navigation.

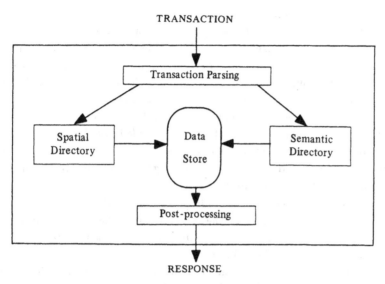

Fig.2. Transaction processing — autonomous land vehicle database. Access to the data store is by means of a spatial directory, or a semantic directory, or both.

4. ORGANIZATION OF SPATIAL INFORMATION

The spatial directory organizes the data tokens into groups determined by spatial location. Because an autonomous vehicle may roam about in an extensive environment, we need a representation of that environment which can deal with its spatial extent. In addition, the representation must be efficient in indexing data when the data are distributed nonuniformly over the environment. Data will need to be accessed at various levels of resolution depending on the task that is being addressed. Route planning needs lower-resolution data than does, for example, landmark identification or obstacle avoidance.

4.1. Spatial Directory

The world is three-dimensional, but a land vehicle is restricted to a two-dimensional surface embedded in this world. Although there are many reasons for choosing a two-dimensional index, such as latitude and longitude, and then representing the third dimension as a data value, we chose to use a three-dimensional index. Our selection was motivated by the advantage such an index gives in encoding spatial relations within the directory, in generating visibility information, and in using this architecture in other spatial domains in which movement is not restricted to a two-dimensional surface (such as for underwater vehicles).

The three-dimensional index selects a volume in space that we represent as *voxels*[3]. The largest voxel is the world, which is subdivided into smaller volumes as needed to represent spatial position with higher precision. The index granularity is fine enough to be able to position an object in a volume that is precise enough for the application. Recall that this is an index into a directory; in the directory cell are pointers to the data tokens associated with the volume of space represented by this index. Data tokens need not be placed in the directory at the finest index available but only at the precision with which their spatial location is known. A building whose position is totally unknown would be placed in the largest voxel; this being the root node that represents the entire world.

The voxel-based directory not only gives a range of position resolutions, it also allows different parts of the world to use different resolutions for storing data. In parts of the world that have little associated data, we may choose to place all the pointers to data tokens representing objects in coarse-grained volumes, while the part of the world in which the vehicle is active can be subdivided into finely partitioned volumes. This approach not only provides for multiple resolution access but also allows us to select resolution relevant to the area concerned.

In selecting a voxel-based representation of space, we have the option of dividing that space into regular voxels in which all voxels, at a given level of subdivision of the space, are of equal size, or choosing to divide the space into irregularly sized chunks. Irregularly sized voxels have some attractions; they allow irregularly shaped objects to be confined, and hence indexed, within a volume that matches them. Uniformly sized voxels often are unnecessarily large when they are large enough to contain an irregularly shaped object. However, if irregularly sized voxels are used, multiple indices are needed to allow for overlapping voxels that are indexing different irregularly sized objects in the same volume of space — thus increasing the computational load. We, therefore, use a regular subdivision of space in which each voxel is subdivided into eight equally sized and shaped smaller voxels.

In making this choice, we must address the problem of indexing objects whose shape does not match this partitioning of space. Generally, it is easy to place stationary compact objects within a voxel that can completely contain them, but objects like linear structures, surfaces, and moving objects require alternative approaches. A linear structure like a road, river, telephone wire, or fence is stored as a single data token, but pointers are placed in all the voxels through which the structure passes. The smallest-sized voxels that are appropriate are used; for example, the voxel size for a road will be determined by the road width so that it is assured that the road "fits" within the voxel. The same approach is taken with other extended objects, such as surfaces: a single data token has pointers to it from the set of voxels through which the surface passes.

The size of the voxel is selected by the process inserting the surface into the database, based on such factors as accuracy of the surface shape, and extent. Recall that this placement in space is to aid retrieval, not to specify exactly where things are. Detailed location information is available within the data token. Usually, a process would place an object in the spatial directory in the smallest voxel possible, although this is not required. When representing terrain patches, for example, placement of the entire patch in a large voxel may be preferable to dividing the patch into more precisely located pieces.

Moving objects are usually compact so they present little problem in placement at their current position, but there may be occasions when it is desirable to represent their track in the directory. The same approach as was adopted for linear structures and extended objects is used: each moving object is represented by a single data token that is pointed to by voxels associated with its track.

An advantage of a multiresolution spatial directory is the ease with which approximate location can be represented. An object is placed in a voxel that is large enough to contain the limits of its possible locations. Object location may be approximate because of image processing errors when detecting objects in imagery, or because of lack of knowledge of a sensor's exact position. The latter is particularly relevant in the case of an autonomous vehicle. Data can be added to the database before its position is known, and then, when better location information becomes available, the directory can be updated by moving the data to a smaller volume. If this is not done, the data will be retrieved and examined whenever requests are processed for data from the original larger voxel. A background process whose task is to move each object to its most precise location within the directory (when processing resources are available) accomplishes the directory update and, thereby, achieves retrieval efficiency. Hence, all data can be directly inserted into one directory whether their location is known accurately or only approximately.

4.2. Retrieval

Having all data, whose position is known or uncertain within one

directory structure allows us to respond easily to data retrieval requests
that seek "all objects that are within a certain volume in space" as well as
"all objects that could possibly be within that particular volume of space."
Clearly, in the task domain of an autonomous vehicle, knowing what *might
be* ahead and what *is* ahead is necessary for competent navigation and obstacle avoidance. For example, a landmark recognition process needs to
know what objects are definitely in some volume, while an obstacle avoidance process is interested in all objects that are possibly in front of the
vehicle. Within the voxel structure, "within a volume" maps to the tree of
voxels below (finer than) the voxel containing the volume while "possibly
within a volume" maps to the tree above (coarser than) the voxel containing
the volume.

When data can be retrieved on the basis of their location, retrievals
on the basis of spatial relations are also possible. The spatial directory
implicitly encodes the spatial relationships between tokens stored in the
database. As objects are moved or their spatial positions refined, these
spatial relations are maintained without additional processing resources.
New objects entered into the database inherently express their spatial relationships with previously entered data. In a mobile robot domain, we
expect to retrieve tokens based on relative position — objects to the right
of the road, trees casting shadows on the road, and so on. Having an
indexing structure that matches the world structure allows this without
the overhead that would be presented by alternative schemes, such as a
relational database.

The reduction of computational resources used to maintain the database
was also instrumental in our treatment of time. The database is always
assumed to represent the world at current time. If historical information
is to be stored, then it must be time-stamped, otherwise it is implied that
the data reflect the state of the world as it currently is. This approach was
adopted so that we could avoid elements of the traditional frame problem:[4]
if time is a parameter of the data token, then this token has to be updated
even when the real data have not changed, but time has passed. We take
the usual approach adopted in conventional databases, in that information
is assumed to be still true if it has not been altered or specifically marked
as applying only to some particular interval of time.

4.3. Implementation

The spatial directory is organized as an *octree* [5] of voxels that span the
world. Specifically, a "pointerless" octree that is implemented by multiple

hash tables is employed. The use of an octree to implement a voxel representation is natural; the selection of the pointerless approach was based on the expectation that many voxels will contain no data, and many voxels will not be subdivided into smaller units. Hence the more usual approach of using cells with explicit pointers to the finer cells will produce many cells containing mainly null pointers. With the pointerless approach, only voxels that contain data tokens are allocated any storage, and null pointers are not used. Figure 3 shows an abstract view (using null pointers) of the way an octree is used to represent the voxel description of the world. The number of levels of hash tables is in fact somewhat less than the number of octree levels, because several octree levels are stored in a single hash table, as shown in Fig. 3.

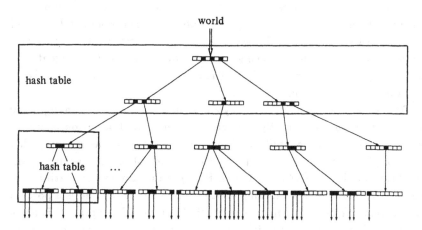

Fig. 3. Octree representation of the voxel description of space. Hash tables are used to implement the octree; more than one level of the octree is stored in a single hash table.

5. ORGANIZATION OF SEMANTIC INFORMATION

A primary feature of the CKS is a capability for characterizing and retrieving information based upon the semantic content of that information. In this regard, the CKS plays two roles within the context of an autonomous community of processes. First, it provides a common vocabulary so that each process can share information with all other processes without concern for the particulars of their implementations. Second, it contains a knowledge base that is used to provide a level of understanding of the terms in its vocabulary. Access to this knowledge is gained either implicitly (as when the CKS attempts to evaluate a query) or explicitly (to give user processes access to that knowledge base). The net result is that the CKS can function alternatively as a knowledge base, a database, or as a knowledgeable data base in its domain of discourse.

5.1. The Vocabulary

The vocabulary is a set of terms that has been constructed through an examination of the communication requirements of processes operating in the ordinary outdoor environment. It is intended to be the primary means of communication between processes and thus forms their common vocabulary. The meaning of each term is intended to be that which is suggested by the word(s) used; of course, communication can only occur to the extent that the processes using the terms agree on the meaning. We make no attempt to define any of the vocabulary terms completely — such a task is truly impossible. Instead, we stipulate certain relations to hold among these terms, thus creating a partial definition that the agents can use as a basis for communication. Their relation to actual English words serves a strictly mnemonic purpose.

Data tokens are given meaning by a user-process through the assignment of a semantic description. Syntactically, a semantic description is simply an unordered list of vocabulary terms. It is interpreted as meaning that all of the terms represent true properties of the token. For example, the semantic description (LARGE POST RED) is tantamount to stating that the data token denotes something which is large and is red and is a post. A formal treatment of the semantics of such "semantic-descriptions" is given in Sect. 6. Issues such as the treatment of contradictory vocabulary terms and the implicit implications of terms are discussed there.

The allowable set of semantic descriptions is restricted to include only those terms listed in the vocabulary. The challenge here is not to provide unlimited flexibility in the language, but rather to identify a moderately sized set of properties that are sufficient for interprocess communication in the domain of interest. If the properties chosen are not adequate, the vocabulary should be modified; it does not imply a fundamental limitation of the database design. The majority of terms in the vocabulary have been chosen on the basis of their value in fostering communication about sensing and navigation in the natural outdoor environment. Some additional terms have been included for the purpose of exploring the limitations of the representation. It is expected that the vocabulary will evolve as domain requirements become more fully understood.

5.2. Attributes

As discussed earlier, a data token can be viewed as a framelike structure composed of slots that represent attributes of the denoted entity. Although the user is free to include any attributes he desires, the CKS identifies some special attributes for each class that will be present on all instances of that class. For example, any object identified as being a member of the class ROADWAY, will have the attributes WIDTH, LANES, SPEED-LIMIT, ROAD-MARKINGS, and so on. These special attributes should be used whenever possible so that the information can be uniformly retrieved by other processes that may be unaware of individual representations.

The CKS also provides default values for the special attributes. The default will appear as an opinion on the value of that slot along with all other opinions for the slot. A process that reads that slot may alternatively choose to use it exclusively, to combine it with the other opinions, or to ignore it completely. An ordinary inheritance mechanism is provided within CKS to infer appropriate defaults.

5.3. Semantic Relationships

The semantic relations among vocabulary words are explicitly described by axioms encoded in a semantic network. These formulas are domain-specific and are carefully chosen to support the types of inference necessary for meaningful communication among independent processes within an autonomous vehicle. They are represented as a collection of machine-readable graph structures. In particular, the semantic network fragment

$$\boxed{A} \xrightarrow{\text{subset}} \boxed{B}$$

encodes the sentence $(\forall x)[A(x) \rightarrow B(x)]$, while

$$\boxed{C} \xleftrightarrow{\text{disjoint}} \boxed{D}$$

encodes $\neg(\exists x)[C(x) \wedge D(x)]$.

These two arcs allow the specification of all possible set relationships. As with the choice of vocabulary terms, the construction of the semantic network is an art that must give careful consideration to the autonomous vehicle's domain and the anticipated uses of the CKS. As a result, we do not expect that the network in its current form will be the final choice for use on an autonomous vehicle. Instead, we anticipate a continual process of revision as experiments are conducted with sensory and navigational

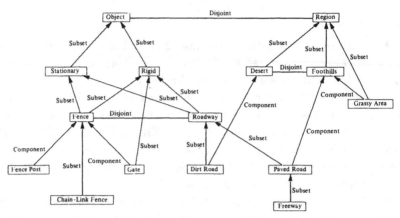

Fig. 4. Semantic Directory. Implemented as a semantic network, it gives access to the database data tokens by means of their semantic type.

processes. An example of a small portion of the semantic network is given in Fig. 4.

A third type of arc is also included in the network. Specifically, the semantic network fragment

$$E \xrightarrow{\text{component}} F$$

encodes the knowledge that F typically has E as a component. For example, a car usually has a wheel as a component and a desert typically has cacti. It is important to recognize that we have not chosen to represent absolute component relationships — such strong statements are truly rare in the outdoor world. For example, we would not want to state that all cars have wheels, because a car without wheels is still a car. Instead, the notion of typical containment is more useful, even if not as clearly defined.

The semantic network represents relations among classes of objects. A relation between an instance and a class is maintained by the semantic directory, which links the data token to the appropriate node in the semantic network. Relations between instances are handled by either of two techniques. If direct access by the name of the relationship is not required, a process may store the information explicitly in the appropriate slot in the data token. For example, a car represented by token201 may have the list (token202 token203 token204 token205) as the value of its COMPONENTS slot, where token202, token203, token204, and token205 are data tokens denoting wheels. For those relations in which direct access may be required, the CKS will employ a relational database to maintain and retrieve the appropriate information.

5.4. The Semantic Directory

The spatial directory provides an indexing scheme that matches the spatial nature of the data in the task domain; the semantic directory provides an indexing scheme that matches the semantic nature of the data in that domain.

Each node of the semantic network is associated with a vocabulary term, and has pointers to all the data tokens in the database that have been labeled with this term. The nodes of the semantic network can be directly accessed by the vocabulary label, and thus provide a directory to data tokens on the basis of the semantic label. Although we view the semantic directory as a graph structure and display the semantic network as a graph, the implementation uses hash tables for speed of access. When tokens are added to the database or when additional labels are added to a token's description, the semantic directory is updated appropriately.

Data tokens are attached to the most specific network nodes possible. If for example, a token had been labeled by a process as being a PAVED-ROAD, then it is attached only to the semantic network node for PAVED-ROAD even though all PAVED-ROADs are known to be ROADWAYs. This approach was adopted to save storage as well as to provide a straightforward implementation of the retrieval request to return all objects that are PAVED-ROADs as opposed to all objects that might be PAVED-ROADs. The second descriptor includes objects in the more general class ROAD-WAY as well as those labeled PAVED-ROAD. Data tokens that represent paved roads are found attached to the nodes of the lattice that form the tree rooted at the node labeled PAVED-ROAD, whereas roadways that *might be* paved are found attached to the nodes of the network tree *above* the node labeled PAVED-ROAD. This arrangement parallels the mechanisms used in the spatial directory to find objects that are at a particular location, as opposed to those that might be at that location. It is the responsibility of the access routines to retrieve the appropriate tokens from the database by means of the semantic network. The ramifications of this approach are described in greater detail in Sect. 6.

6. LOGICAL INTERPRETATION OF THE DATABASE

The CKS database is a storehouse of the *opinions* of many agents. It is not a database of facts. This design gives it some unusual properties — properties that allow it to function as a central repository of information for a community of processes. It also renders much of the research in database

designs inapplicable and has spurred us to develop a new technology for
the storage and retrieval of multiple opinions.

The community of processes architecture adopted for the CKS requires
that processes be able to communicate their opinions with one another
and without undue interference from processes with competing views. The
formalization and use of an opinion base in lieu of a database gives rise to
the following important features.

- The ability to store information that is *inconsistent.*

- The ability to *integrate* multiple opinions and to allow that integration to depend upon the intended use of the information.

- The ability to *separate* one source's opinions from another's.

These goals have been achieved while retaining an ability to incorporate
general knowledge that is universally accepted as being true. An opinion
base appears to us to be a better model of how humans store information
than a conventional database of facts.

Because of the presence of inconsistent information, first order logic is
insufficient for describing the semantics of the database. In what follows
we will resort to a modal logic of belief as a means for interpreting CKS
transactions. This logic is extremely expressive and could be used to specify
a much richer collection of knowledge. However we have purposely limited
the scope of our logic as a concession to the efficiency of implementation. We
are, after all, designing the CKS as the core component of an autonomous
vehicle, and implementation issues cannot be ignored. For this reason, the
ultimate design is a compromise between the ability to express complicated
statements involving beliefs of multiple agents and the ability to retrieve
relevant information quickly. Throughout the design, we have been guided
by the requirements of autonomous vehicles and have adopted what we
feel to be an efficient implementation that does not sacrifice the ability
to express the information that must be communicated among the various
processes of an autonomous system.

6.1. Semantics

Information is stored in the CKS in the form of data tokens. A
data token is a framelike object whose internal structure is related to the
semantic attributes of the object. Among other things, a data token contains information about the spatial location of an object and some domain-
specific properties that are believed to be true about the object. For exam-

ple, a portion of a data token, token01, might contain:

token01
    : SPATIAL-DESCRIPTION   (V1 V2)
    : SEMANTIC-DESCRIPTION (LARGE RED POST)
    : HEIGHT   7.3
    ...

Here the *spatial description* is a list of volume specifications in which the object is presumed to lie. The *semantic description* is a list of properties that the asserting agent believes to be true about token01.

The precise meaning of CKS transactions is specified with the aid of modal logic. This logic consists of the following components:

Object Constants — The collection of all data tokens and potential data tokens in the database.

Function Constants — None.

Predicates — The set of vocabulary words and the set of possible spatial descriptions.

We adopt the usual syntax for forming well-formed formulas (WFFs) over these symbols as well as all the standard axioms of first order logic. In addition, we assume the existence of implicit axioms that allow us to infer that

- $(\forall x)[V_i(x) \to V_j(x)]$
  whenever the volume denoted by V_i is completely contained within the volume denoted by V_j, where V_i and V_j are spatial descriptions.

We employ a modal operator $\mathbf{B}_i$ to be interpreted as meaning "agent i believes that" so that $\mathbf{B}_i[\Phi]$ is interpreted as 'Process i believes Φ is true." This operator is similar to that described by Moore[6] and by Konolige[7]. However, our axiomatization is different, as we only develop here those formulas that are needed to interpret the action of the database.

The following axiom schema provides the modal operator with the semantics we desire:

- $\Phi \to \Psi \Rightarrow \mathbf{B}_i[\Phi] \to \mathbf{B}_i[\Psi]$ — The modal operator $\mathbf{B}_i$ is closed under deductive inference.

Significantly, this axiomatization does not require that $(\mathbf{B}_i[\Phi] \vee \mathbf{B}_i[\neg\Phi])$ is true, nor does it require that $(\mathbf{B}_i[\Phi] \wedge \mathbf{B}_i[\neg\Phi])$ is false. However, it does require $(\mathbf{B}_i[\Phi] \vee \neg\mathbf{B}_i[\Phi])$ to be true and $(\mathbf{B}_i[\Phi] \wedge \neg\mathbf{B}_i[\Phi])$ to be false.

This arrangement allows conflicting beliefs to exist without corrupting the database.

For any proposition Φ, an agent may have any of four states of belief, as listed below. An example is given of an English statement that would been encoded by each of these states of belief. In the example $\Phi \equiv House(\text{object})$:

- $(\mathbf{B}_i[\Phi] \wedge \neg\mathbf{B}_i[\neg\Phi])$ "The object is a house."
- $(\mathbf{B}_i[\Phi] \wedge \mathbf{B}_i[\neg\Phi])$ "The object is a house and it's also a car."
- $(\neg\mathbf{B}_i[\Phi] \wedge \neg\mathbf{B}_i[\neg\Phi])$ "The object is blue."
- $(\neg\mathbf{B}_i[\Phi] \wedge \mathbf{B}_i[\neg\Phi])$ "The object is a car."

6.2.   Insertions

Interaction with the CKS is through insertions and queries. An insertion is of the form

(INSERT-DATA-TOKEN token01)

where token01 is an instance of a data token:

token01
    :SPATIAL-DESCRIPTION   (V1 V2)
    :SEMANTIC-DESCRIPTION (LARGE RED POST)
    :HEIGHT   7.3
    . . .

Executing (INSERT-DATA-TOKEN token01) has the same effect as asserting

$$\mathbf{B}_i[V_1(\text{token01})] \wedge \mathbf{B}_i[V_2(\text{token01})]\wedge$$
$$\mathbf{B}_i[LARGE(\text{token01})] \wedge \mathbf{B}_i[RED(\text{token01})] \wedge \mathbf{B}_i[POST(\text{token01})]$$

Assertions about objects can only be in the form of a conjunction of properties. This approach allows an agent to assert that token02 is a GREEN HOUSE but does not allow him to say, for example, that token02 is either a HOUSE or a BARN. If an agent desires to convey this information, he must rephrase it as, for example, token02 is a BUILDING, with the attendant loss of information. If it is truly important for a process to convey this disjunction precisely, the vocabulary should be extended to include HOUSE-OR-BARN as an acceptable term. The ability to reason with beliefs involving disjunctions requires a combinatoric expenditure of computational resources — a cost we feel is too great for a system designed to support real-time applications. It is our expectation that processes will need to communicate only in terms similar to those that have evolved for human communication, and as a result, that there will be little need to resort to such artificial constructs as HOUSE-OR-BARN. The same mechanism can be employed to circumvent the inability to express beliefs about negations.

6.3. Queries

The CKS query language differs from traditional query languages because the database contains information that is both incomplete and inconsistent. The query language must provide the user with a means for discerning multiple opinions. For this reason, the qualifiers APPARENTLY and POSSIBLY are provided to make these distinctions. Loosely speaking, a WFF is true "APPARENTLY" if there is some agent that believes it. It is true "POSSIBLY" if there is some agent who believes it or there is no agent that believes that it is false. These notions will be formalized shortly.

First, we enumerate the situations in which there is only a single agent. Φ is "APPARENTLY" true for the following combinations of beliefs of an agent:

Belief about Φ / Belief about $\neg\Phi$	$\mathbf{B}_i[\Phi]$	$\neg\mathbf{B}_i[\Phi]$
$\neg\mathbf{B}_i[\neg\Phi]$	Yes	No
$\mathbf{B}_i[\neg\Phi]$	Yes	No

Similarly, Φ, is "POSSIBLY" true for the following combinations of belief:

Belief about Φ / Belief about $\neg\Phi$	$\mathbf{B}_i[\Phi]$	$\neg\mathbf{B}_i[\Phi]$
$\neg\mathbf{B}_i[\neg\Phi]$	Yes	Yes
$\mathbf{B}_i[\neg\Phi]$	Yes	No

Before providing exact formulas for the interpretation of CKS queries, it may be useful to examine when Φ is "APPARENTLY" and "POSSIBLY" true when there are two agents involved.

APPARENTLY

Beliefs of Agent 2 / Beliefs of Agent 1	$\mathbf{B}_2[\Phi]$ $\wedge$ $\neg\mathbf{B}_2[\neg\Phi]$	$\mathbf{B}_2[\Phi]$ $\wedge$ $\mathbf{B}_2[\neg\Phi]$	$\neg\mathbf{B}_2[\Phi]$ $\wedge$ $\neg\mathbf{B}_2[\neg\Phi]$	$\neg\mathbf{B}_2[\Phi]$ $\wedge$ $\mathbf{B}_2[\neg\Phi]$
$\mathbf{B}_1[\Phi] \wedge \neg\mathbf{B}_1[\neg\Phi]$	Yes	Yes	Yes	Yes
$\mathbf{B}_1[\Phi] \wedge \mathbf{B}_1[\neg\Phi]$	Yes	Yes	Yes	Yes
$\neg\mathbf{B}_1[\Phi] \wedge \neg\mathbf{B}_1[\neg\Phi]$	Yes	Yes	No	No
$\neg\mathbf{B}_1[\Phi] \wedge \mathbf{B}_1[\neg\Phi]$	Yes	Yes	No	No

POSSIBLY

Beliefs of Agent 2 / Beliefs of Agent 1	$\mathbf{B}_2[\Phi]$ $\wedge$ $\neg\mathbf{B}_2[\neg\Phi]$	$\mathbf{B}_2[\Phi]$ $\wedge$ $\mathbf{B}_2[\neg\Phi]$	$\neg\mathbf{B}_2[\Phi]$ $\wedge$ $\neg\mathbf{B}_2[\neg\Phi]$	$\neg\mathbf{B}_2[\Phi]$ $\wedge$ $\mathbf{B}_2[\neg\Phi]$
$\mathbf{B}_1[\Phi] \wedge \neg\mathbf{B}_1[\neg\Phi]$	Yes	Yes	Yes	Yes
$\mathbf{B}_1[\Phi] \wedge \mathbf{B}_1[\neg\Phi]$	Yes	Yes	Yes	Yes
$\neg\mathbf{B}_1[\Phi] \wedge \neg\mathbf{B}_1[\neg\Phi]$	Yes	Yes	Yes	No
$\neg\mathbf{B}_1[\Phi] \wedge \mathbf{B}_1[\neg\Phi]$	Yes	Yes	No	No

By extrapolating these results, we are in a position to describe the interpretation of each query in terms of our modal logic.

- (FIND-IDS (APPARENTLY IS W4)) returns a list of those objects in the set

$$\{x|(\exists i)\mathbf{B}_i[W_4(x)]\} \ .$$

  where W4 denotes a vocabulary word. In English, this query corresponds roughly to "Find each data token for which some agent believes W_4 is true of it."

- (FIND-IDS (APPARENTLY IN V3)) returns a list of those objects in the set

$$\{x|(\exists i)\mathbf{B}_i[V_3(x)]\} \ .$$

  where V3 is a spatial description. This query can be interpreted as "Find each data token such that some agent believes it is contained within the volume V_3."

- (FIND-IDS (POSSIBLY IS W4)) returns a list of those objects in the set

$$\{x|[(\exists i)\mathbf{B}_i[W_4(x)] \vee \neg(\exists i)\mathbf{B}_i[\neg W_4(x)]\} \ .$$

This query can be roughly translated as "Find each data token for which some agent believes W_4 could possibly be true." The set of objects which satisfy this query will always include those objects that satisfy the APPARENTLY version.

- (FIND-IDS (POSSIBLY IN V3)) returns a list of those objects in the set
$$\{x|[(\exists i)\mathbf{B}_i[V_3(x)] \vee \neg(\exists i)\mathbf{B}_i[\neg V_3(x)]\} \ .$$

This query can be interpreted to mean "Find each data token such that some agent believes that it could possibly be in the volume denoted by V_3."

- (FIND-IDS (AND Query1 Query2))

$$\{x|x \in (\text{FIND-IDS Query1}) \wedge x \in ((\text{FIND-IDS Query2})\} \ .$$

In English, this can be translated as "Find each data token that satisfies both Query1 and Query2." It can be thought of as the intersection of the sets of tokens that satisfy each query.

- (FIND-IDS (OR Query1 Query 2))

$$\{x|x \in (\text{FIND-IDS Query1}) \vee x \in (\text{FIND-IDS Query2})\} \ .$$

This can be translated as "Find each data token that satisfies either Query1 or Query2. It can be thought of as the union of the sets of tokens that satisfy each query.

- (FIND-IDS (AND-NOT Query1 Query2))

$$\{x|x \in (\text{FIND-IDS Query1}) \wedge x \notin (\text{FIND-IDS Query2})\} \ .$$

This query can be interpreted to mean "Find all data tokens that satisfy Query1 but that do not also satisfy Query2." In set-theoretic terms, it is the set difference of the sets of data tokens that satisfy Query1 and Query2.

In answering negative queries, the database has no Closed World Assumption (i.e. it does not assume that a proposition is false if it cannot be proved true), thus it avoids issues of nonmonotonicity and has no need for circumscription. A negative belief cannot be inserted in the database.

However, a negative belief can be deduced using the deductive inference axiom and the general knowledge incorporated in the vocabulary. For example, a process cannot assert that token03 is not a PINE. But if it does assert that the token is an OAK, (i.e., $\mathbf{B}_i[OAK\ (\text{token03})]$), the database will infer that $\mathbf{B}_i[\neg PINE(\text{token03})]$.

6.4. Discussion

There are several restrictions upon the statements that a process can make about the world and on the types of queries that can be posed. These restrictions were necessary to enable a practical implementation of the database.

The query language only allows a limited variety of queries. Acceptable queries are limited both by their syntax and by the vocabulary of properties. The query language is not intended to be a universal language. We have designed it so that the only queries that can be posed are those that can usually be retrieved efficiently, given our database architecture. It is important to bear in mind that the limitation of the query language is one that restricts only what questions can be answered efficiently; it does not prevent the identification of data tokens that satisfy an unusual query. When faced with a question that cannot be posed as a syntactically legal query, a user can obtain the exact retrieval by first retrieving a superset of the desired data tokens with an acceptable query, and then examining each token in that set individually for satisfaction of the intended query. Empirical evidence will decide if our designs have been made appropriately.

7. PROCESS CONTROL

We have described the various processes that form the system as independent, asynchronous processes that can be activated be means of daemons embedded in the database or by more conventional procedure calls. Each process uses vocabulary terms to interact with the database. Each process is continuously executing, although a process may put itself to sleep only to be awakened when predetermined data conditions exist. Who determines these conditions? Should every process be permitted to determine the conditions needed to interrupt another process? Some processes may be time critical and prefer not to be interrupted. Our approach is to require that the process itself set these conditions within the database.

7.1. Daemons

Any process can attach a daemon to any data slot of any data token, so that the process will be interrupted whenever any new or changed opinion modifies that data slot. Daemons are attached to data slots rather than data tokens because tokens usually represent a complex frame and any one process is probably interested in only some aspects of it; for example, the navigational module of an autonomous vehicle will want to be interrupted if a sensor process gives a new opinion on the position of an obstacle, but it is unlikely to need to be interrupted if the obstacle's color changes. It is, therefore, the responsibility of each process to determine when it is to be interrupted. Daemons may also be placed on vocabulary terms on spatial locations to generate an interrupt whenever an object of a particular class or at a particular location is identified.

Likewise, it is the process that determines what action to take when it is interrupted. The interrupt handler is part of the definition of each process. As processes are quite varied, there is no sense to the notion of a generic interrupt handler. A process may choose to continue with what it is doing rather than to process the interrupt if it assesses the current task to be more relevant to mission success than that associated with the interrupt. Conversely, a process may instead suspend or abandon what it is doing in favor of the interrupt. The overall system concept is that of a loosely coupled system in which all processes work on their goals cognizant of the overall mission of the system. Each process determines how it can best support the mission goals and is responsible for the means to achieve this.

The process architecture parallels that of blackboard systems that were brought to prominence in the building of speech understanding systems[8]. In these systems data are placed on a blackboard; if the combination of data on the blackboard meets the preconditions for a particular procedure to execute, then that procedure is triggered and put on the schedule for computing resources. In an important way, the approach of activating processes using daemons differs from the triggering mechanism used on blackboard systems. There is no pattern matcher whose job is to trigger processes when a particular pattern of data appears in the database (or on the blackboard). For efficiency reasons, the patterns that pattern matchers are to recognize must be predetermined and compiled in at system building time. In a system that is loosely coupled, in which different processes may be present during different executions of the system — in which the

system must function even if some of the processes (or hardware) fail —
an approach to pattern matching that decentralizes the responsibility for
determining whether a process should be triggered seems more manageable.
We have chosen to trigger on an opinion being changed rather than on a
particular pattern in the data itself. In selecting this mechanism, the cost
of the additional processing that is done by the interrupt handler in each
process was weighed against the computational cost of running a generalized
pattern matcher.

7.2. Meta-Level Control

In any system with multiple processes, priority will sometimes need to
be given to processes that perform time-critical tasks. At other times, the
system could be underused. As a result some processes should be scheduled
as foreground jobs, which compete for resources when they request them,
while others should be background processes using only spare resources.
Some of the background processes have already been identified: the module that resolves data inconsistencies, the one that recovers storage space,
and parts of the resource allocator itself. The system should never be idle.
Computational resources are allocated to modules by a separate process,
a meta-level process, that changes the time slice allocated to various processes. A process that produces data, including opinions, that are used by
other processes warrants more resources than a producer of unused data.
In addition, a process can request more resources if it determines such a
need, so that critical processes can ask for priority.

In the current system implementation all the various processes execute
on one computer system, a Symbolics 3600, and all interact through a
common virtual address space. This approach was adopted to eliminate
the system building necessary to run experiments on multiple processors.
However, the conceptual design assumes a virtual environment in which
there are many processors running in parallel, with a communications network between them. This accounts for the design decision of the rather
loose coupling between processes. On a network of parallel processors, we
would expect some processors to be dedicated to particular modules whose
computational task is matched to the particular machine hardware. Other
processes would be allocated among the available processors. Although
we are aware of the bottleneck that might be caused by centralizing the
database, we envisage a system in which the process accepting requests for
database transactions will be centralized, but the database itself and the
procedures that carry out the internal processing may be split across processors.

8. EXTENDED EXAMPLE

As a means of gaining an overview of how the Core Knowledge System interacts with mission tasks we look at the following example. Suppose that an autonomous land vehicle (ALV) is to carry out the mission of finding a suitable landing site for helicopters in terrain for which some reconnaissance data are available. We shall suppose that the reconnaissance data have provided us with topographic information, vegetation cover, feature identification, such as roads and buildings, and so on as shown in Fig 5. Further we shall suppose that this information has been entered into the database using some of the CKS interface tools such as a two-dimensional map interface.

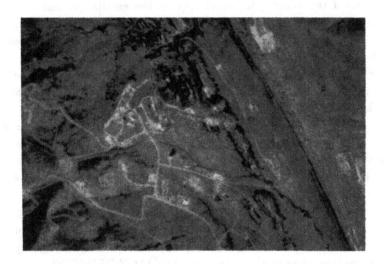

Fig. 5. Aerial photograph of terrain used in helicopter landing site example.

In setting up the mission, the (human) planner needs to specify what needs to be done and to determine if the reconnaissance data are sufficient to support the ALV task. Firstly, he might want to retrieve from the CKS all the information known about the mission area and render this in the form of an aerial "image". The CKS can retrieve data based on spatial location and can render these data on the basis of the description stored within each data token. Figure 6 gives an example of some selected data retrieved from the area portrayed in the aerial photograph and displayed iconically. If the specific description is unknown then a default is used to fill in the "typical" characteristics. Now, the planner may mark an approximate path for the vehicle to take, or he may invoke an automatic planner to find a path from the current location of the vehicle to the approximate area of the landing site. This automatic planner would retrieve terrain data tokens and, using information about the vegetation, determine what areas can be traversed, using topography to determine what areas provide cover from being detected, and using the location of landmarks (maybe pointed out by the human planner) to determine the areas from which the vehicle's sensors can "see" a landmark and hence support navigation. In making its queries, the planner would integrate multiple opinions in a manner suited to each particular task. For example, in deciding whether a bridge will support the weight of the vehicle, it would request the smallest estimate of the bridge's maximum support weight to ensure the safety of crossing. On the other hand, during obstacle avoidance, the maximum width of a potential obstacle would be of interest. When there is a conflict in opinions the planner may prefer data provided manually during a pre-mission briefing. These data can be accessed by naming the provider of that information. Once the path is selected, the CKS can supply data related to that path so that a scene renderer can display the view that the ALV's sensors will detect. On viewing these rendered images, a (human) planner can select locations at which the vehicle's sensors need to be reoriented and daemons can be placed in the CKS database so that the process controlling sensor position will be interrupted when the vehicle is at these locations.

The selection of a particular path may have been made on the assumptions that particular vegetation cover is available. Daemons can be placed on these data tokens so that if their properties are altered (say, by the object recognizer changing the data-slot FOLIAGE-DENSITY), the automatic planner is called to replan a path.

Once the mission is planned, the ALV starts the task of navigating. Nearby objects are retrieved from the database. A process responsible for choosing landmarks would request everything that is "APPARENTLY" in its field of view, so that it would only need to deal with those objects that it should be able to sense. A module whose responsibility is to avoid obstacles would instead request all solid objects that are "POSSIBLY" along the route in order to consider all potential obstacles. The description and properties of these objects can then be used to confirm their presence in the sensor

Fig. 6. Iconic rendering of some selected data stored in the CKS.

data. The CKS data allows much of the bottom-up object recognition to be replaced by model verification. Of course, discovery processes are still needed to deal with the unexpected and the unknown. This information is usually at a finer resolution than that known *a priori*, and its discovery and inclusion into the database can aid in subsequent excursions in this area by the ALV.

The context provided by the stored data can be used to select particular routines to process the data. If the road is asphalt (and confirmed by, say, texture analysis) then this information can be used to determine the method for local navigation (say, by finding road edges). Knowing that the road is asphalt can help in calibrating the raw sensor images to help in material identification. The CKS can supply local information, pieced together by many processes to provide constraints for subsequent processing. Should the image analyzer determine that the expected trees to one side of the road are without leaves and, if these trees were assumed to provide cover from detection in the original plan, then the vehicle's planner will be interrupted and used to determine if an alternative route should be used. This interruption will be triggered by a daemon attached to the tree's density data slot that was inserted during planning.

Daemons will also be triggered when the vehicle nears particular locations and the sensors need to be reoriented to detect landmarks.

Once the ALV nears the approximate location of the proposed landing site, the vehicle needs to change modes into one of search. The sensor processes may now be more bottom-up with object recognition modules using the knowledge in the semantic network to determine that the recognition of a post suggests that a fence or sign post may be present and routines should be invoked to look for these objects in the scene. The required landing site may be described in general terms: flat, no gullies, hidden by the topography from a particular direction, and so on. The routine that is looking at the information known about different locations will need to use the semantic network to infer if these conditions are met from the particulars of the data tokens: grade of two degrees, grass cover, and the like.

On the return journey the ALV can make use of the data inserted in the CKS during the outward journey. Particularly, it can use the fine resolution data acquired previously to aid in the identification of objects that maybe now have only been seen from a different perspective. Planning can use more up-to-date information, context setting is based on more complete information, and so on. During debriefing the CKS can render details of the landing site and provide a simulation of the approaches the helicopters may take. See Fig. 7, for example[10].

9. SUMMARY

The Core Knowledge System plays the role of providing the context in which the task is executed. This may involve setting parameters that a procedure uses, selecting the appropriate procedure, or choosing an appropriate model to be instantiated. The integrating role of the CKS allows knowledge of the domain to be built up incrementally. In the above example on the outward journey some properties of an object may have been determined, but it may only be on the return journey when that object is seen from some different angle that we are able to determine enough information to recognize it. The knowledge embedded in the semantic network allows inferences to be drawn over semantic descriptions. A task that calls for hiding the ALV behind a tree cannot be satisfied by hiding behind a pine tree if the task has no way of determining that pine tree is a subset of tree. The semantic network provides for such inferences. The daemon mechanism provides for data-driven control. Without it a system would be overwhelmed by checking for all types of conditions. The CKS is an integra-

Fig. 7. Synthetic image of terrain with objects from CKS database superimposed (courtesy of L. Quam).

tor of information. Its benefits are realized when there are many processes carrying out interdependent tasks — when one process can determine information that another can use. However, even in the above example where only a few tasks are described, it is natural to divide the problem into a set of modules that have similar functionality to those described. The CKS provides those basic modules and frees the task designer from the need to consider those details. It provides a mechanism for coordinating user provided modules — again freeing the task designer from the need to consider the coordinating details.

The Core Knowledge System provides a rich infrastructure for building autonomous systems. Its major features are the following:

Representation of both knowledge and data — The CKS is a true knowledge-based database. It has the ability to perform inferences at the level of stored knowledge as well as the ability to infer information from newly acquired data. It retains the virtues of database systems in providing for rapid retrieval based upon selected indices and in being a system that persists over time, well beyond the extent of a single execution.

Spatial orientation — Autonomous vehicles operate in the physical world. It is vital, therefore, that a vehicle's information manager have the ability to represent the 3-dimensional world in a natural way. The spatial directory, designed as a volume-based octree, provides the spatial orientation for the CKS database.

Multiple opinions — The need for representations of uncertainty and for combining multiple pieces of evidence has been demonstrated by the many techniques and systems in existence for this purpose. The CKS recognizes this need by providing a mechanism for maintaining multiple, conflicting opinions within its database. This approach affords the opportunity to integrate information according to the demands of the present situation, and also affords the option to forego integration altogether when it is irrelevant to the task at hand.

Mixed-initiative control — Borrowing from the technology of blackboard systems, the CKS is organized as a community of asynchronous processes that communicate by way of a common database. Additional flexibility of control is attained through implementation of a complete daemon facility and through meta-level control processes that oversee the operation of the community.

Versatile user interface — Centralizing all information to be shared in a common database fosters communication between computational processes. Centralization has the additonal benefit of allowing a single display or user interface tool to access all the data. Thus a tool that is constructed for a particular purpose is immediately available for use with data provided by any source. Such a capability is conducive to rapid development and facilitates conversion to new domains.

It is true that none of these features is particularly new. What makes the CKS novel is the integration of all these features in a single, coherent system that allows the implementer of an autonomous vehicle to take advantage of whatever capability is desired at the time. It is our contention that the availability of a core knowledge system will encourage the development of new algorithms that make use of stored knowledge for the purpose of image understanding in particular, and for autonomous vehicle control in general.

References

1. S. Shafer, A. Stentz and C Thorpe, "An architecture for sensor fusion in a mobile robot," in *IEEE Int'l Conf. on Robotics and Automation*, 1986.

2. C. Thorpe et al., "Vision and navigation for the Carnegie Mellon Navlab," *Proc. of the DARPA Image Understanding Workshop*, Vol. 1, Feb. 1987, pp. 143-152.

3. S. N. Srihari, "Representation of three-dimensional digital images," *Computing Surveys* **13** (1981) 399-424.

4. A. Barr and A. Feigenbaum, *The Handbook of Artificial Intelligence*, William Kaufmann, Los Altos, 1981.

5. H. Samet, "The quadtree and related hierarchical data structures," *Computing Surveys* **16** (1984) 187-260.

6. R. Moore and G.G. Hendrix, "Computational models of belief and semantics of belief sentences," SRI Artificial Intelligence Center Technical Note 187, SRI International, Menlo Park, 1979.

7. K. Konolige, "A deduction model of belief and its logic," SRI Artificial Intelligence Center Technical Note 326, SRI International, Menlo Park, Aug. 1984.

8. L. Erman, F. Hayes-Roth, V. R. Lesser and D. Raj Reddy, "The hearsay-II speech understanding system: integrating knowledge to resolve uncertainty," *Computing Surveys* **12** (1980) 213-253.

9. A. J. Hanson, P. Pentland and L. H. Quam, "Design of a prototype interactive cartographic display and analysis environment," *Proceedings IU Workshop*, Vol. II, 1987, pp. 475-482.

10. G. B. Smith and T. M. Strat, "Information management in a sensor-based autonomous system," *Proc. of the DARPA Image Understanding Workshop*, Vol. 1, Feb. 1987, pp. 170-177.

2

PLAUSIBLE REASONING IN CLASSIFICATION PROBLEM SOLVING

Lashon B. Booker

Navy Center for Applied Research in AI
Naval Research Laboratory, Code 5510
Washington, D. C. 20375, USA

A prototype system for classifying complex ship images has convincingly demonstrated that Bayesian reasoning is a valuable tool for making plausible inferences about classificatory hypotheses given impoverished feature data[1]. It remains to be shown that such methods are also useful in handling the large scale, resource-constrained classification problems that are of interest to the Navy. Classifying objects using sensor data in an operational environment is a demanding task. Regardless of the kind of sensor information available — visual, infrared, radar, or sonar — this is a task in which complex inferences must be made reliably under stringent computational constraints, and based on incomplete and uncertain evidence. This paper describes research efforts focused on devising a robust and accurate classification problem solver that meets this challenge.

1.   INTRODUCTION

Knowledge-based techniques for the analysis and interpretation of images have proven to be valuable tools in many practical applications[2]. In almost all of these applications, a key objective is to use extracted features to generate descriptions of the objects in the image, then "classify" the image objects by matching these descriptions with models of known object classes. This classification process is considerably more difficult when the feature information available is incomplete or uncertain. Under such circumstances the comparison of complex descriptions must be flexible and robust, resolving ambiguous interpretations within the constraints of the available domain knowledge.

When the evidence concerning the identity of an image object is incomplete, a classification problem solver must determine the information it needs to know from whatever information is at hand. This requires that the problem solver go beyond the evidence directly available and draw inferences or *reason* about the implications of what it knows. If in addition the evidence is unreliable or imprecise, the problem solver must assure that its infererences are plausible. The reasoning process will then involve procedures for computing a degree of belief for each hypothesis and mechanisms for aggregating and justifying these beliefs. The demands on a reasoning mechanism become even more difficult if the process is also constrained by limited resources. When there is not enough time or memory for an exhaustive feature analysis, intelligent decisions must be made about how to use the resources available to maximum advantage. This means that the reasoning mechanism must be involved in the control of the information extraction activities, as well as the interpretation of the results. Ship classification is an example of one practical application in which all of these problems arise.

Classification of ships in an operational environment is a difficult task regardless of what kind of images are used. This is not always obvious to those who are only familiar with the kind of detailed view of a ship one finds in an intelligence manual or reference book. Observers in the field rarely have such explicit detail to work with. Images are most often obtained during a brief observation interval from a distance that makes high resolution difficult to achieve. The viewing angle is usually a matter of opportunity rather than choice, and the observer must make do with the prevailing visibility, weather, and lighting conditions at sea. Another factor degrading image quality is the fact that sensor platforms are often buffeted by turbulence in the air or the ocean. These difficulties are of course exacerbated when the classification must be done in real time. The quality of images produced in this way is likely to be lower than that attainable using sophisticated enhancement techniques and powerful computing resources. All of this is in addition to the complexity faced when distinguishing among hundreds of classes of vessels, some of which differ only in fine feature details.

Real-time ship classification is a demanding application. It is a task requiring that complex inferences, based on incomplete and uncertain information, be made reliably under stringent computational constraints. In devising a system that meets this challenge, two of the most important research issues are control and inference. Given that resource constraints often preclude an exhaustive feature analysis, which features should be sought after in the time available? Given an uncertain and incomplete feature description, what kind of heuristic reasoning tools provide reliable and computationally inexpensive ship classifications? This paper describes a knowledge-based framework for reasoning in classification problems that successfully manages many of these issues using a probabilistic representation of belief. A prototype developed at the Navy Center for Applied Research in AI (NCARAI) has convincingly demonstrated that such an approach to ship classification is effective and practical[1,3]. Our current research effort builds on this work, and is developing a robust classification problem solver for handling large-scale versions of problems of this kind.

2. SHIP CLASSIFICATION PROBLEMS

Having ship images classified correctly is obviously important to the Navy, which has invested heavily in training personnel to analyze and interpret images under operational conditions. Human observers and sensor operators must be highly trained and experienced. They must know which features are related to which kinds of ships, and make a judgement as to how well various features are manifested in the image. Moreover, they must keep track of the implications of all these judgements — both with respect to their uncertainty and consistency, and with respect to an eventual classification.

Decision aids are critical to the effective use of image data for classification. The classification methods currently available are often extremely labor intensive. Operators sometimes do not have time to make even coarse-grained classifications of all ships being detected. Even experts need a classification aid to help quickly discriminate similar ship types. Clearly the speed, reliability and capability of the classification process must be enhanced to effectively handle large numbers of ships at one time.

In this section we examine the classification process one typically finds in the operational Navy, and then describe a prototype decision aid that computes plausible inferences about complex ship images.

2.1. Typical Ship Classification Procedures

Because of the meager computational facilities available on most military platforms, sensor operators are usually used as a pattern recognition resource in the classification process. Operators can perform at acceptable levels even when the image quality and resolution are less then ideal. Moreover, the operator retains information about a sequence of images that may be important in analyzing any given frame. Computer-based classification tools are therefore most likely to be semiautomated.

A typical configuration is shown in Fig. 1. The operator begins the process by registering the location of certain gross ship components in the image. The computer then uses these points to make various estimates about the physical dimensions of the ship, and compares the results with a database of ship structural descriptions. Those ships that are plausible matches are ranked ordered if possible then displayed to the operator. At this point the operator is on his own and must look for small feature differences to resolve ambiguities. This usually requires the use of classification "keys" for discriminating one kind of ship from another.

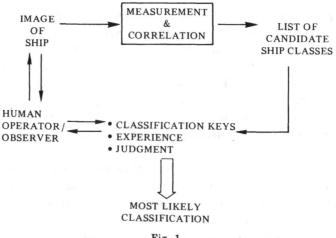

Fig. 1.

The crucial phase of the classification process is the use of the classification keys. These keys are used to refine classificatory hypotheses in a series of steps that is standard for all image data, regardless of the sensor in question:

- Establish a coarse-grained functional classication for the ship image; for example, military combatant versus commercial vessel.

- Establish the *Naval Class* of the ship image, which identifies it as belonging to a group of ships built to the same design and known collectively by the lead ship's name.

- Determine the name or hull number of the ship

The operator is required to make several judgements about the quality of information in the image, which keys to use and when to use them. This requires considerable expertise when difficult discriminations must be made. The information needed to achieve each step is not always available or easy to obtain, and the best sequence of classification keys to use is not always obvious.

2.2. A Prototype Decision Aid

One straightforward way of reducing operator overload and training requirements in this kind of situation is to provide a decision aid that somehow captures the complex reasoning about an image that is characteristic of an expert analyst. A prototype version of this kind of decision aid has been developed and tested at NCARAI[1]. As a simplification, the prototype system was implemented to rely exclusively on operator input. This allows the reasoning and uncertainty management issues of the classification process to be examined without worrying about sensor-specific feature extraction issues.

2.2.1 Knowledge about ships

The knowledge for this system was provided by an expert analyst who picked 10 Naval Classes that have similar imagery and are often difficult to distinguish from one another. Some are similar based on the relative location of masts and superstructure; others, based on feature details as they appear in different kinds of imagery. The similarities between any two classes might be apparent from either a *profile* (or side) view, a *plan* (or top-down) view, or both. Figure 2 shows the kind of features that are

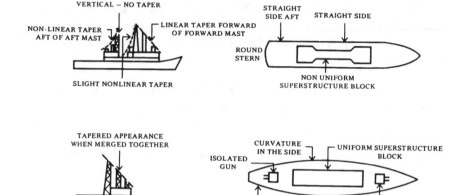

Fig. 2.

considered important. The primary items of interest in analyzing a plan view image, for example, are the shape of the stern, curvature of the sides, location of weapons, etc. Needless to say, not all of this detail is likely to be available in every image; and, when an analyst looks for these things he often has to make uncertain judgements about whether or not they are really there.

The expert also provided feature descriptions for each class. These descriptions were given in tabular form as shown in Table 1 which describes the plan view stern shape for all 10 classes. The descriptions include a subjective weight for each feature attribute and Naval Class combination. This number indicates an expectation about whether that attribute will be manifested in the imagery. The weights are given on a scale of 0 to 10, with 0 meaning the attribute should never be detected and 10 meaning it should always be detected. Two structures with the same weight for a given attribute cannot be distinguished on that basis alone. So, for example, the sterns of Sverdlov and Forrest Sherman are square in the same way.

The knowledge can be organized into a simple hierarchy having four levels: Naval Class, major structural components, features, and observations. At the top of the hierarchy are the hypotheses about how to classify a particular image. This presumably cannot be directly determined, so at the next level are hypotheses about the gross structural components of the ship — the stern, deck, superstructure blocks, etc. Table 1 indicates that there are 5 types of sterns. Sometimes evidence is available that directly bears on knowledge at this level. For instance, the stern of the Sverdlov

Table 1. Plan view Stern descriptions.

Shape Attribute	Stern Type				
	Virginia	Belknap Leahy	Sverdlov	Bainbridge California Coontz Long Beach Truxtun	Forrest Sherman
Square	10	0	1	0	1
Round	0	10	0	5	2
Tapered	0	0	10	0	0

class is very distinctive and can often be recognized immediately. In most cases, though, components have to be determined from their constituent features in the next level of the hierarchy. For the stern components of this set of ships, there are two ways for a stern to be square, three ways to be round, and one way to be tapered. In practice, it is often difficult even to obtain evidence at this level. A poor quality image or non-expert observer might only be able to provide evidence that the stern in the image is somewhat rounded, period. The lowest level in the hierarchy represents these very simple assertions.

2.2.2. Inference networks

Reasoning about possible classifications for a ship image involves determining the diagnostic or causal impact of new evidence on these structural hypotheses. A decision-tree approach to this problem (e.g. Ref. 4) is inadequate because the evidence is not likely to be complete or reliably available. Moreover, it is difficult to interrupt a fixed decision sequence and accept arbitrary evidence volunteered by the operator. The methods of classical statistical pattern recognition can play a useful role, but they cannot solve the entire problem. The complexity of the mapping between sensor manifestations and ship features most likely will preclude the use of any easily computed mathematical function of the feature set as a reliable discriminator. Even if the problem can be decomposed into pieces that are manageable analytically, the formal computations of classical statistics do not provide the kind of easily understood chain of reasoning that a sensor operator would be familiar with.

A much more appropriate framework for this kind of reasoning task is the *inference network*: The nodes in an inference network designate the knowledge variables or hypotheses of interest and each link signifies a direct influence exerted by the belief about one hypothesis on the belief about another. Besides serving as a way of representing knowledge, an inference network also provides a computational framework for reasoning about that knowledge. By maintaining a measure of belief for each node and summarizing the dependencies between nodes with constraints on beliefs, the network structure indicates which beliefs need to be updated when new information is available. In this way, an integrated summary can be maintained of what is known directly about each hypothesis and what can be inferred from their inter-relationships. Furthermore, the sequence of steps followed in this updating process is easily understood and explained in terms of the way one hypothesis is related to another.

Probabilities are very natural measure of belief to use in the ship classification problem. The way each feature partitions the set of Naval Classes is known in advance, so that simple counting arguments can be used initially to quantify the relative beliefs and constraints on beliefs associated with this knowledge. Several probabilistic reasoning schemes have been devised for updating beliefs in inference networks[5]. A version of the PROSPECTOR updating method[6] was developed at NCARAI to solve a resource allocation problem[7], and was available for the ship classification work. Consequently, a PROSPECTOR-style inference engine was used to implement the prototype.

In our version of the PROSPECTOR scheme, the relation between evidence and hypothesis is a rule of inference of the following type[a]

$$\text{If P1 then (to extent } \lambda 1, \lambda 2 \text{) conclude P .}$$

P1 and P are both propositions. P1 is called the *antecedent* of the rule and is a source of evidential support for belief in P. P is called the *consequent* of the rule. The strength of the implication is attenuated by the two numbers $\lambda 1$ and $\lambda 2$: $\lambda 1$ is the conditional probability of P given that P1 is true and $\lambda 2$ is the conditional probability of P given that P1 is false. This information, together with the prior probability of P and P1, is used to compute a posterior belief for P when the truth of P1 is uncertain. When several independent propositions provide evidential support for P, the posterior belief in P is computed using a heuristic generalization of Bayes Rule. See

[a]PROSPECTOR also allows belief to be inferred between propositions related by logical AND, OR and NOT. However, only the Bayesian inference rule was needed for the classification prototype.

Duda et al.[6] for more details. Reasoning is accomplished in this framework by *propagating* changes through the inference network. Data that changes the belief in any given proposition also changes the amount of evidential support that proposition provides to all its consequents. The posterior belief in each consequent must therefore be updated to reflect the modified evidential support. These revisions in turn lead recursively to more belief updates, a process that terminates at the *top-level* nodes in the network which have no consequents. In this way the effects of the initial change spread upward, from antecedents to consequents, to all propositions that directly and indirectly use that data as supporting evidence.

The inference network representation for the ship classification problem has been organized to model the four-level knowledge hierarchy described previously. The structure of these inference networks is illustrated in Fig. 3.

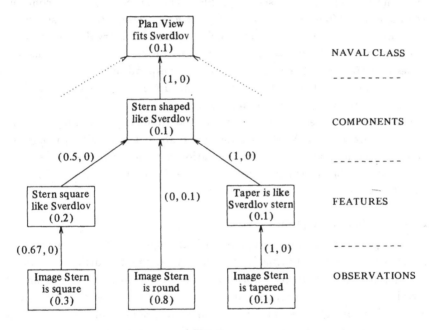

Fig. 3.

This excerpt is a portion of the network for evaluating the hypothesis that a plan view image belongs to the Sverdlov class, based on the feature description in Table 1. It shows how the shape of the stern influences the top-level hypothesis. Each rectangle designates a proposition along with its prior probability (the number in parentheses). The conditional probabilities λ_1 and λ_2 needed to do evidential updating are given as an ordered pair adjacent to each arc. The bottom nodes correspond to the three relevant observations about the shape of the stern in the image. There are two propositions at the feature level, corresponding to the fact that the Sverdlov class is described as both square and tapered in Table 1. At the third level in the hierarchy, belief is computed about whether the overall stern shape fits Sverdlov. An observation that the stern is round is evidence that the stern does not fit Sverdlov, so its influence comes in at this point. It is also at this level that the feature weights are explicitly factored into the computation. The impact of evidence not sure to be detected (i.e. with a weight less than 10) is modeled by reducing the link parameters in proportion to the relative size of the weight.

Networks of this type were constructed for all 10 Naval Classes, one set for plan views and another set for profiles. The plan view network contains 181 nodes and 297 links. Fourteen of these nodes designate propositions at the bottom level in the hierarchy which are directly observable details that any operator can be questioned about. The profile network contains 417 nodes and 767 links. Forty of these nodes correspond to observable details, reflecting the fact that profiles contain more information than plans. The networks were implemented separately because the knowledge contained in the simple feature descriptions is too shallow to manage anything but pure plans or pure profiles. Without information about the physical dimensions of ship structures and their spatial relationships, for example, the system cannot determine which features should be detectable from an arbitrary aspect angle.

2.2.3. System description

The prototype system interacts with the operator to get the feature information in a mixed-initiative fashion. At any point during the session the operator can volunteer information about the presence or absence of certain features in the image. In this way, the operator can direct the program's chain of reasoning in a manner he deems appropriate. When the operator is not volunteering information, the program asks a series of questions about the image. The questioning sequence is dynamically ordered so as to maximize the effectiveness of the evidence in determining a classification.

Perhaps the easiest way to appreciate how the prototype works is by means of an example. The sample session given below is based on an actual classification trial, though modifications have been made to demonstrate various aspects of the system in operation. The information typed in by the user has been italicized and printed in upper-case. Text enclosed in square brackets [...] is an editorial comment, inserted to make the example easier to understand.

Welcome to the NCARAI ship image interpretation aid

Do you wish to see instructions? *YES*

In using this system, you will be asked to answer questions about the presence of various features in the image. Your judgement about a feature is indicated by a number from −5 to 5. Answer 5 if the feature is definitely present, −5 if it is definitely absent, and 0 if you can't tell one way or the other. Keep in mind that positive answers increase the system's estimated probability of the occurrence of a feature; negative answers decrease that probability; and, 0 leaves it at the expert's default value.

You can obtain a list of possible responses to any question or input request by typing '?'.

To print these instructions, type 'help'.

[First, the user tells the system about a new image to be classified]

− Enter command: *ADD*
>> Enter the unique name or t: *IMAGE1*
>> Enter the image type: *PROFILE*
>> Enter the next unique name or t: *T*

[Now the user volunteers information about a prominent feature in the image.

Note that any unique prefix of a command serves as an alias.]

− Enter command: *VOL*
>> Enter the image for volunteering or t: *IMAGE1*

[The system provides a simple keyword search capability to facilitate identifying propositions for volunteering or changing information]

>> Enter the first volunteered property or t: *GAP?AFT?MAST?*
**Relevant items are:
    14) profile-has-a-gap-between-aft-mast-and-aft-superstructure-block
    24) profile-has-linear-taper-with-a-gap-aft-of-aft-mast

**Reply with one of the above items, it's number, or t to terminate **

>> Enter the first volunteered property or t: *14*

To what degree do you believe that

(*profile-has-a-gap-between-aft-mast-and-aft-superstructure-block)? *5*

>> Enter the next volunteered property or t: *T*

[The user now initiates questioning mode. A list of classes to consider can be specified, perhaps based on information from some preliminary analysis. An asterisk means consider all classes in the knowledge base. The cutoff value gives the user control over how extensive the questioning will be]

– Enter command: QUES
>> Enter the image name or t: *IMAGE1*
>> Enter the class name or t: *
>> Enter the confidence value for cutting off questions: *4*

[Upon request the confidence in each ship class will be summarized after every question]

Do you wish to see the results of each question? *NO*

To what degree do you believe that
(*profile-has-no-taper-aft-of-aft-mast)? *-3*

To what degree do you believe that
(*profile-has-slight-non-linear-taper-fwd-of-aft-mast)? *0*

To what degree do you believe that
(*profile-has-thin-pole-mast-fwd)? *-5*

To what degree do you believe that
(*profile-has-isolated-directors-on-aft-superstructure-block)? *5*

To what degree do you believe that
(*profile-has-linear-taper-aft-of-aft-mast)? *-3*

[The user realizes that the answer to the previous question was an error, and changes it to what was intended]

To what degree to you believe that
(*profile-01-level-superstructure-extends-slightly-fwd-of-bridge)? *CH*

>> Enter the fact you want to change or t: *?*

**Valid responses include:
    1) profile-has-linear-taper-aft-of-aft-mast
    2) profile-has-isolated-directors-on-aft-superstructure-block
    3) profile-has-thin-pole-mast-fwd
    4) profile-has-slight-non-linear-taper-fwd-of-aft-mast
    5) profile-has-no-taper-aft-of-aft-mast
    6) profile-has-a-gap-between-aft-mast-and-aft-superstructure-block

**Reply with one of the above items, it's number, or t to terminate **

**To see items relevant to some word xxx, type xxx?

>> Enter the fact you want to change or t: *1*

To what degree do you believe that
(*profile-has-linear-taper-aft-of-aft-mast)? *3*

>> Enter the next fact you want to change or t: *T*

[Note how the changed value results in a different question being selected as most important]

To what degree do you believe that
(*profile-mast-heights-are-equal)? *−4*

[. . . The system asks a few more questions, then determines that the remaining questions are unlikely to change the user's classification decision]

The remaining questions seem unimportant given your cutoff criterion
Do you wish to continue the questioning anyway? *NO*

[The system leaves questioning mode by summarizing its confidence in every ship class considered. This particular trial resulted in the strongest kind of discrimination the system can make: a confidence of near +5 in the correct class and near −5 for all other cases]

***Summary of hypotheses about ***

Image1

Coontz	4.99
California	-4.74
Virginia	-4.84
Sverdlov	-4.88
Truxtun	-4.91
Leahy	-4.92
Forrest Sherman	4.99
Belknap	-5.00
LongBeach	-5.00
Bainbridge	-5.00

I strongly suspect that image1 is Coontz
I strongly doubt that image1 is Forrest Sherman, Bainbridge, Sverdlov, LongBeach, Leahy, Belknap, Truxtun, California or Virginia.

– Enter command: *EXIT*

As in all systems of the PROSPECTOR genre, the interaction between the system and the user involves so-called *confidence values* between −5 and 5. This arbitrary scale is used to make sure the user's input is interpreted consistently. Suppose, for example, the user tries to indicate that some evidence is unlikely to be present by giving a low probability of 0.01 in response to a question. If the expert decided that the prior probability for the given proposition is 0.001, a Bayesian updating scheme will misinterpret the user's response as an encouraging one. By using confidence values, on the other hand, positive answers always mean that the evidence is likely to be present and increase belief in the underlying proposition; negative answers always mean that the evidence is not likely to be present and decrease belief in the underlying proposition; and, an answer of zero always means the user has no opinion, implying the need to use default assumptions about the evidence. Confidence values are converted into probabilities using a simple piecewise linear function that maps a confidence of −5 into a probability of zero, a confidence of zero into the proposition's prior probability, and a confidence of +5 into a probability of one.

A global control strategy is used to select which question to ask. Each proposition is assigned a weight called a *merit* which estimates its ability to alter the value of a top-level proposition. The merit of a proposition H is the ratio $\delta P/\delta C$ where δP is the expected change in the value of the top-level proposition if a value for H is obtained and δC is the expected cost of obtaining a value for H. With this information, an efficient algorithm can be used that finds the proposition with the largest absolute merit value in a network. See Slagle et al.[8] for a complete discussion of how merit values are dynamically calculated and updated. At each stage of the consultation, the user is asked the question having the highest merit value with respect to the chosen top-level node. This amounts to an unconstrained network traversal, selecting the most cost-effective question regardless of where it is in the network. In the ship classification prototype, the user provides a confidence value that defines a threshold above which belief (or disbelief)[b] in a proposition is "strong enough". When a proposition is chosen by the merit control strategy, the system computes the new expected confidence in the top-level proposition. Once the top-level confidence exceeds the threshold, the only questions asked are those that might drop the confidence below threshold. By using this kind of control strategy, ineffective questions

[b]A proposition is "believed" or "disbelieved" to the extent that its confidence value is greater or less than zero.

can be easily identified and suppressed. Moreover, in a time-critical task, the user is assured that the most critical questions are asked first; and, therefore, if questioning must be prematurely terminated, the time has been used to maximum advantage. Additional details about the implementation of the prototype system can be found in Ref. 1.

2.3. Feasibility Test and Evaluation

The classification system has been extensively tested on 119 ship images. These images were photographs of sensor data from various sources, chosen because they are typical of the mediocre quality available from most operational systems. Of this total, 101 images were of ships belonging to one of the 10 Naval Classes represented in the program's knowledge base. The remaining 18 images were ships of other Naval Classes, chosen to test the program's behavior given ships it shouldn't be able to classify. Some of these classes are single masted, whereas all the inference network models describe ships having two masts. These classes were included to severely test the system's ability to make correct inferences given incomplete information.

The test data included 55 plan views, 64 profiles and covered a fairly representative range of aspect angles. The quality of the test images was difficult to assess objectively. What one would really like to measure is the amount of useful information available. The prototype system provides a direct, albeit not perfect, measure of the amount of information in an image. The number of questions about an image an expert analyst answers with high confidence is proportional to the clarity of the feature detail. For every feature that is clearly present or absent, the expert answers the system's questions with a confidence value of ± 4 or ± 5. We can therefore estimate the amount of information in an image by measuring the proportion of these confident answers. Using this measure, the highest rating of 1.0 indicates that all the feature detail is clearly visible. The worst possible rating is 0.0, indicating that no features are clearly discernible. The average quality for the test images was a fairly low 0.325. This is in line with the stated research objective of classifying the typical image one might encounter operationally.

Table 2 summarizes all 119 trials of the system. Three kinds of information are presented: the program's confidence values for the two top ship classes on the average trial; the final rank given to the correct ship class on the average trial; and, the partitioning of classes by the expert — based on the program's confidence values — into three qualitative categories. The labels used for these categories in the table are "Yes" for plausible classification candidates, "No" for implausible candidates, and "Maybe" for the rest.

Table 2. Summary of test results.

Type of Trial	Final Avg. Confidence		Avg. Rank of Correct Class	Avg. Size of Qualitative Categories		
	Top ranked class	2nd ranked class		Yes	Maybe	No
Image Class in Knowledge Base						
•Plan	1.557	−0.603	1.481	1.962	2.462	5.576
•Profile	1.230	−3.818	1.061	1.041	0.469	8.490
•Correct Class Ranked First	1.692	−2.383	1.000	1.400	1.282	7.318
•Correct Class Not First	−0.161	−0.990	2.750	2.125	2.625	5.250
•Overall	1.398	−2.163	1.277	1.515	1.495	6.990
Class not in Knowledge Base						
•Plan	−1.554	−3.063	—	1.000	1.333	7.667
•Profile	−3.459	−4.820	—	0.200	0.200	9.600
•Overall	−3.141	−4.528	—	0.333	0.389	9.278

The results of the 101 trials are summarized in the upper portion of Table 2. For the typical trial, the program had positive confidence in the top ranked ship class and negative confidence in all others. The differences between the confidence in the top ranked ship class and the confidence in the next best alternative were all statistically significant[c]. In this sense, the top ranked class was usually recommended as the only plausible classification. Interestingly, the program was much more "decisive" when the ship class ranked first was in fact the correct one. On those trials, the average confidence in the top ranked ship class was 1.692 and that for the second class was −2.383. This difference was, again, statistically significant. For the trials where the correct ship class was not ranked first, however, the

[c]Statistical significance was determined using a t test with an alpha level of 0.01.

average confidence in the two top alternatives was only −0.161 and −0.990. Not only are these low values, their difference is not statistically significant. This behavior was a useful indication of when the system was wrong. Overall, the program reliably ranked the correct ship class at or near the top of the list. Using the qualitative assessment of confidence values described previously, the analyst was able to eliminate about 7 of the 10 classes on the average trial. Navy experts have reviewed these results and judged them to be excellent given the quality of the test images.

For the 18 trials involving classes not in the knowledge base, the program typically expressed disbelief in all known alternatives. Indeed, in 11 of those trials every alternative was assigned a confidence value between −4 and −5. On four occasions, however, the confidence in the top ranked ship class slightly exceeded zero. The classes involved in those cases all slightly resemble some ship in the knowledge base either in plan or profile. The features needed to definitively conclude that these classes are unknowns were not part of the ship descriptions provided to the system.

These tests also provided the opportunity to obtain empirical validation of the effectiveness of the merit control strategy. In classification problems an important indicator of effective problem solving is the extent to which one class is distinguished from the others. Consequently, a straightforward way to evaluate a questioning strategy is to measure how quickly the correct class is discriminated from the rest. The absolute value of the difference between the confidence in the correct class and the average confidence in the other classes is one measure of discrimination that makes sense here. This measure has its minimum of zero when all classes have the same confidence value and its maximum of ten when the system makes its sharpest discrimination by assigning a confidence of +5 to the correct class and −5 to all the others. For a given classification trial, the effectiveness of a questioning strategy is indicated by the rate at which the discrimination measure achieves its final value: the discrimination level after all questions have been asked. We can consider any deviation from this ultimate value as a discrimination "error" and deem the best questioning strategies to be those that reduce this error most rapidly.

The fairest test of a strategy is in those cases where a strong discrimination is possible given the information available. Accordingly, the only classification trials used to evaluate control strategies were those with a fairly high (> 8) final level of discrimination. This set of trials included 10 plan views and 10 profiles. Figures 4a and 4b show how the root mean square error is reduced for three control strategies: a depth-first traversal of

Profile Views

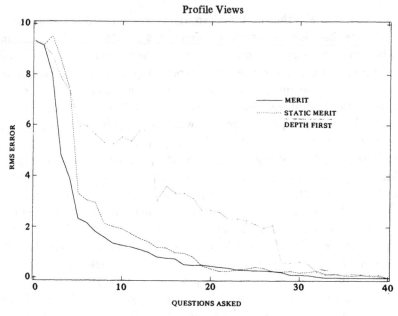

Fig. 4a.

Plan Views

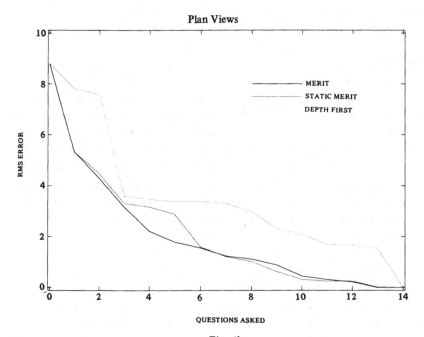

Fig. 4b.

the network in which the nodes have an arbitrary order; a best-first traversal in which the nodes are ordered by *a priori* static merit values; and, the normal dynamic merit control strategy. The depth-first traversal is clearly the worst strategy, reducing the error to negligible levels only after almost all of the questions have been asked. The static best-first strategy is nearly as effective as the merit strategy on this set of data. Merit's advantage shows in the early stages of questioning. Once about half of the questions have been asked, the static merit strategy has closed the performance gap. Part of this is of course due to the fact that once the "important" questions have been asked — in any order — the remaining questions have only a marginal effect on the final confidence values. Nevertheless, the advantages of using merit are not as pronounced as one might expect. One plausible explanation for this is that the independence assumptions made in the merit computation clearly don't hold in this problem. A strong belief that the stern is square, for example, reduces the importance of observations about the round and tapered attributes. Merit does not properly take these kinds of interactions among antecedents into account. Nevertheless, these tests of merit illustrate the importance of using control knowledge[9] to enhance problem solving effectiveness.

3. A BROADER PERSPECTIVE

Because of the interest generated by the performance of the prototype, work on this problem has now moved into a second phase whose goal is a large-scale, realistic classification system. The inference and control concepts in the prototype must be scaled up to manage a more varied and complex problem solving process. Automatically extracted feature data from raw sensor signals and imagery has to be analyzed and interpreted, together with any other evidence that may be available. The system also must have the capacity to represent and reason about any of the approximately 640 military Naval Classes that might be encountered at sea. Clearly, the research issues associated with this larger problem are considerably more difficult than those deal with in the feasibility study.

The issues raised here touch on almost every aspect of the emerging "second generation" expert systems technology. We have focused on the following two issues as important cornerstones of our research program:

- The Navy problem domain is one in which the reliability of machine-drawn inferences is critically important. It is therefore crucial that the uncertainty associated with evidence be managed with representations and rules of combination based on sound theory and clear semantics. Management of uncertainty is a central problem in computing the belief in every classificatory hypothesis and in the overall control of the classification process.

• The kinds of knowledge needed to solve these problems must be explicitly delineated and represented. It is clear, for example, that the system will have to know something about the reliability of the sensor being used, the physical relationships among ship components, and the many taxonomic relations describing the structure and function of ships. Knowledge about the classification process itself would also be useful, so that classification decisions can be made at a level of specificity commensurate with prevailing resource constraints.

3.1. Generic Classification

Scaling up a feasibility prototype to handle the complexities of a realistic problem is a difficult task. Our approach to managing this difficulty is to analyze classification problem solving at the *knowledge level*[10], identifying the information processing requirements common to several Navy classification problems and several kinds of sensors. Such an understanding will provide insights about the kinds of knowledge structures and control regimes that are characteristic of these classification tasks in general. This, in turn, will allow us to develop system building tools that reflect the inherent structure of the classification problems, facilitating system design, knowledge acquisition, and explanation. An added benefit is that these tools can then be used for a wide variety of applications.

This approach builds on work done by Clancey[11] and Chandrasekaran[12], who argue that the inherent structure of any problem solving task can be revealed by decomposing it into elementary organizational and information processing strategies called *generic tasks*. Because many heuristic programs accomplish some form of classification, a considerable amount of work has already been done to analyze classification problem solving in this way. The primary generic task associated with classification problem solving is called *hierarchical classification*[12], which for our purposes can be defined as follows:

Given a set of hierarchically organized categories or hypotheses, together with assertions about these hypotheses based on evidence regarding an unknown object, identify the object as a member of one of the categories.

This task statement makes it clear that classification inherently involves selecting from a pre-enumerated set of solutions (e.g. see Fig. 5). The solutions are organized into hierarchies, pointing to the importance of taxonomic knowledge about categories in classification problem solving. Finally, note that the problem solving process essentially involves interpreting the impact of evidence, establishing which hypotheses should be believed and refining the alternatives to get the most specific solution possible.

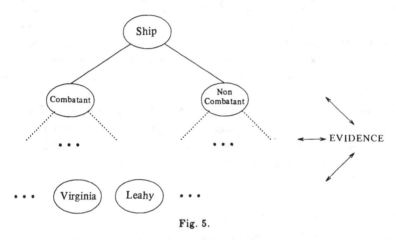

Fig. 5.

In very simple classification problems, heuristic classification is the only generic task required. In most cases, though, the extent to which the data available constitutes evidence for establishing or rejecting a hypothesis cannot be known directly and must be inferred. Two kinds of generic tasks are available to support such inferences. The first is called *data abstraction*. This task accomplishes simple categorical inferences that exploit conceptual relationships in the data such as definitional abstractions, or property inheritance. The need for this kind of reasoning was apparent in the ship classification prototype. For example, the expert wanted to maintain the following two hypotheses about mast height:

The mast heights are equal
The foward mast is higher than the aft mast

The relationship between these two assertions is obvious. Data obtained regarding one of them has clear implications for the other. The required inferences, though, are not classificatory. Trying to accomodate them in a strictly classificatory context, as done in the prototype, leads to awkward implementation-level hacks. This can be avoided by making the proper distinctions at the knowledge level.

When the data available is uncertain, incomplete or only partially matches a hypothesis, the categorical inferences of data abstraction are no longer adequate. The fit between data and hypotheses must then be determined by another generic task called *hypothesis matching*. As the name implies, hypothesis matching is the process of interpreting data as evidence that confirms, rejects or suggests hypotheses. The emphasis is on managing the uncertainty associated with both the data and the knowledge needed to relate it to the hypotheses of interest. Several familiar methods are available for implementing this task: statistical classification algorithms, inference networks, heuristic rules and so on. Since the reasoning associated with this task may be hierarchical, the overall classification process can involve several levels of abstraction, each perhaps having its own reasoning mechanism, all integrated by the primary classification task. From this perspective is it clear that the ship classification prototype only focused on a small portion of the larger problem. It basically implemented hypothesis matching for the small feature details, restricting the hypotheses of interest to those at the Naval Class level.

3.2. Characteristics of the Navy Domain

An analysis of classification problem solving into generic tasks is a major step in designing a system to manage complex classification problems. However, if the system must be concerned with solving only a specific subclass of classification problems, it is also important to examine the characteristics of that subclass. This will help focus the choice of problem solving techniques to those that best fit the constraints of this more restricted problem domain.

Many of the major characteristics of ship classification and related problems have been discussed earlier. The following characteristics are the ones that are most important from the standpoint of their effect on classification problem solving:

Unstructured Environments: There is often little control over or information about the conditions under which the sensor is used. Parameters like aspect angle, scale, scattering properties and so forth may be unknown. This makes it difficult to accurately predict how a hypothesized object should appear in the sensor returns. If its ability to predict is weak, a classification problem solver cannot make good judgements about what evidence will be available or when it will become available. Problem solving strategies must therefore be flexible and opportunistic, capable of suspending work on a hypothesis if the evidence needed to definitively establish or reject it is not available. Control strategies that insist on a rigid establish/refine problem solving sequence[13] are not well suited to handle this situation.

Inherent Ambiguities: For many sensors there is not a one-to-one mapping between manifestations in the sensor domain and features in the object domain. Consequently, patterns of features extracted from the sensor returns might have more than one plausible cause in the object domain. Maintaining consistent beliefs for multiple causes of the same manifestation can be a tricky problem in intercausal reasoning. Many formalisms for uncertain inference either handle this problem awkwardly or cannot handle it at all[14].

Empirical Data: Problems in the Navy domain often come with large amounts of data concerning the structure of objects, how many there are, where they are most frequently found, etc. This data can be used to compute statistical expectations about which manifestations of features and feature combinations will be observed when the object is sensed. Any reasoning mechanism for classification problem solving in this domain should be capable of using this data in some well-understood way.

Limited Resources: Whenever classification is done under operational conditions, resource limitations become a problem. Time and computing capacity may preclude expensive inferences or any information gathering not absolutely necessary to make a decision. Under these circumstances model-driven (or causal) reasoning is crucial for pruning away implausible hypotheses. Moreover, some reasonable theory must be available for converting the beliefs computed by the inference method into cost-effective decisions.

Developing a classification problem solver that meets all of these requirements is a non-trivial task. Our approach to accomplishing this task is to develop a collection of generic software tools to facilitate the construction of such a system. This set of tools will be a "shell" that provides inference procedures, knowledge representation and acquisition facilities, explanation capabilities, etc. all tailored for use in solving these kinds of classification problems. The robustness of this approach will be tested by using the tools to build a knowledge-based system for ship classification using imagery; then, build systems that solve classification problems using sonar data and electromagnetic emissions.

Perhaps the most important issue in classification problem solving is the management of uncertainty. Uncertainty has many potential sources in these problems: sensors are rarely completely accurate or reliable; observations and feature extraction techniques can be flawed; there may be no strong correlations between manifestations and causes; some of the evidence may be contradictory; and so on. The reasoning mechanism will therefore have to perform causal, diagnostic and intercausal inferences in combination. Effective interaction with feature extraction modules will involve decisions about the order to acquire data, the number of image frames to process before making a judgement about some feature, etc. Belief updating therefore must be amenable to a variety of control schemes. Our current research focuses on implementing a generic tool for uncertainty management that satisfies these requirements.

4. MANAGEMENT OF UNCERTAINTY

The PROSPECTOR inference scheme used in the ship classification prototype does not appear to be well suited for the larger problem. Though the method has been used successfully in some applications, it lacks a solid theoretical foundation. The parameters it needs to do belief updating overconstrain the underlying probability distribution, leading to inconsistencies that are more or less ignored[5]. It only provides for data-driven inferences and works best with data driven control strategies. Because of the stringent independence assumptions made in this framework, sets of mutually exclusive and exhaustive multi-valued variables cannot be adequately modeled[15]. Consequently, only true-false propositions were used in the prototype system and the networks only encoded a selected subset of the dependencies among propositions. This meant that the network structure did not correspond very well to the intuitive picture of how the evidence really interacts.

Another concern is that the networks were difficult to maintain. The entire system used 2726 interrelated probabilities, most of which were the conditional probabilities quantifying inferences from manifestations to causes. Probabilities conditioned on manifestations can vary drastically as the relative proportions of the causes change[16]. In the ship classification problem, this meant that every time assumptions about the relative proportions of the Naval Classes were changed, all the probabilities in the system had to be changed. As the domain expert refined the feature descriptions, managing the changes in so many probabilities became extremely difficult. A spreadsheet calculator database was constructed to alleviate some of the computational burden. Nevertheless, this bookkeeping function might become unmanageable in a larger more complex classification problem.

4.1. Alternative Reasoning Schemes

The difficulties encountered using probabilities in the ship classification system are similar to those that have led many AI researchers to seek alternative formalisms for managing uncertainty in knowledge-based systems [e.g. Refs. 17, 18, 19]. Several supposed limitations of probability have been cited as justification for these new approaches: the misleading precision of a single number as a measure of belief, the need for exhaustive data about joint statistics, the need to make unrealistic independence assumptions, etc. If probability is indeed inadequate, what alternatives are available to support the reasoning under uncertainty required in classification problems?

One kind of alternative is to abandon any formal framework for uncertainty management and rely instead on *ad hoc* heuristics. The Radar Target Classifier (RTC)[20] is a successful example of this kind of approach. RTC automatically classifies targets from high-resolution radar images. It uses a model-directed classification strategy that begins with a bottom-up extraction of simple features, followed by repeated cycles in which solutions are hypothesized, features details are predicted, and predictions are tested in the imagery. Final interpretation of an image involves assigning an informal measure of confidence to each hypothesis, indicating how well it explains the evidence found in the image. Confidence is computed under the guidance of simple heuristic rules which merely add to or subtract from the current confidence level. This approach seems to rely heavily on the predictive power of abstract symbolic object models and the inherent redundancy of the radar feature data to make careful assessments of belief unnecessary. The success of RTC is hard to judge because it was tested only with very high resolution imagery, and the test set included several ships that are easy to distinguish from one another. With lower quality imagery, the uncertainty of the evidence increases and the predictive power of the abstract models is diminished. The reasoning needed to classify similar targets under such circumstances will have to account for the tentative nature of the evidence. This is difficult to do reliably without using some well understood computational procedure.

A more systematic approach is taken in the Conceptual Structures Representation Langauge (CSRL)[13,21], which is a programming language for constructing classification problem solvers. The basic premise in this system is that the conditions for applying most uncertainty calculi usually do not hold in practice. Translating expert knowledge into a *normative* calculus therefore becomes a step that unnecessarily introduces uncertainty into the problem solver. The CSRL solution to this problem is to represent uncertainty qualitatively, trying to model as closely as possible the judgements and conceptual structures used by an expert. CSRL hopes to avoid the need for normative methods by using the inherent organization of the problem solving task to make the search for good solutions tractable[21]. There is no experimental evidence, however, that the qualitative uncertainty methods of CSRL are really a better descriptive model of human judgement than numeric methods. Moreover, such an approach only provides decisions about the relative plausibility of solutions. If one has the option not to make any classification decision at all, contingent on whether the most plausible hypothesis is really well established, a strictly qualitative approach is inadequate. Indeed, whenever CSRL has to decide if a hypothesis has been established, the qualitative uncertainty is translated into an *ad hoc* numeric scale of "confidence values". No theory is provided to justify this process or give it a clear semantic interpretation.

Theoretical justifications are provided for an evidential reasoning approach that has been used for image understanding[22,23], multisensor integration[17], and medical diagnosis[24]. These applications use a formal framework for belief maintenance called Dempster-Shafer theory[25] that reduces to a Bayesian model when exhaustive statistics are available; yet, allows consistent inferences to be made even without such complete information. In this theory the belief in a proposition is represented by a subinterval of $[0,1]$. The lower bound of the subinterval designates the total evidential support for the proposition. The upper bound denotes the extent to which the evidence fails to refute the proposition. This representation has the advantage that the amount of evidence for and against a proposition can be readily determined, and the precision of the knowledge about a proposition is directly represented by the size of the subinterval. A shortcoming of this method is that the interval combination scheme, in theory, has an exponential computational complexity. In practice, the method has proven to be computationally tractable but only after carefully organizing computation to take advantage of the structure of the problem[26], or settling for an approximate solution[24]. Another cause for concern is that no effective decision theory is available for this approach.

The certainty-factor calculus[18] is yet another method for uncertain inference that has been applied to hierarchical classification problems [e.g. Ref. 27]. Evidence for and against a proposition is summarized by independently maintained measures of belief and disbelief. In a manner partially based on confirmation theory, these measures are used to determine changes in belief given a new piece of evidence. This method has been used successfully in several applications, but its suitability for the problems of interest here is questionable. Estimates of prior beliefs are not used, a decision that turns out to be equivalent to an assumption of uniform prior beliefs[14]. The intercausal reasoning problem poses severe difficulties for the certainty factor formalism[14]. Finally, the independence assumptions needed to update beliefs in object/class hierarchies[27] do not allow for hypotheses that are mutually exclusive. All of these limitations are significant given the previous discussion about classification problems in the Navy domain.

4.2. Probability Revisited

The fact that the many alternatives for uncertain inference have undesirable or poorly understood properties has led many researchers to re-examine the suitability of probability calculus for knowledge-based systems[14,28,29]. While the debate is far from over, it is clear that many of the common objections to using probability are no longer valid. Coherent probabilistic schemes are now available that avoid the problems associated with earlier attempts to use probability theory. These new approaches make it clear that the difficulties previously encountered were problems associated with particular implementations, not inherent limitations of probability.

Henrion[14] provides a good review of recent ideas about using probability in knowledge-based systems. The following ideas are the ones most relevant to this discussion:

1) The need for exhaustive data about joint statistics can be avoided by using the qualitative structure of the problem. Specifically, the topology of a dependency graph — in which variables directly related are linked together — gives a qualitative representation of the dependencies and conditional dependencies constraining a set of variables. This reduces the task of specifying the complete joint distribution over all variables to a much simpler task of making local quantitative judgements for small clusters of variables. Even though these probability assessments are made locally, their combined effect is guaranteed to be consistent[16]. This use of the inherent qualitative structure of the problem is similar in spirit to the CSRL point of

view, but has the added advantage of a sound theoretical interpretation.

2) A single number representation does not convey the precision of the available knowledge, nor does it indicate the relative amounts of evidence for and against a given belief. However, information about evidential sources of belief and disbelief can be retrieved from the graph structure in a properly constructed probabilistic scheme[28] and there are several ways to derive information about the precision of a probability[29].

3) The problems arising from the kind of unrealistic independence assumptions made in systems like PROSPECTOR can be eliminated by generalizing the notion of propositions to include multivalued variables[5,16]. This change makes the conditional independence assumptions required for a coherent probabilistic approach intuitive and reasonable[30].

Moreover, probability is still the only inference calculus that is closely coupled to a theory of decision making, has well established ways to make use of empirical data, and correctly handles problems in intercausal reasoning[14]. We have therefore determined that a Bayesian approach is the best choice for our classification problems. Furthermore, among the many Bayesian schemes available, the approach championed by Pearl[16,28,31,32] has the required breadth, flexibility and conceptual clarity.

Pearl's framework provides a method for hierarchical probabilistic reasoning in directed, acyclic graphs called *belief networks*. Each node in the network represents a discrete-valued propositional variable[d]. Each link between nodes represents a causal dependence or object-property relationship whose strength is quantified using a matrix of probabilities conditioned on the states of the causal variable. The directionality of the links is from causes to manifestations, each link emanating from a parent node in the graph. It is important to note that numbers used to quantify the links do not have to be probabilities. All that is required is that the matrix entries are correct relative to each other. This is the minimum requirement one can expect for quantifying the relationship between variables, and it must be met by any formalism that attempts to translate evidence from one propositional space to another (e.g Ref. 33).

---

[d]Some capability is also provided to handle continuous variables[34].

The belief updating scheme keeps track of two sources of support for belief at each node: the diagnostic support derived from evidence gathered by descendants of the node and the causal support derived from evidence gathered by parents of the node. Diagnostic support provides the kind of information summarized in a likelihood ratio for binary variables. Causal support is the analogue of *a priori* probability, summarizing the background knowledge lending support to a belief. These two kinds of evidential support are combined to compute the belief at a node with a computation that generalizes the odds/likelihood version of Bayes Rule. Each source of support is summarized by a separate local parameter, which makes it possible to perform diagnostic and causal inferences at the same time. These two local parameters, together with the matrix of numbers quantifying the relationship between the node and its parents, are all that is required to update beliefs. Incoming evidence perturbs one or both of the support parameters for a node. This serves as an activation signal, causing belief at that node to be recomputed and support for neighboring nodes to be revised. The revised support is transmitted to the neighboring nodes, thereby propagating the impact of the evidence. Propagation continues until the network reaches equilibrium. The overall computation assigns a belief to each node that is consistent with probability theory. See Pearl[16] for more details.

4.3. A Bayesian Reasoning Tool

Pearl's approach to uncertain inference has several properties that fit nicely with the requirements for classification problem solving discussed previously:

- Both goal driven and data driven inferences are allowed.

- Updating is done with local asynchronous computations that are independent of the control mechanism that initiates the process.

- The impact of evidence is represented by and computed in terms of likelihood ratios. This makes is possible to clearly specify the level of commitment for a piece of evidence. For example, the same piece of data might confirm some propositions, disconfirm others, and be completely neutral regarding all the rest.

- The computation is amenable to a straightforward implementation in parallel hardware, which makes it attractive for real-time applications.

The belief network updating scheme is directly applicable to the hypothesis matching task. Related mechanisms are available for managing beliefs in object/class hierarchies[31] and for categorical instantiation of variables to help construct explanations[32]. This means that all of the inference needs of the classification problem can potentially be met within a Bayesian context.

We have completed an object-oriented, domain independent implementation of the belief network procedure. It is the inference engine for a Bayesian Reasoning Tool we call BaRT. BaRT is the first of the generic software tools being developed at NCARAI for classification problem solving. When completed it will include a knowledge acquisition interface to facilitate the building, editing and testing of belief networks. It will also have an explanation capability that provides justifications at several levels of detail using meaningful linguistic descriptions. The goal is to provide a state-of-the-art tool for probability that can be used to test the heuristic adequacy[14] of probability for managing beliefs in a large scale problem.

The reasoning capabilities of BaRT have already been tested on the problem formulated for the original classification prototype[3]. Starting with the same feature descriptions, an inference network was constructed for BaRT to reason about plan view images of the 10 Naval Classes. A portion of the network is shown in Fig. 6, which shows the variables required to compute belief about the stern components for all classes at once (cf Fig. 3). Because the nodes can represent multi-valued variables, the evidential interactions among the features can be specified directly in a manner that is intuitively meaningful. The result is a more compact and more easily understood model. This network required only 36 nodes and 35 links, as compared to the 181 nodes and 297 links used in the original version. Since the links in the network point from cause to effect, the conditional probabilities for the links do not depend on the overall proportion of ships of each type. This means that a spreadsheet database is no longer needed to manage changes in the model parameters. When tested on the 52 plan view images, the BaRT version produced results nearly identical to those obtained with the PROSPECTOR version. The correct class was ranked first on exactly the same set of images (39 out of 52). In fact, the two versions assigned slightly different rankings to the correct class on just 4 occasions. Overall, the average rank assigned to the correct class was the same for both systems. This is not too surprising, given that the PROSPECTOR version was supplied with a consistent set of probabilities and the network was really a tree. Under those circumstances, the PROSPECTOR method compiles with the axioms of probability and the weight of diagnostic evidence is properly distributed.

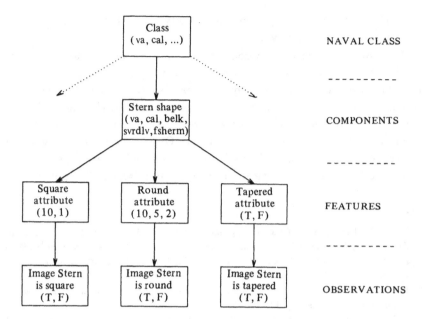

Fig. 6.

5. CONCLUSION

Classification problem solving is a ubiquitous activity in knowledge-based systems[11]. The classification problems found in the unstructured environments of the Navy domain are especially difficult and challenging. These problems involve working with data at several levels of granularity, ranging from raw sensor returns to partially reliable intelligence reports about object identification. Several methodologies are available for transforming this data into evidence useful for classification: signal processing, pattern recognition and feature extraction algorithms, and knowledge-based approaches to feature interpretation. The goal of classification problem solving is to achieve a coherent analysis of sensor returns by selectively applying the methodologies to the data, then choosing the most plausible solution.

Orchestrating this entire process is a complex job. We have used a decomposition of classification problem solving into generic tasks to help manage that complexity. The generic task point of view helps to distinguish between knowledge-level issues and implementation-level issues, thereby making the important research issues easier to identify. It also helps prescribe the architectural requirements for software tools to manage various aspects of the problem solving process.

The application of this approach to a small problem in ship classification has helped us to identify uncertainty management as a key issue in these kinds of problems. Subsequent work led to the development of a domain-independent Bayesian reasoning tool to manage the uncertainty in classification problem solving. Tools for dealing with other aspects of classification are currently under development. One of the important goals of our research is to evaluate whether or not a knowledge-based system built with these tools can be practical and efficient in a large scale application.

References

1. L. B. Booker, "An artificial intelligence (AI) approach to ship classification," in *Intelligent Systems: Their Development and Application, Proc. of 24th Annual Technical Symposium*, Washington D. C. Chapter of the ACM, Gaithersburg, MD, Jun. 1985, pp. 29-35.

2. H. Niemann and Y. T. Chien (eds.), "Knowledge based image analysis," *Pattern Recognition* (special issue), **17** (1984).

3. L. B. Booker and N. Hota, "Probabilistic reasoning about ship images," *Proc. of 2nd AAAI Workshop on Uncertainty in Artificial Intelligence*, Philadelphia, PA, Aug. 1986, pp. 29-36; also to appear in *Uncertainty in Artificial Intelligence*, eds. J. Lemmer and L. Kanal, North-Holland, 1987.

4. R. McLaren and H. Lin, "A knowledge-based approach to ship classification," *Proc. SPIE Conf. on Applications of Artificial Intelligence III*, Orlando, FL, Apr. 1986, pp. 257-267.

5. J. Quinlan, "Inferno: A cautious approach to uncertain inference," *The Computer Journal* **26** (1983) 255-269.

6. R. O. Duda, P. E. Hart and N. J. Nilsson, "Subjective Bayesian methods for rule-based inference systems," Technical Note 124, SRI International, Menlo Park, CA, Jan. 1976.

7. J. Slagle and H. Hamburger, "An expert system for resource allocation problem," *Commun. ACM* **28** (1985) 994-1004.

8. J. Slagle, M. Gaynor and E. Halpern, "An intelligent control strategy for computer consultation," *IEEE Trans. Pattern Analysis and Machine Intelligence* **6** (1984) 129-136.

9. J. A. Barnett, "Some issues of control in expert systems," *IEEE 1982 Proc. of Int. Conf. on Cybernetics and Society*, Seattle, WA, Oct. 1982, pp. 1-5.

10. A, Newell, "The knowledge level," *Artificial Intelligence* **18** (1982) 87-127.

11. W. J. Clancey, "Classification problem solving," *Proc. of 4th National Conf. on Artificial Intelligence*, Austin, TX, Aug. 1984, pp. 49-55.

12. B. Chandrasekaran, "Generic tasks in knowledge-based reasoning: High-level building blocks for expert system design," *IEEE Expert* **1** (1986) 23-30.

13. T. Bylander and S. Mittal, "CSRL: A langauge for classifactory problem solving and uncertainty handling," *The AI Magazine* **7** (1986) 66-77.

14. M. Henrion, "Uncertainty in artificial intelligence: Is probability epistemologically and heuristically adequate?" in *Expert Systems and Expert Judgement*, ed. J. Mumpower, NATO ISI Series, Springer-Verlag, 1987 (in press).

15. R. O. Duda, P. E. Hart, K. Konolige and R. Reboh, "A computed-based consultant for mineral exploration," Final Report, SRI Project 6415, SI Interational, Menlo Park, CA, Sept. 1979.

16. J. Pearl, "Fusion propagation and structuring in belief networks," *Artificial Intelligence* 29 (1986) 241-288.

17. T. Garvey, J. Lowrance and M. Fischler, "An inference technique for integrating knowledge from disparate sources," *Proc. of 7th Int. Joint Conf. on Artificial Intelligence*, Vancouver, B. C., Aug. 1981, pp. 319-325.

18. E. Shortliffe and B. Buchanan, "A model of inexact reasoning in medicine," *Math. Biosciences* 23 (1975) 351-379.

19. L. A. Zadeh, "Fuzzy sets as a basis for a theory of possibility," *Fuzzy Sets and Systems* 1 (1978) 3-28.

20. B. P. McCune and R. J. Drazovich, "Radar with sight and knowledge," *Defense Electronics* 15 (1983) 80-96.

21. B. Chandrasekaran and M. Tanner, "Uncertainty handling in expert systems: Uniform vs task-specific formalisms," *Uncertainty in Artificial Intelligence*, eds. L. Kanal and J. Lemmer, North-Holland, 1986, pp. 35-46.

22. A. Hanson and E. Riseman, "VISIONS: A computer system for interpreting scenes," *Computer Vision Systems*, eds. A. Hanson and E. Riseman, Academic Press, 1978, pp. 303-333.

23. L. Wesley and A. Hanson, "The use of an evidential-based model for representing knowledge and reasoning about images in the VISIONS Systems," *Proc. of IEEE Workshop on Computer Vision: Representation and Control*, Rindge, New Hampshire, Aug. 1982, pp. 14-25.

24. J. Gordon and H. Shortliffe, "A method for managing evidential reasoning in a hierarchical hypothesis space," *Artificial Intelligence* 26 (1985) 323-357.

25. G. Shafer, *A Mathematical Theory of Evidence*, Princeton Univ. Press, 1976.

26. P. Shenoy and G. Shafer, "Propagating belief functions with local computations," *IEEE Expert* 1 (1986) 43-51.

27. J. Kim, "A distributed computational model of plausible classification reasoning," *Proc. of IEEE 2nd Conf. on Artificial Intelligence Applications*, Miami, FL, Dec. 1985, pp. 210-214.

28. J. Pearl, "How to do with probabilities what people say you can't," *Proc. IEEE 2nd Conf. on Artificial Intelligence Applications*, Miami, FL, Dec. 1985, pp. 6-12.

29. D. J. Spiegelhalter, "A statistical view of uncertainty in expert systems," *Artificial Intelligence and Statistics*, ed. W. Gale, Addison-Wesley, 1986, pp. 17-55.

30. J. Kim and J. Pearl, "A computational model for combined causal and diagnostic reasoning in inference systems," *Proc. of 9th Int. Joint Conf. on Artificial Intelligence*, Los Angeles, CA, Aug. 1985, pp. 190-193.

31. J. Pearl, "On evidential reasoning in a hierarchy of hypotheses," *Artificial Intelligence* 28 (1986) 9-15.

32. J. Pearl, "Distributed revision of belief commitment in multi-hypotheses interpretations," *Proc. of 2nd AAAI Workshop on Uncertainty in Artificial Intelligence*, Philadelphia,

PA, Aug. 1986, pp. 201-209.

33. J. Lowrance, T. Garvey and T. Strat, "A framework for evidential-reasoning systems," *Proc. 5th National Conf. on Artificial Intelligence*, Philadelphia, PA, Aug. 1986, pp. 896-903.

34. J. Pearl, "Distributed diagnosis in causal models with continuous variables," Technical Report CSD-860051, Computer Science Dept., Univ. of California, Los Angeles, CA, Dec. 1985.

3

A REGION CORRESPONDENCE APPROACH TO THE RECOVERY OF 3-DIMENSIONAL MOTION AND STRUCTURE IN DYNAMIC SCENES[†]

Seetharaman Gunasekaran and Tzay Y. Young

Department of Electrical Computer Engineering
University of Miami
Coral Gables, FL 33124, USA

Extraction of 3-D motion and structure from a monocular image sequence is considered. The approach is essentially a regional technique and is different from the popular methods that are based on point correspondence. The technique requires that each image in the sequence be first segmented into regions, with each region corresponding to certain visible planar face in the object. The dynamic nature, i.e., the evolution of these shapes are used to extract the 3-D motion parameters, while certain static (*intraframe features*) are utilized to estimate the initial 3-D structure of the object. For orthographic images the shape change is viewed as a linear transformation, while it is nonlinear for the central projection.

A set of methods of computing these shape transformation coefficients are presented. First, a class of iterative methods based on operator formulations are considered. The second approach is based on the moment invariants. A combination of the above two, with reasonably chosen heuristics is also adopted to accelerate the search. In addition, certain mutual constraints among these coefficients are derived, which play the role similar to that of Kanade's results on shape recovery. We present techniques of extracting 3-D orientation and position from three views of one face (region) or from two views of two faces. To emphasize the distinction from the point correspondence approach, we also examine in detail similar regional or contour based approaches that are adopted by others.

[†]This work was supported by the National Science Foundation under Grant DCR85–09737 and by the Florida High Technology and Industry Council under Grant 557A 5594.

1. INTRODUCTION

The recovery of three dimensional (3-D) structure and motion from time varying images has gained increased attention in recent years. Studies on the human visual system have indicated a significant role of motion in the perception process[1,2]. We, humans, are capable of perceiving the 3-D motion of an object from its 2-D image sequence, even the perception of 3-D structure is enhanced by the cue of motion. Kanade[3], Sugihara[4] and Nelson and Young[5], and many others have addressed the problem of 3-D shape recovery from a single image. In this chapter we will be concerned with techniques that extract the 3-D motion, structure and initial orientation information from an image sequence.

We define an image sequence as an ordered set of images, in which each image is a 2-D projection of a more general 3-D scene (space). Differences between any two images drawn from this set could be due to the observer motion, or due to the subject (one or more objects) motion. For example, when the object is in motion we are dealing with a tracking problem. When the observer is in motion we have an instance of stereoscopy.

The goal of motion analysis is to assimilate the 3-D structure, orientation and motion of the objects, from the given image sequence as a whole, which is not available from any single image. The multitude of applications of motion analysis ranges from simple Image Coding to Autonomous Land Vehicles (ALV). Early research in this area was concerned with motion compensated coding and satellite imagery of clouds etc. Also, they were primarily interested in the motion within the image plane, since such simplified 2-D approximations were generally adequate. However, the need for more realistic models concerning the true 3-D motion have become inevitable due to the rapid growth in Robotics, Artificial Intelligence, ALV and such applications.

Investigations on 3-D motion, so far, have progressed in three main directions. Point correspondence methods, optical flow field interpretations and regional approaches have been applied by many authors. We will be concerned mainly with regional techniques. However, for completeness we will briefly introduce the other approaches as well.

In the point correspondence method, the knowledge of a finite number of points located on the surface of a rigid body is assumed to be available. When the rigid body undergoes motion, the images of these points undergo a 2-D displacement in the image plane. The technique essentially involves identifying these points in the given images and comparing their positions in consecutive images. The number of points required and the number of consecutive images required are related, depending on the complexity of the analysis. Roach and Aggarwal[6], considered 5 points in two views to produce a set of 18 nonlinear equations in 18 unknowns. The approach is quite sensitive to noise and to the locations of the points themselves. Mitiche and Aggarwal[7] present the principle of conservation of distance between points on a rigid object for motion analysis. They chose 5 points (of which at least 4 are non coplanar) on the object, and arrived at a set of 10 equations in 10 unknowns. The motion parameters are computed after solving these nonlinear equations.

Tsai and Huang[8] defined a set of eight pure parameters, from which the motion parameters of a planar patch can be recovered. They computed the pure parameters from the spatio-temporal differentials of image intensity[8]. It is shown in Ref. 9 that, given four point correspondence in two images, with no three collinear, the pure parameters can be uniquely computed by a set of linear equations. In both cases the uniqueness of motion parameters is not addressed and in fact it is shown that two solutions exist. Also, the authors have shown in Ref. 10, given four point correspondence in three images, both the pure parameters and the motion parameters are uniquely determined.

Tsai and Huang[11] have also defined a set of eight essential parameters, from which the motion parameters can be uniquely recovered by solving a set of linear equations. They developed a linear algorithm to compute these essential parameters which is applicable for curved surfaces also. In addition, it is shown that eight point correspondence is necessary, for unique estimation from two perspective views. Experimental results[11-12] indicate that the method is quite sensitive to the image resolution. Similar results were developed independently by Longuet-Higgins[13]. He also presented a particular geometrical configuration[14] for which Refs. 11 and 13 failed.

Another popular approach to motion analysis is optical flow[15], which relates spatio-temporal variations in the image planes to the velocity fields. In this approach, the velocity at each pixel is computed by some local operators and thus a velocity field is formed. Often, only a partial computation of local velocity is possible, and some global aggregation process is necessary[15-19]. Many techniques have been proposed to interpret these velocity fields. Adiv[19] employed a more general model, and presented methods of computing the 3-D motion parameters from the optical flow. Mitiche and Aggarwal[6], applied the principle of conservation of distances for the flow field interpretation.

In an effort to utilize regional shape information instead of isolated points, Young and Wang[20] proposed a method based on *region correspondence*. A Rigid Planar Patch (RPP) under motion is considered. It is shown that the shape of its 2-D projection in the image plane undergoes an affine transformation uniquely characterized by the 3-D rotation, orientation and the range of the plane. Given two images of (the 2-D projections) an RPP, Legters and Young[21] discussed an iterative procedure to compute these shape change and 2-D motion parameters, through an operator formulation. In the case of central projection, Wang and Young[22] have shown the significance of quadratic terms to describe the shape changes, which agrees with the Ψ-transformation adopted by Adiv[19] as well.

Young and Gunasekaran[23], adopted the *region correspondence* method for three dimensional tracking, where both the initial orientation and range of the planes were assumed available. The redundant information available within the shape change parameters was noted, but not utilized. Also, the authors have studied the mutual constraints[24] on the shape change parameters and arrived at two methods for extracting the initial orientation of the RPP, from two given images. First, with orthographic projection, a set of constraints in a certain parameter space (actually a scaled gradient space) is developed, which can be transformed into the gradient space, i.e., the (p, q) space. In addition, the concept of *shear ambiguities* due to *skewed symmetry* discussed by Kanade[3] is utilized to solve for the orientation parameters. Also, in the case of central projection it is shown that the motion and orientation parameters can be extracted by solving a set of eight nonlinear equations. However, the translation parameters can be extracted only up to an unknown scale factor.

Kanatani[25,26] highlights the difficulties that are generally associated with the point correspondence methods and the optical flow techniques, and suggests two methods for tracing planar patch motion. The necessary assumption is that the surface is planar, and that there is a closed contour on it. The first method[25] considers the orthographic projection, and it is concerned with pure rotation only. The translation, however, can be computed in x, y directions, while that of the z direction is lost. He defined two feature functions, $f(\theta)$ and $D(\theta)$ associated with a closed contour, and presented methods of numerically computing them from the image. Also, he expressed these functions in terms of certain rotational invariant features C, A_2 and B_2, whose time derivatives are related to the rotation parameters. The method is robust and is reasonably accurate, however, it is only applicable for small rotations, since it involves many approximations.

In addition, the initial orientation of the plane is assumed to be available.

Kanatani[26] presents a method that considers perspective projection, and addresses both rotational and translational motion. Through rigorous analysis, he arrived at a set of 6 linear equations which are exact. The possibility of degeneracy is noted, but not addressed. The formulation is a special case of Amari's theory of invariant feature spaces[27,28]. In addition, he also presented methods to extract the initial conditions, i.e., the orientation of the planar patch itself, from multiple views. Waxman et al.,[29-31] have also proposed methods based on evolution of contours, but they use flow fields, while the framework of analysis in Ref. 26 is entirely different.

Bamieh and De Figueiredo[32] adopted moment invariants, which are invariant under affine transformation of the two dimensional image plane, for 3-D object recognition from a single image. They were interested in estimating the attitude of a rigid planar patch. Given two images of an RPP, it is established that the projection of an RPP transforms in an affine manner when the RPP undergoes rigid motion in space. They were mainly concerned with the determination of attitude, however, their formulations based on moment invariants are related to the techniques we shall present later. Freidberg[33], addressed the need for certain invariants under skew symmetry, and developed analytical constraints on the axis of skewed symmetry based on the second order moments. A salient feature of his work is that of the formation of certain one-dimensional search space.

In this chapter, we shall present a set of techniques available for 3-D motion and orientation parameter extraction by *region correspondence*. For the sake of completeness we will add some important results achieved by the point correspondence approach and the optical flow techniques. However, since it is not our intention to write a survey paper, such addition may not be complete.

2. LITERATURE REVIEW

Several researchers have adopted point correspondence and optical flow approaches for motion analysis. Often, these words involved nonlinear equations with the motion parameters as unknowns. We will be concerned with the linear algorithms due to Tsai and Huang[8-11] and Longuet-Higgins[13,14]. The optical flow field interpretations by Adiv[19], is the first one to consider a fairly complex scene with several moving objects. In addition, as we shall see later, the Ψ transformation developed in Ref. 19 is similar to the nonlinear model adopted in our shape change analysis. Mitiche and Aggarwal[7] applied the principle of conservation of distance which combines both point correspondence and *motion fields*. We will present only the key equations underlying the aforementioned formulations.

2.1. General Point Correspondence Methods and Results

In this section, we review the analysis adopted by Tsai and Huang[11], in which the authors present a linear algorithm for motion parameter extraction. The method involves the computation of a set of essential parameters, from which the motion parameters can be extracted uniquely. A similar approach was also developed by Longuet-Higgins[13,14]. The second algorithm[8-10] employs a set of eight pure parameters from which the motion and orientation parameters can be extracted.

The imaging geometry is sketched in Fig. 1. The image space coordinates are denoted by (x, y) and the camera space coordinates are described by (X, Y, Z). Often $\mathbf{X}$ will be used to specify $(X, Y, Z)^T$ a column vector for convenience and subscript t will be used to specify time. Consider an arbitrary point (X, Y, Z) in space, then from Fig. 1 it follows that,

$$x = F\frac{X}{Z}, \quad y = F\frac{Y}{Z}. \tag{1}$$

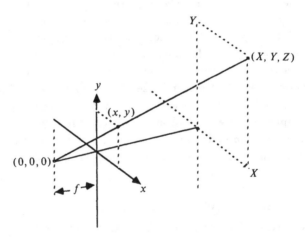

Fig. 1. The basic geometry of a perspective imaging system.

The position of $\mathbf{X}$ after a composite motion can be completely described by an equivalent rotation followed by translation as follows,

$$\mathbf{X}_{t+1} = \mathbf{R}\mathbf{X}_t + \mathbf{T}$$
$$= \begin{bmatrix} r_{11} & r_{12} & r_{13} \\ r_{21} & r_{22} & r_{23} \\ r_{31} & r_{32} & r_{33} \end{bmatrix} \begin{bmatrix} X \\ Y \\ Z \end{bmatrix} + \begin{bmatrix} T_X \\ T_Y \\ T_Z \end{bmatrix}. \tag{2}$$

Then, our aim is to estimate the elements of $\mathbf{R}$ and $\mathbf{T}$ from two given images, $f(x, y; t)$ and $f(x, y; t + 1)$. There are eight different ways[34] of representing the orthonormal rotation matrix $\mathbf{R}$. Irrespective of the choice, it can be shown from basic principles that its intrinsic dimensionality is three. From (1) and (2) it follows that,

$$
\begin{aligned}
x_{t+1} &= \frac{(r_{11}x_t + r_{12}y_t + Fr_{13})Z + FT_X}{(r_{31}x_t + r_{32}y_t + Fr_{33})Z + FT_Z}, \\
y_{t+1} &= \frac{(r_{21}x_t + r_{22}y_t + Fr_{23})Z + FT_Y}{(r_{31}x_t + r_{32}y_t + Fr_{33})Z + FT_Z}.
\end{aligned}
\tag{3}
$$

Therefore,

$$
\begin{aligned}
Z &= \frac{F(T_X - x_{t+1}T_Z)}{-(r_{11}x_t + r_{12}y_t + Fr_{13}) + (r_{31}x_t + r_{32}y_t + Fr_{33})x_{t+1}} \\
&= \frac{F(T_Y - y_{t+1}T_Z)}{-(r_{21}x_t + r_{22}y_t + Fr_{23}) + (r_{31}x_t + r_{32}y_t + Fr_{33})y_{t+1}}.
\end{aligned}
\tag{4}
$$

For simplicity, F is set to be unity. Then, it can be shown from (4) that,

$$
[x_{t+1}, y_{t+1}, 1]
\begin{bmatrix}
0 & -T_Z & T_Y \\
T_X & 0 & -T_X \\
-T_X & T_X & 0
\end{bmatrix}
\begin{bmatrix}
r_{11} & r_{12} & r_{13} \\
r_{21} & r_{22} & r_{23} \\
r_{31} & r_{32} & r_{33}
\end{bmatrix}
\begin{bmatrix}
x_t \\
y_t \\
1
\end{bmatrix}
= 0.
\tag{5}
$$

Then, when (5) is expressed in the form as in (6), leads to the definition of essential parameters $(e_1, e_2, e_3, \ldots, e_9)$ such that,

$$
[\mathbf{x}_{t+1}^T, 1]
\begin{bmatrix}
e_1 & e_2 & e_3 \\
e_4 & e_5 & e_6 \\
e_7 & e_8 & e_9
\end{bmatrix}
(\mathbf{x}_t^T, 1)^T = 0.
\tag{6}
$$

Thus,

$$
\begin{aligned}
x_{t+1}x_t e_1 + x_{t+1}y_t e_2 + x_{t+1}e_3 + y_{t+1}x_t e_4 + y_{t+1}y_t e_5 \\
+ y_{t+1}e_6 + x_t e_7 + y_t e_8 + e_9 = 0.
\end{aligned}
\tag{7}
$$

Then, by choosing eight points in the image plane $(x_t, y_t)_i$ and their respective correspondent points $(x_{t+1}, y_{t+1})_i$, Eq. (7) can be solved for $e_i s$ to within an unknown scale factor. A minimum of eight point correspondence is necessary. When, $\mathbf{T} = 0$, Eq. (7) becomes degenerate, hence not solvable. Longuet-Higgins[13,14] and Haralick[35] present the spatial structure of the candidate points, for which Eqs. (7) become insoluble. The structure is as follows: Consider an environment where the points are chosen from a generalized quadratic surface, and that the camera undergoes motion while the curved surface remains stationary. If the surface under inspection passes through the origin before and after the motion, then Eqs. (7) becomes degenerate. In such instances, if the surface is planar, then the RPP tracking algorithm of Tsai and Huang[8-10] may be considered. If the structure at hand is not a plane, then the nonlinear methods in Refs. 6-8 may be resorted. If both are not possible, then the problem cannot be solved at all. For a detailed study on the extraction of the actual motion parameter from the essential parameters $e_i s$, the reader is referred to Ref. 11.

The rigid planar patch (RPP) tracking algorithms of Tsai and Huang[8-10], will be described below. The imaging geometry is essentially the same as that of Fig. 1 and the basic equations (2) remain the same as well. Since we are concerned with a planar patch, the feature points are chosen such that,

$$\mathbf{g} = (a, b, c)^T \quad \text{and} \quad \mathbf{g}^T \mathbf{X} = 1 . \tag{8}$$

Then,

$$\mathbf{T} = \begin{bmatrix} T_X \\ T_Y \\ T_Z \end{bmatrix} = \mathbf{T}[a, b, c] \begin{bmatrix} X \\ Y \\ Z \end{bmatrix} \tag{9}$$

and

$$\mathbf{X}_{t+1} = \begin{bmatrix} r_{11} + aT_X & r_{12} + bT_X & r_{13} + cT_X \\ r_{21} + aT_Y & r_{22} + bT_Y & r_{23} + cT_Y \\ r_{31} + aT_Z & r_{32} + bT_Z & r_{33} + cT_Z \end{bmatrix} \mathbf{X}_t . \tag{10}$$

Then, from (1) and (10) one can express x_{t+1} and y_{t+1} in a simple form,

$$
\begin{aligned}
x_{t+1} &= \frac{a_1 x_t + a_2 y_t + a_3}{a_7 x_t + a_8 y_t + a_9} , \\
y_{t+1} &= \frac{a_4 x_t + a_5 y_y + a_6}{a_7 x_t + a_8 y_t + a_9}
\end{aligned}
\tag{11}
$$

where, $a_1, a_2, \ldots, a_9$ are expressed in terms of r_{ij}'s, a, b, c, T_X, T_Y and T_Z, and are defined as the pure parameters. Therefore,

$$
\begin{aligned}
a_1 x_t + a_2 y_t + a_3 - a_7 x_{t+1} x_{t+1} - a_8 x_{t+1} y_t - a_9 x_{t+1} &= 0 , \\
a_4 x_t + a_5 y_t + a_6 - a_7 y_{t+1} x_t - a_8 y_{t+1} y_t - a_9 y_{t+1} &= 0 .
\end{aligned}
\tag{12}
$$

It is apparent that, by suitably choosing four corresponding point pairs over two image frames, the linear Eq. (12) can be solved for $a_i s$ (to within an unknown scale factor). Tsai et al.[9] present an elegant method for extracting the motion parameters from A. First, given A, one can find a singular value decomposition such that,

$$A = \begin{bmatrix} a_1 & a_2 & a_3 \\ a_4 & a_5 & a_6 \\ a_7 & a_8 & a_9 \end{bmatrix} = U \begin{bmatrix} \lambda_1 & 0 & 0 \\ 0 & \lambda_2 & 0 \\ 0 & 0 & \lambda_3 \end{bmatrix} V^T \qquad (13)$$

where

$$UU^T = I_3 = VV^T = I_3 \quad \text{and} \quad \lambda_1 \geq \lambda_2 \geq \lambda_3 \geq 0 \ .$$

Then, there are three cases: First, when all the $\lambda_i s$ are distinct, $\mathbf{R}, \mathbf{T}$ and $\mathbf{g}$ are determined from $\lambda_i s$, U and V. However, two solutions exist. The second case: when $\lambda_1 = \lambda_2 \neq \lambda_3$, it is shown that $\mathbf{R}, \mathbf{T}$ and $\mathbf{g}$ can be computed uniquely. Finally, when $\lambda_1 = \lambda_2 = \lambda_3$, only $\mathbf{R}$ can be computed uniquely, but $\mathbf{T}$ and $\mathbf{g}$ cannot be computed at all. Also, in Ref. 10 it is proved that, given four point-correspondence over three consecutive image frames, the motion parameters can be computed uniquely.

2.2.   Motion Analysis via Optical Flow Interpretations

Motion analysis based on optical flow techniques consists of two phases: First, an optical flow field i.e., the velocity or displacement field describing the instantaneous velocity at each element, is computed over the image plane. The second stage involves the interpretations of these fields. The basic principle is that, a rigid motion in the 3-D space induces a connected set of flow vectors in the velocity field such that the vectors within a set are consistent in some metric[19]. First, the given flow field is partitioned into several segments, each one satisfying the above criterion. Then these segments are grouped such that each group represents a single 3-D motion. For example, consider a multifaced 3-D object in motion, then for each of its visible faces we have one affine metric governed by the 3-D motion and the orientation parameters. Hence many segments in the flow field corresponding to its visible faces represent the same 3-D motion forming a consistent group of segments. Many such groups indicate the presence of several independently moving objects in the scene. The basic equations are given below: Consider the imaging geometry given in Fig. 2. Let the instantaneous motion (relative to the camera) of an object be decomposed into a rotation $\mathbf{\Omega}$, followed by translation $\mathbf{T}$. It is important to note, that $\mathbf{\Omega}$ is a small rotation-angle approximation of the non-orthonormal rotation of the co-ordinate frame as shown in Fig. 2. Then,

$$X_{t+1} = \mathbf{X}_t + \mathbf{\Omega} \times \mathbf{X}_t + \mathbf{T}$$

$$= \begin{bmatrix} 1 & -\omega_Z & \omega_Y \\ \omega_Z & 1 & -\omega_X \\ -\omega_Y & \omega_X & 1 \end{bmatrix} \begin{bmatrix} X_t \\ Y_t \\ Z_t \end{bmatrix} + \begin{bmatrix} T_X \\ T_Y \\ T_Z \end{bmatrix} . \qquad (14)$$

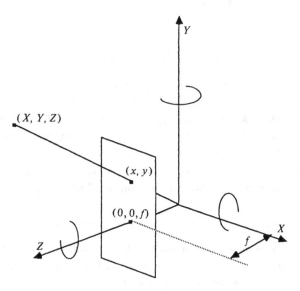

Fig. 2. A central projection imaging system, with the rotational components of the instantaneous velocity being illustrated.

Also,

$$x_t = \frac{X_t}{Z_t}, \quad y_t = \frac{Y_t}{Z_t}, \quad x_{t+1} = \frac{X_{t+1}}{Z_{t+1}} \quad \text{and} \quad y_{t+1} = \frac{Y_{t+1}}{Z_{t+1}} . \qquad (15)$$

Let $(\alpha, \beta)^T = \mathbf{x}_{t+1} - \mathbf{x}_t$, then it can be shown that,

$$\alpha = \frac{(T_X - xT_Z)}{Z} - xy\omega_X + (1 + x^2)\omega_Y - y\omega_Z ,$$

$$\beta = \frac{(T_Y - yT_Z)}{Z} - (1 + y^2)\omega_X + xy\omega_Y + x\omega_Z \qquad (16)$$

when $|\frac{T_Z}{Z}| \ll 1$ and the field of view of the camera is small. When a roughly planar patch in motion is considered, Eq. (15) takes the form of a Ψ transformation that describes the 2-D motion in the image plane by eight parameters $b_1, b_2, \ldots, b_8$, as follows: First, let the planar surface be defined by the equation,

$$k_X X + k_Y Y + k_Z Z = 1 \tag{17}$$

or,

$$\frac{1}{Z} = k_X x + k_Y y + k_Z . \tag{18}$$

Then,

$$\begin{aligned} \alpha &= b_1 + b_2 x + b_3 y + b_7 x^2 + b_8 xy , \\ \beta &= b_4 + b_5 x + b_6 y + b_7 xy + b_8 y^2 \end{aligned} \tag{19}$$

where

$$\begin{aligned} b_1 &= \omega_Y + k_Z T_X , & b_2 &= k_X T_X - k_Z T_Z , \\ b_3 &= -\omega_Z + k_Y T_X , & b_4 &= -\omega_X + k_Z T_Y , \\ b_5 &= -\omega_Z + k_X T_Y , & b_6 &= k_Y T_Y - k_Z T_Z , \\ b_7 &= -\omega_Y - k_X T_Z & b_8 &= -\omega_X - k_Y T_Z . \end{aligned} \tag{20}$$

A multipass segmentation algorithm using Hough Transform technique is developed to combine the flow vectors that are consistent with an affine transformation. Then, the components that are compatible with the same optimal Ψ transform are merged into segments, using a multipass multi resolution search combined with least squared error verification. Those segments that satisfy the same 3-D motion are grouped to represent a rigid object. Many groups of segments, each group representing a 3-D rigid object, are derived from the scene to determine the structure of the scene. The ambiguities due to noisy flow fields are noted to be inherent and its effect on the final interpretations is significant.

In a recent paper Mitiche and Aggarwal[7] applied the principle of conservation of distance to optical flow field. In particular, this approach blends both point correspondence and optical flow. Consider the imaging geometry given in Fig. 2 and let $\mathbf{P}_1$ and $\mathbf{P}_2$ be two arbitrary points located on a rigid object in motion. Then, the principle states that,

$$\frac{d}{dt}\|\mathbf{P}_1 - \mathbf{P}_2\| = 0 .$$

Assuming a stationary viewing system, the instantaneous velocity of a point in motion is given by

$$\mathbf{P}' = \mathbf{T} + \mathbf{\Omega} \times \mathbf{P} .$$

Let (u_i, v_i) be the instantaneous velocity (or displacement) measured at the point (x_i, y_i) in the image plane. Then, it can be shown that,

$$
(a - dx_1\omega_Y + dy_1\omega_X)Z_1^2 + (c - e(x_1 + x_2)\omega_Y + e(y_1 + y_2)\omega_X)Z_1Z_2
$$
$$
+ (b - fx_2\omega_Y + fy_2\omega_X)Z_2^2 + (d + e)T_Z Z_1 + (f + 3)T_Z Z_2 = 0
$$
$$(21)$$

where,

$$
\begin{aligned}
a &= -u_1 x_1 - v_1 y_1 \ , \\
b &= -u_2 x_2 - v_2 y_2 \ , \\
c &= u_1 x_2 + v_1 y_2 + u_2 x_1 + v_2 y_1 \ , \\
d &= -x_1^2 - y_1^2 - 1 \ , \\
e &= x_1 x_2 + y_1 y_2 + 1 \ , \\
f &= -x_2^2 - y_2^2 - 1 \ .
\end{aligned}
\qquad (22)
$$

Then, given a set of four point correspondence, or given the optical flow at four points in the image plane, we can solve Eq. (21) for $\mathbf{T}$ and $\mathbf{\Omega}$.

3. REGIONAL APPROACHES TO MOTION ANALYSIS

There are several reasons to expect, that motion analysis, based on *region correspondence*, could be more accurate and robust than the foregoing methods. Establishing point correspondence in the images, in general, is a difficult task and it is more susceptible to noise. In addition, the location and separation of these points influence the computational error in the overall system[11], and some kind of averaging over a large number of points is necessary. Also, the computation of optical flow has certain difficulties when smooth surfaces are encountered, and requires iterative techniques to form the consistent velocity field, which is more susceptible to local noise. On the other hand, identifying a region correspondence is relatively easier and is more accurate. The inherent integration involved in forming the regions from a collection of pixels makes it less sensitive to noise and other causes of inaccuracy. The physical meaning of shape changes of a region is much clearer than that of the changes in position of a few isolated points. Studies on human visual systems indicate that humans can perceive the shape and orientation of an object from the shapes of its visible faces. Nonetheless, the performance of the region correspondence method depends on the accuracy of the segmentation process, and is also limited to objects with at least one visible planar face.

3.1. Motion and Regional Shape Changes

As stated earlier the main theme of this chapter is to perform motion analysis from the regional shape changes. It is assumed that the object of interest has been segmented and the background has been set to zero. Then, Young and Wang[20] introduced the basic relationship between the 2-D shape changes of the segmented face and the 3-D *object centered* rotation that induces the change. It is suggested that the algorithms for 2-D translation and rotation developed by Schalkoff and McVey[36] and Legters and Young[21], among others can be generalized and applied to estimate the linear shape change parameters.

Consider a point $\mathbf{X}_t = (X, Y, Z)$ that is projected onto (x, y) in the image plane by an orthographic projection. Let the image of this point after motion i.e., $\mathbf{X}_{t+1}$ be (x', y'). Then, it is understood that an affine transformation can be established such that,

$$\begin{bmatrix} x' \\ y' \end{bmatrix} = \mathbf{A} \begin{bmatrix} x \\ y \end{bmatrix} + \mathbf{C} \tag{23}$$

where, $\mathbf{A}$ can be decomposed into a sequence of 2-D rotation, 2-D angular deformation and a 2-D dilation in the form:

$$
\begin{aligned}
\mathbf{A} &= \mathbf{A}_S \mathbf{A}_A \mathbf{A}_R \\
&= \begin{bmatrix} \sigma_x & 0 \\ 0 & \sigma_y \end{bmatrix} \begin{bmatrix} \cos\alpha & \sin\alpha \\ \sin\alpha & \cos\alpha \end{bmatrix} \begin{bmatrix} \cos\theta & -\cos\theta \\ \sin\theta & \cos\theta \end{bmatrix} .
\end{aligned}
\tag{24}
$$

Let the planar face of interest be defined by,

$$Z = -pX - qY - s \tag{25}$$

and the 3-D motion (pure rotation only) of the form,

$$\begin{bmatrix} X' \\ Y' \\ Z' \end{bmatrix} \begin{bmatrix} r_{11} & r_{12} & r_{13} \\ r_{21} & r_{22} & r_{23} \\ r_{31} & r_{32} & r_{33} \end{bmatrix} \begin{bmatrix} X \\ Y \\ Z \end{bmatrix} . \tag{26}$$

In addition, since we are concerned with orthographic projection, we have $(x, y) = (X, Y)$. Then it can be shown that,

$$\begin{bmatrix} x' \\ y' \end{bmatrix} = \begin{bmatrix} r_{11} - pr_{13} & r_{12} - qr_{13} \\ r_{21} - pr_{23} & r_{22} - qr_{23} \end{bmatrix} \begin{bmatrix} x \\ y \end{bmatrix} + \begin{bmatrix} -sr_{13} \\ -sr_{23} \end{bmatrix} . \tag{27}$$

By using the methods that we will present later in this chapter, the elements of $\mathbf{A}$ and $\mathbf{C}$ can be computed from two images that have been segmented already. Then from these shape change parameters $\mathbf{A}$ and $\mathbf{C}$ we can recover the $\mathbf{R}$ matrix partially as follows:

$$r_{11} = a_{11} - \frac{p}{s}c_1 , \quad r_{21} = a_{21} - \frac{p}{s}c_2 ,$$

$$r_{12} = a_{12} - \frac{q}{s}c_1 , \quad r_{22} = a_{22} - \frac{q}{s}c_2 ,$$

$$r_{13} = -\frac{c_1}{s} , \qquad r_{23} = -\frac{c_2}{s} . \tag{28}$$

It is also shown that, assuming the $\mathbf{R}$ matrix as a sequence of Eulerian rotations, the rotation angles can be uniquely extracted as will be shown later.

3.2. Motion Analysis from Regional Features

Kanatani[25,26] highlights the problems that are generally associated with the point correspondence methods and suggests two methods for tracking planar faces in motion. The first method is concerned with orthographic projection and considers rotation and 2-D translation only. The method is robust, reasonably accurate and involves many approximations; also it is applicable for small rotations only. We are particularly interested in his second method[26], since it is exact. Generally speaking, the following formulation is an example of Amari's[28,29] feature spaces that accept transformations in the feature domain. We are interested in tracking the rigid motion of a planar patch. Consider the imaging geometry given in Fig. 3. The perspective projection projects an arbitrary point $\mathbf{X} = (X, Y, Z)$ into $(x, y, 0)$ in the image plane, such that,

$$x = \frac{lX}{l+Z} , \quad y = \frac{lY}{l+Z} . \tag{29}$$

Also, we assume that the plane of interest is defined by,

$$Z = pX + qY + r . \tag{30}$$

It is assumed that the given planar face is available in the form of a closed contour in the image plane. Also, it is required that the values of p, q and r are explicitly known for the first frame. A feature I_k of the contour is defined as line integral along the closed contour C such that,

$$I_k = \oint_C F_k(x, y) ds \tag{31}$$

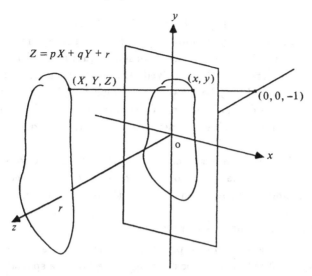

Fig. 3. A generalized perspective imaging geometry. Note, when $l \to \infty$, the system becomes orthographic.

where $ds = \sqrt{dx^2 + dy^2}$ measured along the contour C. Then, by using Stoke's theorem it is established that its time derivative is of the form,

$$\frac{d}{dt}I = C_1 T_X + C_2 T_Y + C_3 T_Z + C_4 \omega_X + C_5 \omega_Y + C_6 \omega_Z \qquad (32)$$

where $C_1, C_2, \ldots, C_6$ are expressed in terms of in $p, q, r, \frac{dF}{dx}, \frac{dF}{dy}, \frac{dx}{ds}$ and $\frac{dy}{ds}$. In particular they are linear in p, q and r. For the exact expressions, the reader is referred to Ref. 26. It is then required to choose six linearly independent functions $F_1(x, y), F_2(x, y), \ldots, F_6(x, y)$ and compute the six feature functions, $I_1, I_2, \ldots, I_6$ over two frames. Also, for each feature function $F_k(x, y)$ the six $C_{kj}s$ are computed as in Ref. 26. Then a set of six linear equations in six unknowns are formed as given in Eq. (33), and can be readily solved by standard methods,

$$[C_{kj}](T_X, T_Y, T_Z, \omega_X, \omega_Y, \omega_Z)^T = (I_1, I_2, \ldots, I_6)^T . \qquad (33)$$

Once the motion parameters are available from Eq. (33), the values of p, q, r can be computed for the second frame to facilitate tracking over the subsequent frames.

From the fact that C_1, C_2 and C_3 are linear in p, q and r, Kanatani suggested a method by which the initial orientation can be extracted from multiple views of the initial static scene. The planar face is assumed to be stationary, and the camera is moved by a known distance in X, Y and Z directions and three new images are recorded. Again a set of 3 linear equations in p, q and r are formed and solved. However, this method requires at least three views, and may be viewed as a region based stereoscopy. As we will show later, the dynamic nature of the scene can be utilized to extract the initial orientation by different methods, which do not require such extra images.

It should be noted that the choice of the feature functions is crucial since a wrong choice may lead to degeneracy in Eq. (33). For example, x, y, x^2, xy, y^2 and x^2y^2 have been chosen as the feature functions in Ref. 26.

3.3. Role of Shape Changes in Perception

We, humans are able to interpret the 3-D structures and the depth informations from 2-D images. It is exciting to see how the spatial structures of the scenes readily lend themselves to our visual perception process. As Gibson[37,38] has eloquently pointed out, humans are mobile creatures exploring the three-dimensional world. At the higher levels of perception, particularly when dynamic environments are considered, what matters is the structure of the entire system and not the nature of its atomic elements. Also, it is remarkable that, at the lower level the peripheral process readily identifies the areas of persistent changes at a rather subconscious manner (see Jain[39]). The cognition phase, however, is guided by the transformational expectations, which is mainly what a particular human *"knows"* by *experience* about the transformational structures induced by physical events. In addition, the cognition phase is capable of steering an inquisitive inspection of the scene (attentive process) in search of additional cues to resolve any ambiguities it encounters (see Ullman[2] and Martin et al.[40]).

In his interesting review on the psychology of perceptual organization, Palmer[41] presents many psychophysical evidences of the role of *shape constancy,* in image understanding. *Shape constancy* refers to the ability of people to perceive two figures as having the same "shape" or "form" even when they differ in orientation, size and sense. An example of the shape constancy is *shear ambiguities* due to *skewed symmetry* that has been thoroughly treated by Kanade[3] for recovering the 3-D shapes from 2-D projections. It is noted in Ref. 41 that shape perception explicitly or implicitly involves the "feature set theories" of pattern recognition.

From the preceding discussion, it is intuitive that motion analysis based on shape changes is somewhat more realistic than the other approaches.

The experimental results on extracting the 3-D shape from static scenes by Kanade[3], Sugihara[4], Nelsson and Young[5], Woodham[42], Banard[43], Lin and Fu[44], Bameih et al.[32] and several others show the evidence of *shape constancy* in some sense. Hence, as we will show later, it is reasonable to expect that shape constancy over many frames should add up to what can be extracted from a static scene.

In essence, we can conclude that among other things, the dynamic nature of the shapes contain more information than static shape constancy, and that it is possible to extract not only the 3-D shape or structure but also the motion parameters as well from an image sequence. Conversely, in the next section we shall present some methods that extract the orientation parameters while attempting to extract the motion parameters. In particular, the theme of the present chapter is to recover motion parameter from 2-D shape changes in a space-time image sequence.

4. MOTION ANALYSIS FROM ORTHOGRAPHIC IMAGES

In this section we present a set of methods to extract the 3-D structure and motion parameters from orthographic image sequences. It was shown earlier, that when an RPP undergoes a 3-D rotation, the induced changes in the shape of its image within the image plane is described by an affine transformation. In the following sequel we present two methods for computing these parameters, from two given images. We assume that the images have been segmented beforehand and that the region correspondence have been established earlier. This nontrivial task is outlined in Sect. 6 and explained in Ref. 24.

To facilitate an easy understanding of the proposed techniques, it is useful to outline the steps involved in the actual implementation. First, the given images $f(x, y; t)$, $t = 1, 2, \ldots, N$ are segmented to form a set of regions $R_1, R_2, \ldots, R_k$. An array $V(x, y; t)$ is created such that $V(x, y; t) = k$, if $(x, y) \in R_k$ at time t. Assume that at least two segments, among others, have been identified to be the images of two distinct RPPs in the scene, in two consecutive image frames, i.e. in $f(x, y; t)$ and $f(x, y; t + 1)$. We shall call one of these faces as *primary face* and the others *secondary faces*. An *object centered* co-ordinate system in 3-D motion is considered such that its origin is located at the center of the *primary face* and its axes remain parallel to the corresponding axes of the camera or absolute co-ordinate system. Then, the 3-D translation of the object with reference to the stationary observer is simply the translation of the origin of the moving frame. In addition, the rotation of the rigid body is readily described by Eulerian angles, with reference to the moving frame. In practice, such models are adopted in astronomy where several independently moving objects are commonplace. The *primary face* is used mainly for the choice of the origin of the moving frame. A *one-point correspondence* can be used as well.

Furthermore, if the absolute position of the origin with reference to the observer system is known, one can completely interpret the 3-D motion. However, due to the inherent nature of the orthographic imaging systems, both the distance between the camera and the object and the z-component of the 3-D translation cannot be recovered from the given images alone. Additional information is necessary.

First, we present two techniques for computing the shape change parameters from two given images. It is assumed that the images have been segmented already, as explained in Sect. 6. The first method is essentially a one-dimensional search in a parameterized space and the second is an iterative technique developed by Legters and Young[21] and adopted in Ref. 24. When the initial orientation of the plane under inspection is available, the motion parameters can be extracted from the shape change parameters directly.

Secondly, three methods for extracting the 3-D orientation parameters of the RPP under inspection are developed. The orthogonality of the rotation matrix **R** will be used to show the underlying mutual constraints between the linear shape change parameters. These relationships are presented in a parameter space, which is in fact a scaled gradient space. The permissible set of solutions is confined to a line segment in that parameter space. When the constraint is transformed into the gradient space it results in a nonlinear curve $\phi(p, q) = 0$, which we shall call as *solution curve*. The solution curve is essentially a specific form of gradient ambiguities, similar to that of the hyperbolic curves derived by Kanade[3] based on *skewed symmetries*. However, in forming this *solution curve*, no explicit assumption is made about the shape of the planar face.

In addition to the above *solution curve*, by suitably choosing one more constraints in the gradient space, the 3-D structures can be extracted. Three such cases are presented as given below: 1) Given three images of two planar faces (segmented), or 2) two images of three planar faces, the 3-D structure and the motion parameters can be found. Finally, 3) when two images of two planar faces are available, with at least one of them having certain skewed symmetry, the 3-D structure and the motion parameters can be extracted. The rotation and the orientation parameters (including the s term) are extracted with reference to a conveniently chosen *object centered* co-ordinate system. It is to be noted that the absolute measure of the s term in the 3-D orientation cannot be extracted due to the intrinsic nature of orthographic projection.

4.1. Linear Shape Change Parameter Estimation

Affine transformations have many interesting implications to shape changes and *shape constancy*. For instance, rectangles and parallelograms are transformed into parallelograms. Similarly, circles and ellipses transform into ellipses, triangles into triangles and conic sections into conic sections of the same type. Clearly, it can be shown that the centroids of the shapes at two given instants correspond to each other and that the vector c in Eq. (23) represents the linear displacement between these centroids. Also, it is observed that the shape change is fully described by the information contained in the matrix $\mathbf{A}$.

From the physical interpretation of 2-D shape changes, it is easy to show that $\mathbf{A}$ can be decomposed into a rotation, angular deformation and a linear dilation all in that order, as in Eq. (24). Basically, the estimation of $\mathbf{A}$ involves finding four unknowns.

Let $f(x, y; t)$ be the segmented image of the scene at time t. Let S_t be a connected set of points such that $\forall (x, y) \in S_t$ corresponds to the image of the RPP under inspection. Also, since the image has been segmented already one can represent a segment by an associated binary image, $s(\mathbf{x}; t)$ defined as follows:

$$s(x, y; t) = \begin{cases} 1 & \text{if } \mathbf{x} \in S_t \\ 0 & \text{otherwise .} \end{cases}$$

Such binary representations are of two fold: First, it simplifies further computations. Secondly, the shapes are well emphasized by binary representations.

There are basically two approaches to the estimation of the shape change parameters. In the first method, we start with a particular value of the forward transformation i.e., $(\widehat{\mathbf{A}}, \widehat{c})$, hence express the shape of the segment at time t, in terms of its shape at time $t + 1$ in a functional form. Then, a suitably devised correction mechanism is applied to reduce the deviations between the starting values of $(\widehat{\mathbf{A}}, \widehat{c})$ and the actual values of the underlying forward transformation. The method is essentially a time-reversal technique, since it basically analyzes the shape changes from $t + 1$-th image to the t-th image. The second approach follows the fact that the shape change can be interpreted as the co-ordinate system undergoing an inverse transformation. In contrast to the time reversal paradigm, one can start with a particular value of the inverse transformation of the coordinate system and express the shape at time $t + 1$ in terms of the shape at time t. Clearly, a suitable correction is to be applied to the starting value, repeatedly until the resolved shape at time $t + 1$ agrees with the actual shape at time $t + 1$.

Then, it is clear that the time reversal process seeks the value of $\mathbf{A} = \widehat{\mathbf{A}}$ and $\mathbf{c} = \widehat{\mathbf{c}}$ that minimize the mean squared error, $\varepsilon^2(\widehat{\mathbf{A}}, \widehat{\mathbf{c}})$, defined below:

$$\varepsilon^2(\widehat{\mathbf{A}}, \widehat{\mathbf{c}}) = \int \|s(\mathbf{x}; t) - \widehat{s}(\mathbf{x}; t)\|^2 d\mathbf{x} \tag{34a}$$

where,

$$\widehat{s}(\mathbf{x}; t) = s(\widehat{\mathbf{A}}\mathbf{x} + \widehat{\mathbf{c}}; t + 1) \ . \tag{34b}$$

In a similar manner, the operator formulation method seeks the value of $\widehat{\phi}^{-1}(\mathbf{x})$ for which the mean squared error defined below is minimized. The mean squared error $\widehat{\phi}^{-1}(\mathbf{x})$ is defined as follows:

$$\varepsilon^2(\widehat{\phi}^{-1}(\mathbf{x})) = \int \|s(\mathbf{x}; t + 1) - \widehat{s}(\mathbf{x}; t + 1)\|^2 d\mathbf{x} \tag{35a}$$

where,

$$\widehat{s}(\mathbf{x}; t + 1) = s(\widehat{\mathbf{A}}^{-1}(\mathbf{x} - \widehat{\mathbf{c}}); t) \ . \tag{35b}$$

Consider the time reversal technique. In general, due to the finite sampling of the images and due to any of the errors introduced in the segmentation process, the integral in Eq. (34a) may not be zero. In practice, we shall be concerned with minimizing the nonzero mean squared error ε^2, defined in Eq. (36) below:

$$\varepsilon^2 = \sum_{\mathbf{x}} \|s(\mathbf{x}; t) - \widehat{s}(\mathbf{x}; t)\|^2 \ . \tag{36}$$

For a given $\mathbf{x}_t$ the computed $\widehat{\mathbf{x}}_{t+1}$ may not necessarily fall on to a point on the sampling grid. Therefore a simple bilinear interpolation is adopted to evaluate $s(\widehat{\mathbf{A}}\mathbf{x} + \widehat{\mathbf{c}}; t + 1)$. Accordingly, the function $\widehat{s}$ is preferred to be left continuous than thresholded to binary values.

4.2.   Reduced-Space One-Dimensional Search

In this section we present a method based on moments, that will be used to extract the elements of the $\mathbf{A}$ matrix. First, $\mathbf{c}$ is computed readily from the difference between the centroids of the shapes under examination.

For convenience, we choose to solve the problem based on central moments. Let μ_t be the centroid of S_t and μ_{t+1} be the centroid of S_{t+1}. Then,

$$\mathbf{c} = \mu_{t+1} - \mu_t . \tag{37}$$

Let the central moments of the patches be computed as follows:

$$
\begin{aligned}
\mathbf{M} &= E\big[(\mathbf{x} - \mu_t)(\mathbf{x} - \mu_t)^T\big] , & x \in S_t , \\
\mathbf{N} &= E\big[(\mathbf{x} - \mu_{t+1}(\mathbf{x} - \mu_{t+1})^T\big] , & x \in S_{t+1} .
\end{aligned}
\tag{38}
$$

It is easily shown that,

$$N = \mathbf{A}\mathbf{M}\mathbf{A}^T \tag{39a}$$

and

$$n_{ij} = \sum_{k=1}^{2} \sum_{l=1}^{2} a_{ik} a_{jl} m_{kl} . \tag{39b}$$

We observe that Eq. (39) represents 3 nonlinear equations in four unknowns $a_{ij}s$ and that it cannot be solved directly. One way of solving Eq. (39) for $a_{ij}s$ is to parametrize the elements of the matrix $\mathbf{A}$, based on one variable and conduct a systematic search for an optimal $\mathbf{A}$ that results in the least mean squared error. An element of $\mathbf{A}$ or some suitably chosen indirect variable can be used for that purpose. In general, $\mathbf{M}$ is not necessarily a diagonal matrix. However, since $\mathbf{M}$ is an auto covariance matrix, it can be decomposed into a form $\mathbf{U}\mathbf{A}\mathbf{U}^{-1}$. In addition, the properties of $\mathbf{M}$ require that $\mathbf{U}$ be orthonormal, i.e., $\mathbf{U}^{-1} = \mathbf{U}^T$. Therefore,

$$\mathbf{N} = \mathbf{A}\mathbf{U}\mathbf{A}\mathbf{U}^T A^T = \mathbf{B}\mathbf{A}\mathbf{B}^T \tag{40}$$

$$\mathbf{A} = \mathbf{B}\mathbf{U}^T . \tag{41}$$

Also, for convenience $\mathbf{B}$ is represented as in Eq. (42) below,

$$
\mathbf{B} = \begin{bmatrix} b_{11} & b_{12} \\ b_{21} & b_{22} \end{bmatrix} = \begin{bmatrix} \sigma_1 \cos \alpha & \sigma_1 \sin \alpha \\ \sigma_2 \sin \beta & \sigma_2 \cos \beta \end{bmatrix}
\tag{42}
$$

where

$$
\begin{aligned}
\sigma_1 &= \sqrt{b_{11}^2 + b_{12}^2}, & \alpha &= \tan^{-1}(b_{12}, b_{11}) , & -\pi \geq \alpha \geq \pi , \\
\sigma_2 &= \sqrt{b_{21}^2 + b_{22}^2}, & \beta &= \tan^{-1}(b_{21}, b_{22}) , & -\pi \geq \beta \geq \pi .
\end{aligned}
$$

Then, with further simplifications, we arrive at Eq. (43) which can be readily implemented to compute $\mathbf{B}$ as a function of α.

$$(\lambda_1 \cos^2 \alpha + \lambda_2 \sin^2 \alpha)\sigma_1^2 = n_{11} ,$$
$$(\lambda_2 \sin^2 \beta + \lambda_2 \cos^2 \beta)\sigma_2^2 = n_{22} , \qquad (43)$$
$$(\lambda_2 \cos \alpha \sin \beta + \lambda_2 \sin \alpha \cos \beta)\sigma_1\sigma_2 = n_{12} .$$

Thus, for a given value of α, $\mathbf{A}$ can be computed from Eqs. (40)–(43) followed by a mean squared error evaluation. Then, the search technique essentially involves computing the mean squared error $\varepsilon^2(\alpha)$, over the entire range of α and selecting the one that corresponds to the least mean squared error.

Another way of solving Eq. (39) is to suitably adopt the constraint Eq. (53) to be derived later, relating the elements of $\mathbf{A}$ matrix and $\mathbf{c}$ vector. Then one has four nonlinear equations in four unknowns which can be solved by standard methods. The mean squared error measure may be used to select the desired roots among the multiple solutions obtained from such methods.

4.3.   Iterative Estimation of $(\mathbf{A}, \mathbf{c})$ via an Operator Formulation

The operator formulation developed by Legters and Young[21] has been adopted by the authors[24] for iterative computation of the linear shape change parameters. The shape change of the face is viewed as the co-ordinate system undergoing an inverse transformation. For example, consider a 2-D shape undergoing a simple 2-D translation in a certain direction (parallel to the image plane), then it is equivalent to the co-ordinate system of the image plane moving in the opposite direction. In a similar manner, the shape of a patch at time $t+1$ can be expressed in terms of its functional form at t, as follows:

$$S(\mathbf{x}; t+1) = L(t)S(\mathbf{x}; t) \qquad (44)$$

where, $L(t)$ is an operator describing the evolution of the shape in time. Then, from Eq. (23) we see that,

$$S(\mathbf{x}; t+1) = S(\mathbf{A}^{-1}(\mathbf{x} - \mathbf{c}; t))$$
$$= (\mathbf{B}, \mathbf{d})S(\mathbf{x}; t) \qquad (45)$$

where

$$\mathbf{B} = \mathbf{A}^{-1} - \mathbf{I}_2 \quad \text{and} \quad \mathbf{d} = \mathbf{A}^{-1}\mathbf{c} \qquad (46)$$

and

$$L(\mathbf{B}, d) = \exp^{[(B\boldsymbol{x}-d)^T \nabla]} . \qquad (47)$$

Without the loss of generality, it is assumed that $c = 0$, hence $d = 0$. Then, the iterative algorithm developed in Ref. 24 seeks the value of $\widehat{\mathbf{B}}$ which results in the least mean squared error defined by:

$$\varepsilon(\widehat{\mathbf{B}}) = \sum_x [\widehat{S}(\mathbf{x}; t+1) - S(\mathbf{x}; t+1)0^2$$

where

$$\widehat{S}(\mathbf{x}; t+1) = L(\widehat{\mathbf{B}})S(\mathbf{x}; t) . \qquad (48)$$

The algorithm begins with a suitably estimated value of $\mathbf{B} = \widehat{\mathbf{B}}_0$ and evaluates

$$\frac{\partial}{\partial \widehat{\mathbf{B}}} \widehat{S}(\mathbf{x}; t+1) = \nabla \widehat{S}(\mathbf{x}; t+1)\mathbf{x}^T , \qquad (49)$$

and iteratively refines $\widehat{\mathbf{B}}_k$ such that,

$$\widehat{\mathbf{B}}_{k+1} = \widehat{\mathbf{B}}_k - \rho_k \frac{\partial}{\partial \widehat{\mathbf{B}}_k} \varepsilon(\widehat{\mathbf{B}}_k) . \qquad (50)$$

Since the algorithm is a gradient based scheme, the convergence is not assured. Also, the method may be sensitive to the initial estimate, i.e., the starting value of $\mathbf{B}_0$.

4.4. Gradient Ambiguities: A Mutual Constraint in $(\mathbf{A}, \mathbf{c})$

From the orthogonal property of the rotation matrix $\mathbf{R}$, we shall develop certain auxiliary equations constraining p, q, s, a_{ij}'s and c_k's as follows: Consider the basic equation (28). Since $\mathbf{R}$ is an orthogonal matrix, it follows that,

$$\sum_{k=1}^{3} r_{ik} r_{jk} = \begin{cases} 1 & \text{if } i = j \\ 0 & \text{otherwise} . \end{cases} \qquad (51)$$

Then, Eq. (28) can further be reduced to show that,

$$\begin{aligned}
\left(\frac{p}{s} - \frac{a_{11}}{c_1}\right)^2 + \left(\frac{q}{s} - \frac{a12}{c_1}\right)^2 &= \frac{1}{c_1^2} - \frac{1}{s^2} \\
\left(\frac{p}{s} - \frac{a_{21}}{c_2}\right)^2 + \left(\frac{q}{s} - \frac{a_{22}}{c_2}\right)^2 &= \frac{1}{c_2^2} - \frac{1}{s^2}
\end{aligned} \qquad (52)$$

and

$$\left(\frac{p}{s} - \frac{a_{11}}{c_1}\right)\left(\frac{p}{s} - \frac{a_{21}}{c_2}\right) + \left(\frac{q}{s} - \frac{a_{12}}{c_1}\right)\left(\frac{q}{s} - \frac{a_{22}}{c_2}\right) = -\frac{1}{s^2} . \qquad (53)$$

A simple geometric interpretation of the above equations is possible. Consider a plane, spanned by the scaled gradient space by a factor $\frac{1}{s}$ and call it a parameter space. Note that s is also varying, and not to be thought of as a constant. Then, in the parameter space Eq. (52) represent a pair of intersecting circles, which, in a limiting case touch each other, when $s \to \sqrt{c_1^2 + c_2^2}$. The circles are shown in Fig. 4 for $s = \infty$, which correspond to the circles with the largest possible radii. It can be easily shown that the third equation is linearly dependent, since it defines the line of intersection of the above circles. Also, it can be shown that,

$$\left(\frac{a_{11}}{c_1} - \frac{a_{21}}{c_2}\right)^2 + \left(\frac{a_{12}}{c_1} - \frac{a_{22}}{c_2}\right)^2 = \frac{1}{c_1^2} + \frac{1}{c_2^2} \tag{54}$$

and

$$0 \le \frac{1}{s^2} \le \frac{1}{c_1^2 + c_2^2} . \tag{55}$$

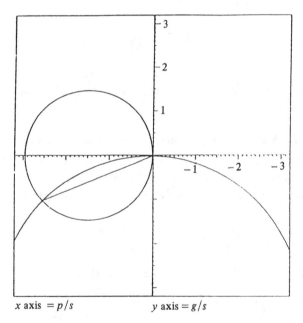

x axis $= p/s$ y axis $= g/s$

Fig. 4. A pair of intersecting circles defined by Eq. (52) illustrated in the $\left(\frac{p}{s}, \frac{q}{s}\right)$ space. Also, the results from experiment 6.2.1.

For a given value of $\frac{1}{s}$ within the permissible range, the value of $\frac{p}{s}$ and $\frac{q}{s}$ can be readily computed, hence (p, q). In addition, it can be proved[24] that the permissible range of s corresponds to the points located on the common chord of the two largest circles in the parameter space, defined by a straight line given below:

$$\frac{p}{s}\left(\frac{a_{11}}{c_1} - \frac{a_{21}}{c_2}\right) + \frac{q}{s}\left(\frac{a_{12}}{c_1} - \frac{a_{22}}{c_2}\right) = \frac{a_{11}^2 + a_{12}^2 - 1}{c_1^2} - \frac{a_{11}a_{21} + a_{12}a_{22}}{c_1 c_2}.$$

(56)

A practical way is to sample this straight line very densely and to compute s at each sample point, hence p and q.

The solution curve developed above is nonlinear, and a closed form expression would be extremely useful. It has interesting applications as that of Kanade's[3] results based on skewed symmetry. Also, it is important to note that the gradient ambiguities are constrained from dynamic shape change parameters only and no assumptions are made on the shape of the object. In the following sections, we present few methods that take advantage of the *solution curve* in the gradient space or the *constrained line segment* in the parameter space, to extract the 3-D orientation parameters of the given plane(s).

4.5. Two Region Correspondence from Three Images

In this section we will be concerned with extraction of (p, q, s) from three time sequential images of a rigid body in motion. It is assumed that the images have been segmented beforehand and that at least two-region correspondence have been identified. The *primary face* is used mainly for the choice of the origin of the moving frame. A *one-point correspondence* can be used as well. Given $F(\mathbf{x}; t-1), F(\mathbf{x}, t)$ and $F(\mathbf{x}; t+1)$, for brevity we will represent them as F_{-1}, F_0 and F_1. We take a point of view of time inverse motion, which takes an object from its final position $\mathbf{F}_0$ to its initial position $\mathbf{F}_{-1}$ marching backward in time. It is readily seen that such motion can also be represented by a unique rotation matrix $\widetilde{\mathbf{R}}$ followed by a translation $\widetilde{\mathbf{T}}$. Also, it is to be noted that the "*initial orientation*" is the same for both these motions i.e., $M^+(\mathbf{R}, \mathbf{T}) : F_0 \rightarrow \mathbf{F}_1$ and $M^-(\widetilde{\mathbf{R}}, \widetilde{\mathbf{T}}) : \mathbf{F}_{-1} \leftarrow \mathbf{F}_0$. Let $(\mathbf{A}, \mathbf{c})$ and $(\mathbf{B}, \mathbf{d})$ describe the shape changes induced by M^+ and M^- respectively. Then in the parametric space $\left(\frac{p}{s}, \frac{q}{s}\right)$, the following four equations will hold.

$$\left(\frac{p}{s} - \frac{a_{11}}{c_1}\right)^2 + \left(\frac{q}{s} - \frac{a_{12}}{c_1}\right)^2 = \frac{1}{c_1^2} - \frac{1}{s^2},$$

$$\left(\frac{p}{s} - \frac{a_{21}}{c_2}\right)^2 + \left(\frac{q}{s} - \frac{a_{22}}{c_2}\right)^2 = \frac{1}{c_2^2} - \frac{1}{s^2},$$

$$\left(\frac{p}{s} - \frac{b_{11}}{d_1}\right)^2 + \left(\frac{q}{s} - \frac{b_{12}}{d_1}\right)^2 = \frac{1}{d_1^2} - \frac{1}{s^2},$$

$$\left(\frac{p}{s} - \frac{b_{21}}{d_2}\right)^2 + \left(\frac{q}{s} - \frac{b_{22}}{d_2}\right)^2 = \frac{1}{d_2^2} - \frac{1}{s^2}.$$

The first two of the four and the remaining two form a set of two intersecting circles, whose common chords, individually represent loci of solution points. The point of intersection of these two common chords is found by solving the above four into two straight lines.

$$\frac{p}{s}\left(\frac{a_{11}}{c_1} - \frac{a_{21}}{c_2}\right) + \frac{q}{s}\left(\frac{a_{12}}{c_1} - \frac{a_{22}}{c_2}\right) = \frac{a_{11}^2 + a_{12}^2 - 1}{c_1^2} - \frac{a_{11}a_{21} + a_{12}a_{22}}{c_1 c_2},$$

$$\frac{p}{s}\left(\frac{b_{11}}{d_1} - \frac{b_{21}}{d_2}\right) + \frac{q}{s}\left(\frac{b_{12}}{d_1} - \frac{b_{22}}{d_2}\right) = \frac{b_{11}^2 + b_{12}^2 - 1}{d_1^2} - \frac{b_{11}b_{21} + b_{12}b_{22}}{d_1 d_2}.$$

$$(57)$$

The computation of (p, q, s) is then carried out simply by substituting the intersection point (α, β), in the $(\frac{p}{s}, \frac{q}{s})$ plane, into any of the above four equations.

Some combinations of $\mathbf{R}_1, \mathbf{T}_1, \tilde{\mathbf{R}}$ and $\tilde{\mathbf{T}}$ may cause these lines to be parallel in the $(\frac{p}{s}, \frac{q}{s})$ space.

4.6.   Three Region Correspondence over Two Images

In this subsection we shall be concerned with two views of two faces of a 3-D body in motion. It is assumed that the segmented image represents at least three planar faces present in the object. Since the rotation and translation will be resolved with reference to the centroid of the primary face, the remaining two faces should have the same rigid motion parameters governing their shape deformations. It is assumed that these two faces are adjacent, and that they are not parallel in the 3-D space. The *primary face* is used mainly for the choice of the origin of the moving frame. A *one-point correspondence* can be used as well.

Let (p_1, q_1, s_1) and (p_2, q_2, s_2) represent two planar faces under observation. Let $(\mathbf{A}, \mathbf{c})$ and $(\mathbf{B}, \mathbf{d})$ describe the shape change parameters of these two planes. Then, from Eq. (28) we note that the following equations hold:

$$\frac{s_1}{s_2} = \frac{c_1}{d_1} = \frac{c_2}{d_2} \ . \tag{58}$$

From Eq. (52) it readily follows that,

$$\left(\frac{p_1}{s_1} - \frac{a_{11}}{c_1}\right)^2 + \left(\frac{q_1}{s_1} - \frac{a_{12}}{c_1}\right)^2 = \frac{1}{c_1^2} - \frac{1}{s_1^2} \ ,$$

$$\left(\frac{p_1}{s_1} - \frac{a_{21}}{c_2}\right)^2 + \left(\frac{q_1}{s_1} - \frac{a_{22}}{c_2}\right)^2 = \frac{1}{c_2^2} - \frac{1}{s_1^2} \ ,$$

$$\left(\frac{p_2}{s_2} - \frac{b_{11}}{d_1}\right)^2 + \left(\frac{q_2}{s_2} - \frac{b_{12}}{d_1}\right)^2 = \frac{1}{d_1^2} - \frac{1}{s_2^2} \ , \tag{59}$$

$$\left(\frac{p_2}{s_2} - \frac{b_{21}}{d_2}\right)^2 + \left(\frac{q_2}{s_2} - \frac{b_{22}}{d_2}\right)^2 = \frac{1}{d_2^2} - \frac{1}{s_2^2} \ .$$

Notice that the above equations are written in terms of $\left(\frac{p_1}{s_1}, \frac{q_1}{s_1}\right)$ and $\left(\frac{p_2}{s_2}, \frac{q_2}{s_2}\right)$. Also, from Eq. (56) we see that,

$$\frac{p_1}{s_1}\left(\frac{a_{11}}{c_1} - \frac{a_{21}}{c_2}\right) + \frac{q_1}{s_1}\left(\frac{a_{12}}{c_1} - \frac{a_{22}}{c_2}\right) = \frac{a_{11}^2 + a_{12}^2 - 1}{c_1^2} - \frac{a_{11}a_{21} + a_{12}a_{22}}{c_1 c_2} \ , \tag{60a}$$

$$\frac{p_2}{s_2}\left(\frac{b_{11}}{d_1} - \frac{b_{21}}{d_2}\right) + \frac{q_2}{s_2}\left(\frac{b_{12}}{d_1} - \frac{b_{22}}{d_2}\right) = \frac{b_{11}^2 + b_{12}^2 - 1}{d_1^2} - \frac{b_{11}b_{21} + b_{12}b_{22}}{d_1 d_2} \ . \tag{60b}$$

In contrast to the previous example, the point of intersection of these lines does not necessarily signify the solution. However, such an instance simply indicates a possibility that $\frac{p_1}{q_1} = \frac{p_1}{q_2}$.

Let L_1 be the solution line segment in the parameter space satisfying Eq. (60a), for valid ranges of s_1. Also, let L_2 be the line segment in the parameter space satisfying Eq. (60b) for valid ranges of s_2. For an arbitrary s_1 one can compute the corresponding s_2 from Eq. (58). Then, the points $(\alpha_1, \beta_1) \in L_1$ and $(\alpha_2, \beta_2) \in L_2$ within the parameter space can be readily calculated corresponding to s_1 and s_2 respectively.

A careful inspection of the problem reveals that we need one more constraint to recover the initial orientations of the two planes. It is shown by Kanade[3] that the image of the line of interface between two arbitrary planes in space satisfies the following relationship: let two planes defined by (p_1, q_1, s_1) and (p_2, q_2, s_2) intersect in the 3-D space at a line, whose image in the image plane subtends an angle γ, then it is required that:

$$(p_1 - p_2, q_1 - q_2) \cdot (\cos\gamma, \sin\gamma)^T = 0 \ . \tag{61}$$

Then, a one-dimensional search algorithm, parameterized by s_1 can be devised, to extract the initial orientation of both the planar faces as follows:

Step 1.   Identify the image of the line of interface L_3 between the two secondary faces within the image plane and measure its slope. Let this slope be γ.

Step 2.   Choose an arbitrary value of s_{1_i}, in the valid range and compute the corresponding s_{2_i}.

Step 3.   Compute the corresponding orientation parameters (p, q) in the gradient plane, as explained in the foregoing sections and call them as $\mathbf{p}_{i1}$ and $\mathbf{p}_{i2}$ respectively.

Step 4.   Check if the vector joining $\mathbf{p}_{i1}$ and $\mathbf{p}_{i2}$ is perpendicular to the line L_3. If so, we have arrived at the solution, and exit to step 6, else continue.

Step 5.   If the entire range of s_1 has been exhausted, then exit with failure message, else choose another value of s_1 and go to step 3.

Step 6.   Label the solution values as $\mathbf{p}_{i1}, s_1$ and $\mathbf{p}_{i2}, s_2$ and exit with success message.

An iterative scheme, however, seems to be possible, and is left for further investigation.

4.7.   Two Region Correspondence in Two Images

In practice, most of the vision systems employed for industrial applications deal with objects of certain geometrical regularities (symmetries). In such cases, as stated earlier the skewed symmetry observed in the image enables us to compute the gradient ambiguities, as developed by Kanade[3]. The two axes of skewed symmetry observed in the image are assumed to represent two perpendicular lines in the 3-D space. Let the two axes of skewed symmetry subtend the angles β_1 and β_2 respectively, with the x-axis. Then, Kanade[3] arrives at a hyperbolic equation relating p and q in the (p, q) plane, from the basic equation:

$$\cos(\beta_1 - \beta_2) + (p\cos\beta_1 + q\sin\beta_1)(p\cos\beta_2 + q\sin\beta_2) = 0 \ . \tag{62}$$

Basically, Eq. (62) constrain an infinite number of (p, q) pairs that can result in the same image, similar to our *solution curve*. With β_1, β_2 measured from the image, the 3-D orientation of the given planar face (p, q, s) can be computed by solving Eqs. (62) and (52).

5. MOTION ANALYSIS FROM PERSPECTIVE IMAGES

In this section, we deal with the recovery of 3-D orientation parameters and motion parameters from perspective image sequences. A rigid object in motion consisting of at least one planar face is considered. First, it is shown that as the rigid body undergoes motion, the associated shape changes of its image is described by a nonlinear (quadratic) transformation. The analysis assumes a *viewer coordinate* system with its origin located at the focus of the camera and hence a central projection model of imaging. Given a region correspondence in two perspective images, the iterative algorithm developed by the authors[24] can be applied for estimating the non-linear shape change parameters. Also, we present certain heuristics to improve the initial estimates and the convergence of the iterative algorithm developed in Ref. 24.

When the initial orientation of the RPP is available, the motion parameters can be computed directly from the shape change parameters by solving a set of linear equations. Also, when the 3-D structure is not known, a method developed in Ref. 24 can be applied to estimate the initial orientation, followed by the computation of rotation parameters. The translation terms, however, can be extracted up to an unknown scale factor. The method involves solving a sixth order nonlinear equation and deals with an instance of one-region correspondence over two images. We also present an extension of the above method to provide an elegant graphical result.

Finally, the basic equations governing the recovery of 3-D structures are emphasized in this section and other possibilities are discussed: Given two-region correspondence in two images, or given one-region correspondence in three images, one arrives at a set of 10 nonlinear equations in 9 unknowns. At the time of writing, these methods have not been completed, and the preliminary results indicate that the solution exists. Further investigation is in progress.

5.1. Quadratic Shape Change Analysis

The perspective imaging system shown in Fig. 2 is considered for the analysis. Let (X, Y, Z) represent an arbitrary point in the camera coordinate system, and let (x, y) represent its image in the image plane. With F as the focal length, the central projection equations can be written as follows:

$$x = F\frac{X}{Z}, \quad y = F\frac{Y}{Z}. \tag{63}$$

An arbitrary motion of a rigid body in space can be represented by a rotation followed by translation as follows:

$$X_{t+1} = RX_t + (\mu_x, \mu_y, \mu_z)^T .$$

(64)

Then, it is readily seen that,

$$x_{t+1} = F \frac{r_{11}x_t + r_{12}y_t + r_{13} + F\frac{\mu_x}{Z_t}}{r_{31}x + t + r_{32}y_t + r_{33} + F\frac{\mu_z}{Z_t}} ,$$

$$y_{t+1} = F \frac{r_{21}x_t + r_{22}y_t + r_{23} + F\frac{\mu_x}{Z_t}}{r_{31}x_t + r_{32}y_t + r_{33} + F\frac{\mu_z}{Z_r}} .$$

(65)

In particular, we adopt the small rotation model of **R** that represents the instantaneous angular velocity. It is known that the angular velocity matrix is a skewed symmetric as shown below.

$$R = \begin{bmatrix} 1 & r_{12} & r_{13} \\ r_{21} & 1 & r_{23} \\ r_{31} & r_{32} & 1 \end{bmatrix} , \quad r_{ij} = -r_{ji}, \quad j \neq i .$$

(66)

In order to emphasize the significance of the linear and quadratic terms in describing the shape changes, we defer the suppression of focal length F from the equations. Let the planar face in the rigid body be described by

$$Z = -pX - qY - s .$$

(67)

The 2-D velocity of the image point in the image plane, is given by $x_{t+1} - x_t = (x_{t+1} - x_t, y_{t+1} - y_t)^T$. Consider the x component of the 2-D velocity,

$$x_{t+1} - x_t = \frac{F^2 r_{13} + F r_{12}y_t - r_{31}x_t^2 - r_{32}x_t y_t - \frac{(px_t + qy_t + F)(F\mu_x - \mu_z x_t)}{s}}{F\left[\left(1 + \frac{\mu_z}{Z_t} + \left(\frac{r_{31}x_t + r_{32}y_t}{F}\right)\right)\right]} .$$

(68)

Under certain conditions, where $\left|\frac{\mu_z}{Z_t}\right| \ll 1$ and $\left|\frac{r_{31}x_t + r_{32}y_t}{f}\right| \ll 1$, we can approximate the above expression into the following form:

$$x_{t+1} - x_t = F\left(r_{13} - \frac{\mu_x}{s}\right) + \left(\frac{\mu_z - p\mu_x}{s}\right)x_t + \left(r_{12} - \frac{q\mu_x}{s}\right)y_t$$
$$+ \left(r_{13} + \frac{p\mu_z}{s}\right)\frac{1}{F}x_t^2 + \left(r_{23} + \frac{q\mu_z}{s}\right)\frac{1}{F}x_t y_t$$

(69a)

similarly, one can show that,

$$y_{t+1} - y_t = F\left(r_{23} - \frac{\mu_y}{s}\right) + \left(r_{12} - \frac{p\mu_y}{s}\right)x_t + \left(\frac{\mu_z - q\mu_y}{s}\right)y_t$$
$$+ \left(r_{13} + \frac{p\mu_z}{s}\right)\frac{1}{F}x_t y_t + \left(r_{23} + \frac{q\mu_z}{s}\right)\frac{1}{F}y_1^2 .$$

(69b)

Then, it is readily seen that,

$$\mathbf{x}_{t+1} = \mathbf{x}_t + \mathbf{G}\,\xi_t \tag{70}$$

where ξ is an augmented vector defined such that $\xi^T = (1, x, y, x^2, xy, y^2)$ and $\mathbf{G}$ is a 2×6 matrix whose coefficients are given below:

$$g_{10} = F\Big(r_{13} - \frac{\mu_x}{s}\Big), \qquad g_{20} = F\Big(r_{23} - \frac{\mu_y}{s}\Big),$$

$$g_{11} = \Big(\frac{\mu_z - p\mu_x}{s}\Big) \qquad g_{21} = \Big(r_{21} - \frac{p\mu_y}{s}\Big),$$

$$g_{12} = \Big(r_{12} - \frac{q\mu_x}{s}\Big), \qquad g_{22} = \Big(\frac{\mu_z - q\mu_y}{s}\Big),$$

$$g_{13} = \frac{1}{F}\Big(r_{13} + \frac{p\mu_z}{s}\Big), \qquad g_{23} = 0,$$

$$g_{14} = \frac{1}{F}\Big(r_{23} + \frac{q\mu_z}{s}\Big), \qquad g_{24} = \frac{1}{F}\Big(r_{13} + \frac{p\mu_z}{s}\Big),$$

$$g_{15} = 0, \qquad g_{25} = \frac{1}{F}\Big(r_{23} + \frac{q\mu_z}{s}\Big). \tag{71}$$

Note that there are only eight distinct parameters that describe the nonlinear shape changes of the image of an RPP in motion. The nonlinear shape change matrix is similar to the Ψ-transformation developed by Adiv[19].

If p, q and s are known, then one has a set of eight linear equations in six unknowns. Also, if the initial orientation of the planar face is not available, then one has eight equations in nine unknowns. At this point, it is worthwhile to recall the results on pure parameters defined by Tsai and Huang[8-10]. It is interesting to note that, we have started with a different approach and have arrived at a set of eight indirect parameters to describe the dynamic nature of the image of an RPP in motion. In the following section, we present the iterative procedures to estimate the shape change parameters, when we are given a region correspondence over two images.

5.2. Estimation of the Quadratic Shape Change Parameters G

In the case of affine transformations associated with linear shape changes it was possible to interpret the change in shapes as the co-ordinate system undergoing an inverse transformation. Unlike the linear transformations the nonlinear transformations do not lend themselves to such interpretations, since their inverse transformations, in general are not unique. Therefore, the estimation process essentially follows the time reversal technique,

defined in Sect. 4.1. The method examines the shape changes of the visible
face backwardly from the $(t + 1)$-th image to the t-th image in a tractable
form. Given a particular value of $\mathbf{G}$, say $\widehat{\mathbf{G}}$, the shape of the visible face
at time t is expressed in a functional form as follows:

$$\hat{s}(\mathbf{x}; t) = s(\mathbf{x} + \widehat{\mathbf{G}}\xi; t + 1) \ . \tag{72}$$

Then, our objective is to find the $\widehat{\mathbf{G}}$ such that the mean squared error,

$$\varepsilon^2(\widehat{\mathbf{G}}) = \sum_{\mathbf{x}} \|\hat{s}(\mathbf{x}; t) - s(\mathbf{x}; t)\|^2 \tag{73}$$

is minimized. Then, the iterative algorithm,

$$\widehat{\mathbf{G}}_{k+1} = \widehat{\mathbf{G}}_k - \rho_k \frac{\partial}{\partial \widehat{\mathbf{G}}} \varepsilon^2(\widehat{\mathbf{G}}) \tag{74}$$

seeks the value of $\widehat{\mathbf{G}}$ for which ε^2 is minimum, where

$$\frac{\partial}{\partial \widehat{\mathbf{G}}} \varepsilon^2(\widehat{\mathbf{G}}) = 2 \sum_{\mathbf{x}} [\hat{s}(\mathbf{x}; t) - s(\mathbf{x}; t)][\nabla \hat{s}(\mathbf{x}; t)]\xi^T \ .$$

Generally speaking, it is possible that the algorithm converges into a local
minimum instead of the true minimum. The nature and the existence of
multiple extrema in the objective function are not clearly known. The
experimental results indicate that the iterative method is sensitive to the
initial estimates, i.e., $\widehat{\mathbf{G}}_0$ and that oscillations are inevitable if ρ_k is not
chosen carefully.

5.3. Estimation of the Initial Value $\widehat{\mathbf{G}}_0$

In order to improve the convergence performance, it is desired to have
a good estimate of the initial value $\widehat{\mathbf{G}}_0$ for the iterative procedure. In this
section we suggest a few methods to approximate $\widehat{\mathbf{G}}_0$. The methods to be
described below essentially involve finding the best linear terms first, which
is then followed by a suitable estimation of the quadratic terms i.e., g_{13} and
g_{14}.

The first method relies on the assumption that at larger values of x_t,
the computation of x_{t+1} is mainly dominated by the quadratic terms, i.e.,

$$\max_{x}(x, y) \in S_t \implies \max_{\hat{x}}(\hat{x}, \hat{y}) \in S_{t+1}$$

and similarly,

$$\max_{y}(x, y) \in S_t \implies \max_{\hat{y}}(\hat{x}, \hat{y}) \in S_{t+1} .$$

In a sense the formulation captures the essence of the point correspondence method. It is assumed that $\tilde{G}$ is available, in which the linear terms have been estimated to a reasonable accuracy. First, we find the maximum value of x, say η_t and η_{t+1} contained in S_t and S_{t+1} respectively. Let $\bar{y}_t$ and $\bar{y}_{t+1}$ be their y coordinates. If there are many points with the same η values we take the average of their y values in choosing $\bar{y}$. Then one can approximate that,

$$\eta_t^2 \tilde{g}_{13} + \eta_t \bar{y}_t \tilde{g}_{14} \simeq \eta_{t+1} - \tilde{g}_{10} + \tilde{g}_{11}\eta_t + \tilde{g}_{12}\bar{y}_t .$$

Similarly one can form another linear equation as follows,

$$\bar{x}_t \kappa_t \tilde{g}_{13} + \kappa_t^2 \tilde{g}_{14} \simeq \kappa_{t+1} - \tilde{g}_{20} + \tilde{g}_{21}\bar{x}_t + \tilde{g}_{22}\kappa_t .$$

Then by solving the above expressions for $\tilde{g}_{13}$ and $\tilde{g}_{14}$, we complete the estimation of the initial value G_0, the starting value for the iterative procedure. Other techniques used in establishing point correspondences can be suitably adopted.

The second approach for estimating G_0 is to exploit certain mutual constraints on the elements of the G matrix. It can be shown from Eq. (71) that,

$$
\begin{aligned}
g_{13}F &= \frac{g_{10}}{F} + \frac{g_{11}p(q^2 - 1) - (g_{12} + g_{21})q(p^2 + 1) + g_{22}p(p^2 + 1)}{p^2 + q^2} , \\
g_{14}F &= \frac{g_{20}}{F} + \frac{g_{11}q(q^2 + 1) - (g_{12} + g_{21})p(q^2 + 1) + g_{22}q(p^2 - 1)}{p^2 + q^2} .
\end{aligned}
\tag{75}
$$

If the initial orientation of the RPP i.e., (p, q) is known, one can estimate the quadratic terms from the linear terms of the partially estimated $\tilde{G}$ matrix. It is assumed that the linear terms have been computed to a reasonable accuracy. Once the quadratic terms are estimated, then the iterative estimation algorithm is activated with the suitably initialized $\hat{G}$ matrix. In situations where (p, q) is not known, a large number of candidate points at the vicinity of most likely orientations of that plane in the (p, q) space may be chosen, such that $(p - \hat{p}^2) + (q - \hat{q}^2) \geq \delta^2$, where the radius of search δ is experimentally chosen. Once again the method requires at least a rough estimate of (p, q).

5.4.   Extraction of 3-D Orientation Parameters

In this section we will be concerned with certain methods of extracting the 3-D orientation and the depth information of a rigid, planar-faced object from its perspective image sequence. Unlike the *gradient ambiguity* experienced with the orthographic images explained earlier, an easy interpretation of the underlying relationships is not available at present. The methods to be described follow a set of nonlinear equations developed from Eq. (71).

Consider the basic equations describing the nonlinear shape changes as given in Eq. (71). When one is concerned with tracking, it is assumed that p, q and s are known at time t, and the $\widehat{G}$ matrix has been evaluated as explained in the previous sections. Thus, Eq. (71) represents a set of 8 linear equations in $r_{12}, r_{13}, r_{23}, \mu_1, \mu_2$ and μ_3. Then, one can solve these overdetermined equations by a standard linear least-square techniques and extract the motion parameters.

If p, q and s at time t are not known, we notice that Eq. (71) represents 8 nonlinear equations in 9 unknowns. Through simple manipulations, one can eliminate the r_{ij} terms and arrive at a set of 5 equations in 6 unknowns given below:

$$
\begin{aligned}
p\mu_3 + \mu_1 - h_1 s &= 0, \\
p\mu_1 - \mu_3 + g_{11}s &= 0, \qquad & h_1 &= \left(F g_{13} - \frac{g_{10}}{F} \right), \\
p\mu_2 + q\mu_1 - h_2 s &= 0, \quad \text{where} \quad & h_2 &= -(g_{12} + g_{21}), \qquad (76) \\
q\mu_2 - \mu_3 + g_{22}s &= 0, & h_3 &= \left(F g_{25} - \frac{g_{20}}{F} \right). \\
q\mu_3 + \mu_2 - h_3 s &= 0,
\end{aligned}
$$

Equations (76) play an important role in extracting the 3-D structure of a dynamic scene of rigid objects. With properly chosen conditions, a system of nonlinear equations can be formulated and solved as will be described in the following. Three cases will be considered as follows: 1) One region correspondence in two perspective images, 2) one region correspondence in three consecutive images, and 3) two region correspondence in two consecutive images.

Consider an application where one is provided with a pair of perspective images, with a one region correspondence established beforehand. The situation is essentially the same as in Eqs. (76). In a restricted sense the problem can be thought of as an instance of dynamic stereo. The emphasis is placed on the unknown nature of the relative position between the cameras, or alternatively the motion parameters themselves. We observe in Eq. (76) that s is essentially a scale factor and that the translation parameters can be extracted up to an unknown scale factor. By substituting $\nu_i = \mu_i/s$, $i = 1, \ldots, 3$ we see that,

$$(p^2 + 1)\nu_3 - ph_1 = g_{11} ,$$
$$(q^2 + 1)\nu_3 - qh_3 = g_{22} , \tag{77}$$
$$ph_3 - 2pq\nu_3 + qh_1 = h_2 .$$

By eliminating ν_3 in the above, we can show that,

$$p = \frac{(q^2 + 1)(h_1 q - h_2)}{(h_3 q^2 + 2g_{22} q - h_3)} ,$$

$$\tag{78}$$

$$q = \frac{(p^2 + 1)(h_3 p - h_2)}{(h_1 p^2 + 2g_{11} p - h_1)} .$$

Further reductions of (78) is possible by substituting q in the first equation from the second expression. Such a reduction results in an 8-th degree polynomial equation in p whose roots can be found by standard numerical methods. A closer look at (78) reveals two solutions, $(p = \frac{h_2}{h_3}, q = 0)$ and $(p = 0, q = \frac{h_2}{h_1})$, that are meaningless. After eliminating these two roots by a factorization process, however, we are still left with a sixth degree polynomial equation in p to be solved numerically.

It is expected from the fundamental works of Tsai and Huang[8-10] that there are only one (repeated) or two distinct roots of the sixth order polynomial in p. We note that in arriving at Eq. (76) from Eq. (71), only a set of linear substitutions were made at each step, hence there exists only one set of q, ν_1, ν_2, ν_3 and r_{ij}'s corresponding to each one of the six roots of the polynomial equation in p.

To facilitate an easy understanding of the underlying solutions of Eq. (76) a graphical solution is desired. By substituting $\alpha = \tan^{-1} p$ and $\beta = \tan^{-1} q$ we can rewrite Eq. (76) such that,

$$\alpha = \tan^{-1}\left[\frac{(\tan^2 \beta + 1)(h_1 \tan \beta - h_2)}{h_3 \tan^2 \beta + 2g_{22} \tan \beta - h_3}\right]$$
$$\quad \text{where} \quad -\frac{\pi}{2} \leq \alpha, \beta \leq \frac{\pi}{2} .$$
$$\beta = \tan^{-1}\left[\frac{(\tan^2 \alpha + 1)(h_3 \tan \alpha - h_2)}{h_1 \tan^2 \alpha + 2g_{11} \tan \alpha - h_1}\right]$$

$$\tag{79}$$

It is to be noted that the graphical solution plotted in (α, β)-plane is essentially a different form of gradient ambiguities in which two loci of permissible orientations intersect at the expected solution points. The experimental results indicate that the performance still leaves much to be desired.

There are alternative ways to determine the initial orientations. A recent work by Nelsson and Young[5] indicates that for 3-D objects that are rich in parallel lines, the surface orientations can be determined from single perspective view. If there is only one set of parallel lines, however, a linear constraint equation in p and q can be developed through the vanishing point of the images of the parallel lines. Then the linear constraint in conjunction with Eq. (78) can answer the uniqueness considerations.

Another possibility of extracting the 3-D orientation is to observe two or more visible faces (planar faces) in two or more images and analyze their quadratic shape change parameters. Let us assume that we are given the image with a visible planar face in three consecutive images. The problem is quite similar to what we have seen in Sect. 4.5 with the exception of orthographic projection. For convenience, we represent the three images as $\mathbf{F}_{-1}, \mathbf{F}_0$ and $\mathbf{F}_1$. Let $\mathbf{G}^+ : \mathbf{F}_0 \rightarrow \mathbf{F}_1$ and $\mathbf{G}^- : \mathbf{F}_{-1} \leftarrow \mathbf{F}_0$, describe the shape changes of the visible face in time. Also, let the 3-D translation components of the underlying forward and inverse motion be described by μ_i^+ and μ_i^- respectively. Then one can easily formulate a set of nonlinear equations in $p, q, s, \mu_i^+ s$ and $\mu_i^- s$ such that,

$$
\begin{aligned}
p\mu_3^+ + \mu_1^+ - h_1^+ s &= 0 , & p\mu_3^- + \mu_1^- - h_1^- s &= 0 , \\
p\mu_1^+ - \mu_3^+ + g_{11}^+ s &= 0 , & p\mu_1^- - \mu_3^- + g_{\bar{1}1}^- s &= 0 , \\
p\mu_2^+ + q\mu_1^+ - h_2^+ s &= 0 , & p\mu_2^- + q\mu_1^- - h_2^- s &= 0 , \\
q\mu_2^+ - \mu_3^+ + g_{22}^+ s &= 0 , & q\mu_2^- - \mu_3^- + g_{\bar{2}2}^- s &= 0 , \\
q\mu_3^+ + \mu_2^+ - h_3^+ s &= 0 , & q\mu_3^- + \mu_2^- - h_3^- s &= 0 , & (80)
\end{aligned}
$$

where

$$
\begin{aligned}
h_1^+ &= \left(F g_{13}^+ - \frac{g_{10}^+}{F} \right) & h_1^- &= \left(F g_{13}^- - \frac{g_{10}^-}{F} \right) \\
h_2^+ &= -(g_{12}^+ + g_{21}^+) \quad \text{and} & h_2^- &= -(g_{12}^- + g_{21}^-) \\
h_3^+ &= \left(F g_{25}^+ - \frac{g_{20}^+}{F} \right) & h_3^- &= \left(F g_{25}^- - \frac{g_{20}^-}{F} \right) .
\end{aligned}
$$

We notice that Eq. (79) exhibits 10 nonlinear equations in 9 unknowns and is expected to give a unique physically acceptable solution among others.

Consider the instance where we are given a two region-correspondences in two images. It is assumed that the faces belong to the same rigid object, therefore their individual shape changes are governed by the motion parameters of a single rigid motion. Let $\mathbf{G}^{(1)}$ and $\mathbf{G}^{(2)}$ be the two sets of shape change parameters of the two visible faces under inspection, and let (p_1, q_1, s_1) and (p_2, q_2, s_2) be the orientation parameters. Then, using (76) one can arrive at a set of nonlinear equations in $p_1, q_1, s_1, p_2, q_2, s_2, \mu_1, \mu_2$ and μ_3.

In addition to these equations, three more independent constraints on μ_1, μ_2, μ_3, s_1 and s_2 can be developed. Furthermore, if these two faces are assumed to be adjacent in 3-D space, i.e., if they intersect in space within the field of view, one can develop a quadratic constraint in p and q. Thus, a system of overdetermined non-linear equations in 9 variables can be formulated and solved using any of the standard techniques.

6. EXPERIMENTAL RESULTS

In this section we describe the experimental systems for extracting motion and orientation parameters from image sequences. Two fairly complex scenes of an automobile in motion and two simulated image sequences of a solid rectangle in motion are considered. In order to apply the region correspondence method of motion analysis, each image in the given image sequences has to be segmented individually, followed by a region matching process that identifies the corresponding region pairs. A multistage segmentation system adopted in Ref. 24 is described in Sect. 6.1. The technique is a combination of the region-growing and boundary tracing methods.

Generally speaking, it is easier to establish region correspondence in two segmented images than to establish point correspondence. However, additional information may be required if the individual faces within each image are almost similar to each other. Such an instance is an example of the problems associated with feature selection in the area of pattern recognition. Problems of the same nature are inevitable in point correspondence as well.

A brief description on segmentation will be given in Sect. 6.1, followed in Sect. 6.2 by motion parameter extraction on two nearly real-world images. To demonstrate the moment based methods for shape change extraction two simulated image sequences are considered and dealt with in Sect. 6.3.

6.1. Segmentation

The purpose of image segmentation is to divide the given image into connected subsets of points or pixels, such that each subset (segment) represents a certain entity present in the scene.

In practice, most of the segmentation systems follow either a region-growing method or an edge detection and boundary tracing method. A combination of the above two methods, with suitably chosen data structures can be of much use, as will be explained later. The multi-stage segmentation method adopted by the authors[24] is considered for the current study. The method is divided into four phases:

1. Preprocessing to reduce noise and fine textures in the image data using an edge-preserving, smoothing method.
2. Edge detection and evaluation including non-maxima suppression and relaxation.
3. Boundary formation which connects edge elements to form lines, and a boundary interaction graph.
4. Finally a region adjacency graph formation that facilitates a recursive split and merge operation to refine the initial segmentation obtained from the third stage.

The edge preserving filter described by Prager[48] is applied for the smoothing of the images. Let N_0 be the point at which we are interested in smoothing the image, and define a set S of neighbouring pixels contained in the 3×3 square block centered at N_0. Then select only those N_i's, $i = 0, 1, 2, \ldots, 9$, whose absolute difference with N_0 is less than a previously chosen threshold value T, and replace the value of N_0 by the average of these N_i's. Statistical techniques are available to choose optimal values of T from the spatial statistics of the image. However, its value was chosen experimentally on a trial and error basis.

An edge by definition is a representation of spatial discontinuities in the gray values of the image function. Due to the finite size of the pixels, and the nature of the associated discrete geometry, the edges can be represented by different methods. The connectivity paradox associated with rectangular grids is explained in Refs. 45 and 46 and suitable canonical representations are suggested in Ref. 47. We consider the interpixel representation of edges in the main directions. From this standpoint one needs to evaluate the edge strength at a given pixel by computing its components in the horizontal and vertical directions. A modified Sobel mask was employed for this purpose. In order to consolidate the raw edge from the data obtained above, the edge tracing and relaxation methods are applied to the previous result.

The system consolidates the edge elements into meaningful sequences of edge elements. A Boundary Interaction Graph (BIG), representing the partial segmentation is developed in which each node corresponds to the end point of a connected edge sequence, and an arc represents the corresponding boundary. A region based approach is then applied to recursively split and/or merge the pseudo regions through a Regional Adjacency Graph

(RAG). Whenever a split or merge operation is carried out, both the RAG and BIG are suitably updated. The last step is to eliminate segments of insignificant size, especially the "holes", which are totally surrounded by another region.

The final result of our segmentation is a set of regions, each corresponding to one node in the region adjacency graph, and a set of boundaries connecting any two regions. Associated with each segment is the centroid, the average gray value, the variance and the list of all pixels that it contains, are available at the output. Also, associated with each boundary, i.e., interface between any two regions, are the values such as the slope, endpoints, the variance of the edge values etc. In essence, both the BIG and RAG carry information of a complementary nature that can be used by the techniques developed for motion analysis. For a detailed description of the complete segmentation system the reader is referred to Ref. 24, Pavlidis[45,46], and Hanson[47].

6.2. Parameter Extraction from Real Images

Two fairly complex image sequences are considered to demonstrate the applicability of the proposed methods. The first sequence assumes orthographic images while the second considers perspective projections. Both the sequences contain a pair of images of an automobile in motion recorded at two different time instants.

6.2.1. Orthographic projections

The images in Figs. 5a and 5b represent the image sequence of an orthographically recorded scene. The images were segmented as described in Sect. 6.1 and the segmented images are given in Figs. 5c and 5d. The segments corresponding to the leftside view and the one corresponding to the hood of the car were chosen for the subsequent analysis.

The centroid of the leftside view was chosen to be the origin of the moving coordinate system. Thus the translation was found by computing the shift in its position in time. Also, the vector **c** was computed by subtracting the translation from the shift in the centroids of the segment corresponding to hood. The choice of the above segments was two fold: First, the above two are the largest two non-occluded faces in the given image pairs. Secondly the hood segment exhibits skewed symmetry, hence is suitable for extracting Kanade's gradient ambiguities, used for extracting the initial orientation.

a) The image of the automobile
under composite motion at time T_1.

b) The image of the automobile
under composite motion at time T_1.

c) The segmented image of Fig. 5a.

d) The segmented image of Fig. 5b.

Fig. 5. The orthographic image sequence of an automobile in composite motion from
time T_1 to T_2.

Two binary image functions $s(\mathbf{x}; t)$ and $s(\mathbf{x}; t + 1)$ were generated such
that: $s(\mathbf{x}; t) = 1$ if $\mathbf{x}$ at time t was contained within the hood segment
at time t; and $s(\mathbf{x}; t) = 0$ otherwise. The iterative parameter estimation
algorithm described in Sect. 4.1 was applied over $s(\mathbf{x}; t)$ and $s(\mathbf{x}; t + 1)$,
in order to estimate the linear shape change parameters. The values thus
obtained are:

$$A = \begin{bmatrix} 1.0061 & 0.0004 \\ 0.015 & 1.000 \end{bmatrix}, \qquad \mathbf{c} = \begin{bmatrix} -6.736 \\ -2.829 \end{bmatrix}.$$

The consistency of these values was verified with (54), and the estimated
values of A and $\mathbf{c}$ given above agree with (52), to a reasonable accuracy. The
partial information contained in A and $\mathbf{c}$ is best revealed in the parametric
$(p/s, q/s)$ space, as illustrated in Fig. 4.

For any given point on the line-segment L_1 in the parametric space, the values of p, q and s were computed as described in Sect. 4. The resulting loci of (p, q) are presented in Fig. 6. In addition to the above, from BIG and RAG the angles of skewed symmetry, β_1 and β_2, of the hood segment were extracted. The values were: $\beta_1 = 14°$ and $\beta_2 = 152.5°$. The hyperbolic gradient ambiuity described in Ref. 3 for these values is also illustrated in Fig. 6. Clearly, from the figure, the solution curve and the hyperbola intersect at two points, which are negatives of each other, corresponding to the $\pm$ values of s. Thus, the initial orientation obtained above was:

$$(p, q, s) = (\pm 1.4, \pm 3.4, \quad 278) \, ,$$
$$= (\pm 1.4, \pm 3.4, -278) \, .$$

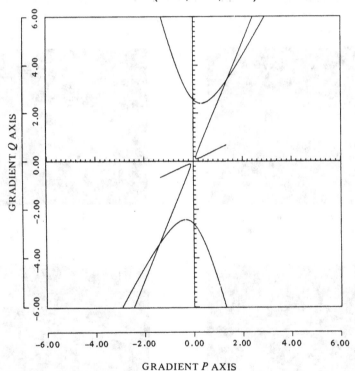

GRADIENT P AXIS

Fig. 6. The *solution curve* and Kanade's *hyperbolic* constraint, showing the solution of Eqs. (62) and (52).

These values were then substituted (23) to compute the elements of the rotation matrix R. The resulting rotation angles are:

$$(\phi, \theta, \Phi) = (22.8°, 1.5°, -22.1°) \, .$$

Most of the computations described above was toward the computation of the initial orientation parameters which is required to be computed only once during tracking.

6.2.2. Perspective projections

Two perspective images of an automobile in motion are given in Figs. 7a and 7b. It is considered that the orientation parameters (p, q, s) are unknown. The purpose of the experiment was to determine the initial orientation (p, q), with s treated as scaling parameter. First, the nonlinear shape change parameters, $\hat{G}$ was determined by the iterative algorithm described in Sect. 5.2. It is to be borne in mind that the analysis involves many approximations and therefore accuracy is limited by many factors. In addition, the extracted values of (p, q) were found to be very sensitive to the values of $g_{ij}s$, due to the underlying nonlinear models.

a) The image of the automobile under composite motion at time T_1.

b) The image of the automobile under composite motion at time T_2.

c) The segmented image of Fig. 7a.

d) The segmented image of Fig. 7b.

Fig. 7. The perspective image sequence of an automobile in composite motion from time T_1 to T_2.

The experimental studies have indicated that the iterative G parameter estimation algorithm is more sensitive to the starting value of the first iteration, i.e., $\hat{G} \simeq \hat{G}^{(0)}$. On certain simulated images, we were able to observe that the algorithm was prone to convergence at some false local minima; however, no meaningful conclusions could be conceived. Furthermore, in the real world images there are no methods available to easily determine such conditions. Similar to the previous experiment, we chose the hood-segment for further analysis. For the scene under consideration the estimated shape parameters were,

$$G = \begin{bmatrix} 0.0884 & 0.0073 & -0.1498 & 0.0536 & 0.1796 & 0.000 \\ 0.0730 & 0.1944 & 0.0186 & 0.0000 & 0.0536 & 0.1796 \end{bmatrix}.$$

With the above values of G, Eqs. (78) was solved for (p, q) using the standard IMSL package, and the extracted orientation parameters were, $(p, q) = (-1.67, 5.39)$. Contrary to the fact, the values appear to be questionable. In order to assert the fact, it was desired to see the possible ranges of (p, q), if it could be derived from other methods. One such method is to take advantage of the set of parallel lines that form the hood segment. Due to the fact that the perspectiveness is not very well pronounced in these images, it is possible to adopt Kanade's basic equations and to inspect the possible ranges of (p, q). With $\beta_1 \simeq 20°$ and $\beta_2 \simeq 155°$ measured from the figure, the (p, q) values extracted above were observed to be in the reasonable range. In other situations, methods developed by Young and Nelsson[5] may be considered. Nevertheless, such methods are used only for estimating the expected ranges of (p, q) values and not for the extraction itself.

6.3. Simulated Images

The results obtained in the previous experiments do not answer the questions related to the accuracy and sensitivity of the estimated orientation parameters. It is understood that the success of the overall system depends upon the accuracy to which one can determine the shape-change parameters. Then, in the case of orthographic images, one can see that it is possible to improve the overall system by estimating more accurately A and c. The moment based one-dimensional search technique is adopted to show the improvement in the performance. The nonlinear shape-change parameter estimation algorithm on the other hand indicates that the iterative algorithm is inevitable. In order to examine the accuracy of the estimated values, we considered simulated images for the two experiments described in the following sections.

6.3.1. Linear shape-change parameter estimation

An image sequence of a solid rectangle consisting of four frames is presented in Figs. 8a–d. The centroid of the right side was considered as the moving origin, while the top face was considered for subsequent shape change analysis. First, the 2-D shift in the centroid of the primary face was found and taken as the translation. Then, c was evaluated directly by finding the 2-D shift in the centroids of the secondary face i.e., *top face* with reference to the moving frame. Both the iterative algorithm and the 1-D search techniques were applied to the images, to facilitate a comparison of the results. The least mean-squared error $\varepsilon_{\min}^2(\alpha)$ obtained was less than 5%, while the iterative technique resulted in 11%. It is understood that the finite sample-spacing and the adopted bilinear interpolation do place a lower bound on the least mean squared error that can be obtained.

Two conclusive evidences were observed: First, the moment based approach is more robust, but requires more computational efforts. Secondly, even when the exact values of **A** and **c** were known accurately, the corresponding values of mean-squared error due to discrete sampling was somewhat closer to the $\varepsilon_{\min}^2(\alpha)$ obtained by the 1-D search algorithm. Also, it is noted that within the moving coordinate system, a visible surface is generally associated with the negative values of s. This is due to the fact that the positive values of s denote planes that intersect the Z-axis at a point behind the primary face, hence a slope (3-D orientation) that leaves the plane not visible.

6.3.2. Nonlinear shape changes in simulated images

The purpose of this experiment is two fold: First, it exhibits the improvement in performance of the iterative algorithm, when the starting value of the first iteration is a fairly accurate approximation of the true value. Secondly, this demonstrates the feasibility of a two-step procedure in which the linear terms in the shape change parameters are estimated first followed by heuristic computation (Sect. 5.3) of the two quadratic terms, in evaluating the starting value of the iterative procedure. In addition, we present a graphical solution of the (p, q) extraction.

The image sequence under inspection is shown in Figs. 9a–b. The images were generated with $F = -1, \Delta X = \Delta Y = 0.0016$ and the field of view was chosen such that $-0.2048 \leq (x, y) \leq 0.2047$, i.e., $-128 \leq (i, j) \leq 127$.

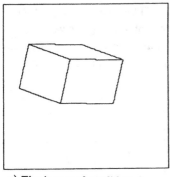

a) The image of a solid under composite motion at time T_1.

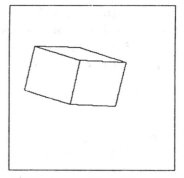

b) The image of the solid under composite motion at time T_2.

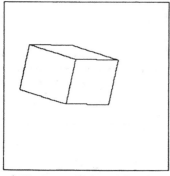

c) The image of the solid under composite motion at time T_3.

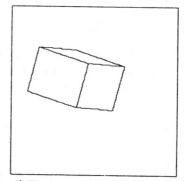

d) The image of the solid under composite motion at time T_4.

Fig. 8. The orthographic image sequence of a solid rectangle in composite motion from time T_1 through T_4.

First, using the reduced 1-D search algorithm used in the linear case was adopted to find the linear terms, which was reasonably close to the actual values. Then, using the heuristics described in Sect. 5.3, g_{13} and g_{24} were computed with the use of the linear terms computed earlier. The iterative algorithm demonstrated a fast convergence and converged to the values within 20 iterations. The least mean squared error evaluated during this experiment was 6%. The estimated values of G are given in Fig. 10. Also, the extraction of (p, q) described in Eqs. (79) is illustrated as a graphical solution shown in Fig. 10. The plots indicate that there are 4 real solutions in the permissible range. The two insignificant roots $\left(p = 0, q = \frac{h_1}{h_3}\right)$ and $\left(p = \frac{h_2}{h_3}\right)$ are shown in the figure. Also, there are two more real roots to the given eighth order nonlinear equation, one of which is our solution. The actual values of p and q were, $(1.08, 4.59)$, whilst the computed values of (p, q) are $(\tan 45°, \tan 78°) = (1.0, 4.7)$. The exact interpretation of the other solution is not available at the time of writing, however, given a sequence of three images, the experiments have indicated the two sets of plots intersect at only one solution point, hence a unique extraction.

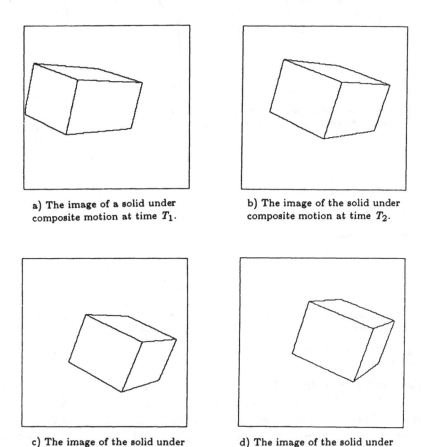

a) The image of a solid under composite motion at time T_1.

b) The image of the solid under composite motion at time T_2.

c) The image of the solid under composite motion at time T_3.

d) The image of the solid under composite motion at time T_4.

Fig. 9. The perspective image sequence of a solid rectangle in composite motion from time T_1 through T_4.

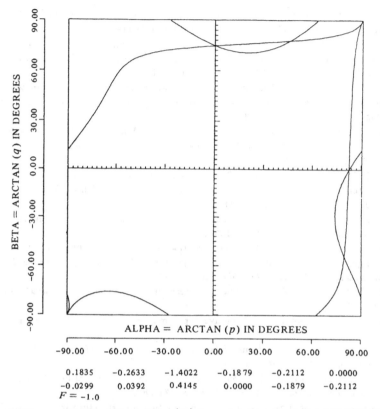

ALPHA = ARCTAN (p) IN DEGREES					
-90.00	-60.00	-30.00	0.00	30.00	60.00	90.00
0.1835	-0.2633	-1.4022	-0.1879	-0.2112	0.0000
-0.0299	0.0392	0.4145	0.0000	-0.1879	-0.2112

$F = -1.0$

Fig. 10. The graphical solution of Eq. (78) for extracting the 3-D orientation in the $\left(\tan^{-1}p,\ \tan^{-1}q\right)$ space.

References

1. Gibbson et al., "Motion parallax as a determinant of perceived depth," *J. Exp. Psychol.* **58** (1959) 40–51.
2. S. Ullman, "The interpretation of visual motion," MIT Press, 1979.
3. T. Kanade, "Recovery of the three-dimensional shape of an object from a single view," *Artificial Intell.* **17** (1981) 409–460.
4. K. Sugihara, "An algebraic approach to shape-from-image problems," *Artificial Intell.* **23** (1984) 58–95.
5. R. N. Nelson and T. Y. Young, "Determining three dimensional object shape and orientation from a single perspective view," *Opt. Engineering* **25** (1986) 394–401.
6. J. W. Roach and J. K. Aggarwal, "Determining the movement of objects from a sequence of images," *IEEE Trans. on Pattern Anal. Mach. Intell.* **6** (1980) 554–562.
7. Amar Mitiche and J. K. Aggarwal, "Analysis of time varying imagery," *Handbook of Pattern Recognition and Image Processing*, eds. T. Y. Young and K. S. Fu, Academic Press, 1986, pp. 311-332.

8. R. Y. Tsai and T. S. Huang, "Estimating three dimensional motion parameters of a rigid planar patch," *IEEE Trans. on ASSP* **29** (1981) 1147–1152.

9. R. Y. Tsai, T. S. Huang and W. L. Zhu, "Estimating three dimensional motion parameters of a rigid planar patch, II: Singular value decomposition," *IEEE Trans. on ASSP* **30** (1982) 525–534; errata, **31** (1983) 514.

10. R. Y. Tsai and T. S. Huang, "Estimating 3-dimensional motion parameters of a rigid planar patch, III: Finite Point correspondences and three views problem," *IEEE Trans. on ASSP* **32** (1984) 213–220.

11. R. Y. Tsai and T. S. Huang, "Uniqueness and estimation of three dimensional motion parameters of rigid objects with curved surfaces," *IEEE Trans. on Pattern Anal. Mach. Intell.* **6** (1984) 13–26.

12. J. Q. Fang and T. S. Huang, "Some experiments on the estimation of motion parameters of a rigid body from two consecutive image frames," *IEEE Trans. on Pattern Anal. Mach. Intell.* **6** (1984) 545–554.

13. H. C. Longuet-Higgins, "A computer algorithm for reconstructing a scene from two projections," *Nature* **293** (1981) 133–135.

14. H. C. Longuet-Higgins, "The reconstruction of a scene from two projections – A configuration that defeats the 8 point algorithm," *Proc. 1st Conf. on Artificial Intell. and Applications*, Denver, CO, 1984, pp. 395–397.

15. B. K. P. Horn and B. G. Schunck, "Determining optical flow," *Artificial Intell.* **17** (1981) 1855–2203.

16. K. Prazdny, "Egomotion and relative depth map optical flow," *Biol. Cybernetics* **36** (1980) 87–102.

17. E. C. Hildreth, "Computations underlying the measurement of visual motion," *Artificial Intell.* **23** (1984) 304–354.

18. W. B. Thompson et al., "Dynamic occlusion analysis in optical flow fields," *IEEE Trans. on Pattern Anal. Mach. Intell.* **7** (1985) 374–383.

19. G. Adiv, "Determining three dimensional motion and structure from optical flow generated by several objects," *IEEE Trans. on Pattern Anal. Mach. Intell.* **7** (1985) 384–401.

20. T. Y. Young and Y. L. Wang, "Analysis of three dimensional rotation and linear shape changes," *Pattern Recognition Lett.* **2** (1984) 239–242.

21. G. R. Legters, Jr. and T. Y. Young, "A mathematical model for image tracking," *IEEE Trans. on Pattern Anal. Mach. Intell.* **4** (1982) 583–594.

22. T. Y. Young and Y. L. Wang, "Analysis of linear and nonlinear shape changes," Internal report, Dept. of Elect. Eng., Univ. of Miami, 1982.

23. T. Y. Young and S. Gunasekaran, "Three dimensional motion analysis using shape change information," *Proc. SPIE Conf. on Applications of Artificial Intell. III*, Orlando, 1986, pp. 318–326.

24. T. Y. Young and S. Gunasekaran, "A regional approach to tracking 3-dimensional motion in an image sequence," in *Advances in Computer Vision and Image Processing* Vol. 3, ed. T. S. Huang, JAI Press, 1987, pp. 63–99.

25. K. I. Kanatani, "Tracing planar surface motion from a projection without knowing the correspondence," *Computer Vision, Graphics and Image Processing* **29** (1985) 1–12.

26. K. I. Kanatani, "Detecting motion of a planar surface by line and surface integrals," *Computer Vision, Graphics and Image Processing* **29** (1985) 13–22.

27. S. Amari, "Invariant structures of signal and feature spaces in pattern recognition problems," R.A.A.G., *Memoirs* **4** (1968) 553–556.

28. S. Amari, "Feature spaces which admit and detect invariant signal transformations," in *Proc. 4th Int'l Joint Conf. on Pattern Recognition*, 1978, pp. 452–456.

29. A. M. Waxman et al., "An image flow paradigm," *Proc. 2nd IEEE Workshop on Computer Vision: Representation and Control*, Annapolis, MD, 1984, pp. 49–57.

30. A. M. Waxman and S. Ullman, "Surface structure and 3-D motion from image flow: kinematic analysis," *Int'l. J. Robotics Research* **4** (1985) 72–94.

31. A. M. Waxman and K. Wohn, "Contour evolution, neighborhood deformation and global flow: planar flow in motion," *Int'l J. Robotics Research* **4** (1985) 95–108.

32. B. Bamieh and R. De Figueiredo, "A general moment-invariants/attributed-graph method for three dimensional object recognition from a single view," *IEEE Trans. on Robotics and Automation* **2** (1986) 31–41.

33. S. A. Friedberg, "Finding axes of skewed symmetry," *Computer Vision, Graphics and Image Processing* **34** (1986) 138–155.

34. G. A. Korn and T. M. Korn, *Mathematical Handbook for Engineers and Scientists*, McGraw-Hill, New York, 1968.

35. X. Zhuang and R. Haralick, "Two view motion analysis," *Proc. of the ICASSP*, 1985, Tampa, FL.

36. R. J. Schalkoff and E. S. McVey, "A model and tracking algorithm for a class of video targets," *IEEE Trans. on Pattern Anal. Machine Intell.* **4** (1982) 2–10.

37. J. J. Gibson, *The Senses considered as Perceptual Systems*, Houghton Mifflin, Boston, 1966.

38. J. J. Gibson, *The Ecological Approach to Visual Perception*, Houghton Mifflin, Boston, 1979.

39. R. Jain, "Extraction of motion information from peripheral processes," *IEEE Trans. Pattern Anal. Mach. Intell.* **3** (1981) 489–503.

40. W. N. Martin and J. K. Aggarwal, "Dynamic scene analysis," *Computer Vision Graphics and Image Processing* **7** (1978) 356–374.

41. S. E. Palmer, "The psychology of perceptual organization: A transformation approach," in *Human and Machine Vision*, eds. J. Beck et al., Academic Press, 1983, pp. 269–339.

42. R. J. Woodham, "Analyzing images of curved surfaces," *Artificial Intell.* **17** (1981) 117–140.

43. S. T. Banard, "Interpreting perspective images," *Artificial Intell.* **21** (1983) 435–462.

44. W. C. Lin, K. S. Fu and T. Sederberg, "Estimation of three dimensional object orientation for computer vision system with feedback," *J. Robotic Systems* **1** (1984) 59–82.

45. T. Pavlidis, *Structural Pattern Recognition*, 2nd edition, Springer-Verlag, 1980.

46. S. L. Horowitz, "Picture Segmentation by a Tree Traversal Algorithm," *J. ACM* **23** (1976) 368–388.

47. R. Hanson and E. M. Riseman, "Computer Vision Systems," in *Computer Vision Systems*, eds. A. R. Hanson and E. M. Riseman, Academic Press, 1978, pp. 128–163.

48. J. M. Pragger, "Extracting and Labeling boundary segments in natural scenes," *IEEE Trans. on Pattern Anal. Mach. Intell.* **2** (1980) 16–27.

4

SPHERICAL ANALYSIS IN COMPUTER VISION AND IMAGE UNDERSTANDING

Michael A. Penna

Department of Mathematical Sciences
Purdue University at Indianapolis
1125 East 38th Street
Indianapolis, IN 46223, USA

Su-shing Chen

Department of Computer Science
University of North Carolina at Charlotte
Charlotte, NC 28223, USA

Human perception has long inspired computer vision and image understanding research. In this paper we present a spherical vision model which is inspired by human perception and which is useful in the study of computer vision and image understanding. More precisely, we discuss spherical geometry, creating and displaying spherical images, and applications of spherical methods to problems in surface recovery, motion analysis, and optical flow.

1. INTRODUCTION

Human perception has long inspired computer vision and image understanding research. In this paper we present a spherical vision model which is inspired by human perception and which is useful in the study of computer vision and image understanding. Applications of spherical vision have already been made, for example, in the compilation of camera mosaics (see Batson and Larson[1]), in surface orientation and edge detection (see Clocksin[2]), in 3-dimensional motion and scene analysis (see Magee and Aggarwal[3] and Yen and Huang[4]), in 3-dimensional object representation (see Roach et al.), in pattern recognition and image processing (see Chen[6]), in shape from shading (see Penna and Chen[7]), and in optical flow (see Chen and Penna[8]). (See also Chazelle et al.[9] for an application to computational geometry.) More precisely, in this paper we discuss spherical geometry, creating and displaying spherical images, and applications of spherical methods to problems in surface recovery, motion analysis, and optical flow.

The cornerstone of spherical vision is spherical perspective projection. Humans perceive objects in two different ways: nearby objects are seen in perspective, and distant objects are seen orthographically. Although orthographic projection is satisfactory in the analysis of distant objects, planar perspective has several well known limitations in the analysis of nearby objects. Perhaps the most noticeable problem with planar perspective is distortion over a wide viewing angle. Other problems with planar perspective are illustrated by a variety of well known illusions that are documented in the literature of psychology (see Coren and Girgus[10], Gibson[11], Luckeisch[12], and Murch[13]). Spherical perspective projection is radial projection onto a 2-dimensional sphere S_f whose radius is $1/f$ where f represents focal length. Spherical perspective projection avoids many of the problems of planar perspective in the same way human eyes do (see Snyder et al.[14]).

Not only is spherical perspective more appropriate than planar perspective in many applications, but it is also just as easy (if not easier) to use. This is because much is known about analytic spherical geometry. Spherical geometry originated, historically, in conjunction with the study of astronomy, navigation, and geodesy. Consequently a great number of analytic techniques have been developed in spherical geometry (see Ayres[15], for example). In this paper we present a simple framework that allows these techniques to be applied in the study of computer vision and image understanding.

Analytic spherical geometry is not only similar to analytic projective geometry, but, in many ways, it is also more natural. Perhaps the most well known application of analytic projective geometry occurs in the analysis of transformations of Euclidean space — transformations of 3-dimensional world space and of 2-dimensional image space, and the viewing operations that transform 3-dimensional world space to 2-dimensional image space. Handling such transformations is frequently only a small part of a larger problem, however, and after applying the techniques of analytic projective geometry, such a problem is frequently recast in the language of Euclidean geometry. The goal of Penna and Patterson[16] is to illustrate that there are a number of techniques of analytic projective geometry that allow further analysis of problems in the realm of analytic projective geometry. There are, however, still restrictions on the use of analytic projective geometry in solving real world problems: The projective plane is nonorientable, so the concept of betweeness — as in "B is between A and C" — is not a projective concept nor are there metric concepts in projective geometry — there is no concept of the measure of a line segment or the angle between two lines that is invariant under projective transformations. (As discussed in Penna and Patterson[16], the concepts of distance between points and angle between lines are affine concepts, not projective concepts.)

Analytic spherical geometry is similar to analytic projective geometry, in that the equations of lines are linear (recall, from geography, that a line — or a geodesic — on a sphere is part of a great circle), there are simple formulas for computing the intersection of two lines, the line determined by two points, and whether or not three points are collinear, and there is a natural concept of duality. Unlike projective geometry, however, in spherical geometry there are also concepts of distance between points and angle between lines, and simple formulas for computing them. Just as important as these results, however, is the fact that they are based on familiar surfaces. The projective plane (the surface upon which the study of projective geometry and planar perspective projection are based) is not a familiar surface to most people: the projective plane cannot be embedded in Euclidean 3-space, it is not orientable, and the metric on it — the cross ratio — is not frequently used in applications. Spheres, on the other hand, are familiar surfaces: they can be visualized, they are orientable, and they are easy to work with.

The goal of this paper is to discuss spherical techniques, not to try to supplant planar techniques by spherical ones. While spherical techniques are superior to planar techniques in some applications, planar techniques are superior to spherical techniques in others. Indeed, where spherical and planar techniques both apply, they tend to complement, rather than oppose, each other.

This paper is organized as follows.

The first part of this paper is aimed at establishing the foundations of spherical computer vision and image understanding. In Sect. 2 we describe the three vision models — the orthographic, planar perspective and spherical perspective vision models — discussed in this paper. In Sect. 3 we describe some of the limitations of the orthographic and planar perspective models. In Sect. 4 we present the fundamentals of analytic spherical geometry, including an explanation of the relationship between analytic spherical geometry and analytic projective geometry. In Sect. 5 we discuss the process of creating and displaying theoretically defined bit oriented spherical images, in Sect. 6 we discuss the process of creating and displaying real bit oriented spherical images, and in Sect. 7 we discuss the process of creating and displaying object oriented spherical images. (A bit oriented image — whether it be spherical or planar — is defined by a function that associates to each picture element a number representing a level of color, brightness, and/or tint; an object oriented image — whether it be spherical or planar — is defined by geometric figures such as curves.)

The second part of this paper is aimed at some specific applications of spherical techniques to problems in computer vision and image understanding. In Sect. 8 we discuss photometric stereo — the process of recording multiple images in rapid succession using a fixed camera and multiple light sources — and recovery of variations in depth from photometric stereo. In Sect. 9 we discuss recovery of the geometric features of a surface. In Sect. 10 we discuss motion analysis. In Sect. 11 we discuss optical flow. These applications all have two aspects in common. First, they are all based on a shading analysis that uses information provided by photometric stereo. Second, on the basis of such a shading analysis alone, none of these problems has a unique solution; given initial depth information, however, they all have unique solutions.

PART I — FOUNDATIONS

2. THE THREE VISION MODELS

In this section we describe the three vision models — the orthographic, planar perspective and spherical perspective models — discussed in this paper. There are two major components to each model: the first is a technique for parametrizing surfaces in space; the second is a technique for projecting three dimensions into two. These components are, in some sense, inverses of each other, and the utility of a vision model can be measured by how well these components complement each other in analyzing real problems.

A *Monge surface* S is the graph (see Fig. 1) of a parametrized surface $\mathbf{x} : U \to R^3$ of the form

$$\mathbf{x}(x_1, x_2) = \big(x_1, x_2, h(x_1, x_2)\big)$$

where U is an open subset of the $x_1 x_2$-coordinate plane and $x_3 = h(x_1, x_2)$ is a differentiable function defined on U. In other words, a Monge surface is a parametrization of the graph of a differentiable function $h : U \to R$.

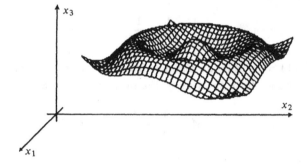

Fig. 1. A Monge surface.

The *orthographic vision model* uses Monge surfaces and orthographic projection as illustrated in Fig. 2. The image plane Π is the plane whose equation is $x_3 = 1/f$ where f represents focal length; the X_1- and X_2-coordinate axes of Π are the lines of intersection of Π with the $x_1 x_3$- and $x_2 x_3$-coordinate planes, respectively. Orthographic projection π_0 from an arbitary surface S to Π is defined by

$$\pi_0(x_1, x_2, x_3) = (X_1, X_2) = (x_1, x_2) \ .$$

There is a natural relationship between Monge surfaces and orthographic projection: if S is the Monge surface associated to $\mathbf{x} : U \to R^3$ then $\pi_0 \circ \mathbf{x}$ is the identity on U and $\mathbf{x} \circ \pi_0$ is the identity on S. Thus the image I in Π of S under π_0 is U.

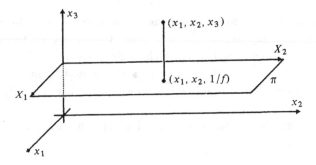

Fig. 2. Orthographic projection.

(Our use throughout this paper f as focal length is really an abuse of terminology; actually $f = (M + 1)F$ where F is focal length and M is the factor by which a negative image is magnified in creating a positive image: The focal length equation is

$$\frac{1}{d} + \frac{1}{f} = \frac{1}{F}$$

where F is focal length, d is the distance from the lens to a negative image, and f is the distance from the lens to the positive image. Since

$$M = \frac{1}{N} = \frac{f}{d}$$

it follows that $d = f/M$, so

$$\frac{M}{f} + \frac{1}{f} = \frac{1}{F} \ .$$

This relation implies that $f = (M + 1)F$.)

The *planar perspective vision model* uses Monge surface and planar perspective projection as illustrated in Fig. 3. The viewer is located at the origin $O(0, 0, 0)$. The image plane Π is, again, the plane Π whose equation is $x_3 = 1/f$ where f represents focal length, and the X_1- and X_2-coordinate axes of Π are the lines of intersection of Π with the $x_1 x_3$- and $x_2 x_3$-coordinate planes, respectively. Planar perspective projection π_p maps the point $P(x_1, x_2, x_3)$ to the point $Q(X_1, X_2)$ in Π defined by intersecting the ray from 0 to P with Π; it follows that

$$\pi_p(x_1, x_2, x_3) = (X_1, X_2) = (x_1/f x_3, x_2/f x_3) \ .$$

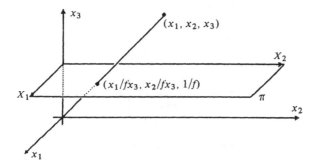

Fig. 3. Planar perspective projection.

We let I denote the image in Π of S under π_p. In general, U and I are different in this model.

A *spherical coordinate surface* S is the graph (see Fig. 4) of a parametrized surface $\mathbf{x} : U \to R^3$ of the form

$$\mathbf{x}(\theta, \phi) = \big(\rho(\theta, \phi) \sin \phi \cos \theta, \rho(\theta, \phi) \sin \phi \sin \theta, \rho(\theta, \phi) \cos \phi\big)$$

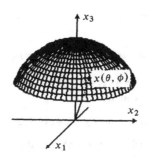

Fig. 4. A spherical coordinate surface.

where U is an open subset of the $\theta\phi$-coordinate plane and where $\rho = \rho(\theta, \phi)$ is a differential function defined on U. (Recall — see Fig. 5 — that the spherical coordinates (ρ, θ, ϕ) of the point whose Cartesian coordinates are (x_1, x_2, x_3) are given by

$$\rho = \sqrt{x_1^2 + x_2^2 + x_3^2}$$

$$\theta = \begin{cases} \tan^{-1}(x_2/x_1) & \text{if } x_1 > 0 \\ \pi + \tan^{-1}(x_2/x_1) & \text{if } x_1 < 0 \end{cases}$$

$$\phi = \cos^{-1}\big(x_3/\sqrt{x_1^2 + x_2^2 + x_3^2}\big)$$

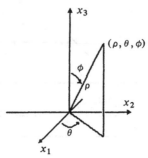

Fig. 5. Spherical coordinates.

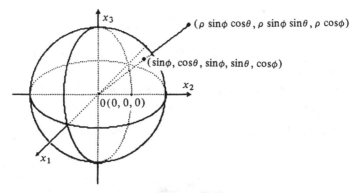

Fig. 6. Spherical perspective projection.

and the Cartesian coordinates (x_1, x_2, x_3) of the point whose spherical coordinates are (ρ, θ, ϕ) are given by

$$x_1 = \rho \sin \phi \cos \theta, \ x_2 = \rho \sin \phi \sin \theta, \ x_3 = \rho \cos \phi \ .$$

If $\rho = 1$, the angles θ and ϕ represent longitude and latitude for points on the unit sphere S^2.) For brevity we write $\mathbf{x} = \rho \mathbf{s}$ where

$$\mathbf{s} = \mathbf{s}(\theta, \phi) = (\sin \phi \cos \theta, \sin \phi \sin \theta, \cos \theta) \ .$$

The *spherical perspective vision model* uses spherical coordinate surfaces and spherical perspective projection as illustrated in Fig. 6. The viewer is located at the origin $O(0,0,0)$. The image sphere is the 2-dimensional sphere S_f whose center is the origin and whose radius is $1/f$ where f represents focal length. Spherical perspective projection π_s from a point P on a spherical surface S to a point Q on S_f is defined by intersecting the ray from 0 to P with S_f. If we use Cartesian coordinates on S_f then

$$\pi_s(x_1, x_2, x_3) = (x_1, x_2, x_3)/f\sqrt{x_1^2 + x_2^2 + x_3^2}$$

or

$$\pi_s\left(\rho \sin\phi\cos\theta,\ \rho\sin\phi\sin\theta,\ \rho\cos\phi\right) = \left(\sin\phi\cos\theta,\ \sin\phi\sin\theta,\ \cos\phi\right)/f$$

and if we use spherical coordinates on R^3 and S_f then

$$\pi_s(\rho,\theta,\phi) = (1/f,\theta,\phi)\ .$$

As with orthographic vision, $(\pi_s \circ \mathbf{x})(\theta,\phi) = (1/f,\theta,\phi)$, and $\mathbf{x} \circ \pi_s$ is the identity on S_f. Thus, as with orthographic projection, the image I in S_f of S under π_s is U.

3. SOME LIMITATIONS OF ORTHOGRAPHIC AND PLANAR PERSPECTIVE PROJECTION

In this section we compare human vision with the orthographic, planar perspective, and spherical perspective vision models.

Looking at objects around us, we find that humans perceive objects in two different ways: nearby objects are seen in perspective, and distant objects are seen orthographically. Although orthographic projection is satisfactory in the study of distant objects, it is not satisfactory in the study of nearby objects.

To illustrate the difficulty in obtaining accurate images of nearby objects using orthographic projection, consider Fig. 7. Despite the fact that this figure is drawn under orthographic projection to produce an accurate view

Fig. 7. Orthographic distortion.

of one face, the other visible faces are distorted so the figure does not accurately reflect the shape of the entire object. Orthographic projection is normally used to produce figures that accurately reflect the shape of individual faces of an object; but having a figure accurately relate the details of individual faces of an object is not the same as having a figure that accurately relates the shape of the object as a whole. In fact, multiview orthographic projections (see Fig. 8) accurately relate the details of all faces, but the only way to obtain an accurate idea of the shape of the entire object is by incorporating high level object recognition.

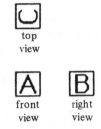

Fig. 8. A multiview orthographic projection.

Related problems with orthographic projection are illustrated by a variety of well-known illusions which are documented in the psychology literature (see Coren and Girgus[10], Gibson[11], Luckeisch[12], and Murch[13]. Such problems are illustrated, for example, by the Necker cube illusion, the Mach open book illusion, the Schroeder reversible staircase, and Thiery's illusion (see Fig. 9.).

An illustration of the inaccuracy of orthographic projection in scene analysis is depicted in Fig. 10. Although three walls are seen in a human perspective view of the hall, at most two are seen in an orthographic view. In general, orthographic views do not accurately portray human views.

Planar perspective projection solves the problem of obtaining accurate views of moderately sized objects, but planar perspective projection has several well known limitations in the analysis of large objects or scenes (objects or scenes that span a wide viewing angle). To illustrate this, consider the sequence of planar perspective images of a cube as the cube is translated parallel to the viewplane away from the observer, illustrated in Fig. 11(a). Note the distortion (as well as the artificial accretion and deletion of faces) that occurs as the cube moves farther and farther away from the observer. With human vision, objects do not become distorted like this as they move away from an observer. (Think about what you see as you stand by a street watching a car move past and away from you.) When a human looks at an object, the object is projected onto an imaginary sphere centered at the human's eye(s), thus creating a spherical image. As the position of the object changes, the human changes viewing position. Figure 11(b) is a corresponding sequence of spherical perspective images of the same cube. Note the lack of distortion as the cube moves farther and farther away from the observer. Similar distorted images of a sphere as the sphere is translated parallel to the viewplane away from the observer are illustrated in Fig. 12(a), and a corresponding sequence of spherical perspective images of the same sphere are illustrated in Fig. 12(b).

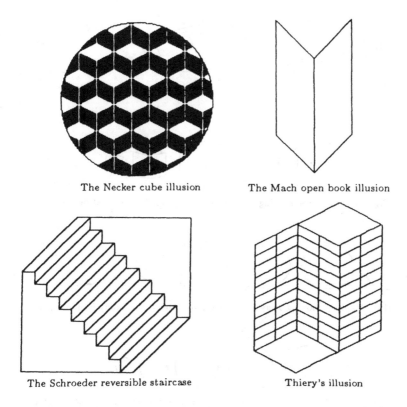

The Necker cube illusion   The Mach open book illusion

The Schroeder reversible staircase   Thiery's illusion

Fig. 9. Orthographic illusions.

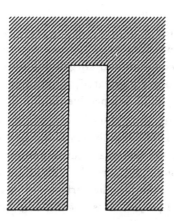

Fig. 10. A problem with orthographic projection in scene analysis.

Fig. 11(a). A cube moving away from the viewer (viewpoint fixed) in planar perspective.

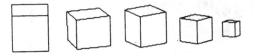

Fig. 11(b). A cube moving away from the viewer in spherical perspective.

Fig. 12(a). A sphere moving away from the viewer (viewplane fixed) in planar perspective.

Fig. 12(b). A sphere moving away from the viewer in spherical perspective.

Related problems with planar perspective projection are also illustrated by a variety of well known illusions which are documented in the psychology literature (again, see Coren and Girgus[10], Gibson[11], Luckeisch[12], and Murch[13]. Such problems are illustrated, for example, by Hering's illusion, Ponzo's illusion, and Gibson's perspective illusion (see Fig. 13).

There are also analytic difficulties involved in using planar perspective projection in the analysis of large objects and scenes. One set of such difficulties centers around the fact that planar perspective analysis requires Monge patch descriptions of surfaces. In a situation such as the one illustrated in Fig. 14(a), for example, the surface visible to an observer at the origin under perspective projection is not a Monge surface (a vertical line

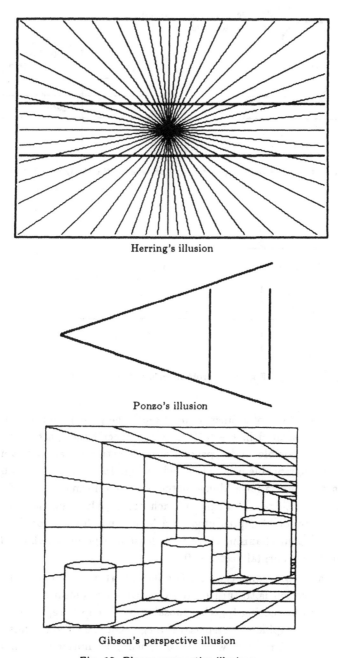

Herring's illusion

Ponzo's illusion

Gibson's perspective illusion

Fig. 13. Planar perspective illusions.

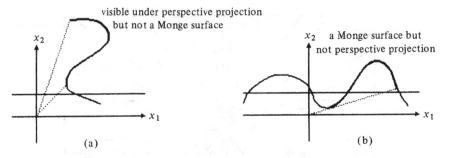

Fig. 14. Monge surfaces are not appropriate for the study of perspective.

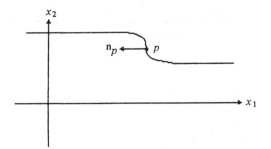

Fig. 15. A problem with differentiability.

intersects the graph of a function in at most one point). In a situation such as the one illustrated in Fig. 14(b), on the other hand, part of the Monge surface is not visible under perspective projection to an observer at the origin. Another problem is illustrated in Fig. 15. The differentiability (or smoothness) criteria for a Monge patch require a normal vector of the form $(-\partial h/\partial x_1, -\partial h/\partial x_2, 1)$ to exist at each point. Although the surface S is smooth, it cannot be represented by a Monge patch since for any position of the viewing mechanism, there is at least one point at which the third component of a normal vector is 0.

One way to overcome the shortcomings of orthographic and planar perspective projection is to turn to mosaics. Classical mosaics are planar images obtained by piecing together mosaic tiles, each tile representing an individual orthographic or perspective image. On the surveyor missions, for example, classical mosaics were made by using an initial wide angle sweep to pick up general landscape features, and then, after landscape features were identified, using narrow angle sweeps to produce individual mosaic tiles. (In this paper we are concerned with mosaics that subtend large viewing angles both vertically and horizontally as well as with mosaics that subtend large viewing angles horizontally but not vertically and mosaics that subtend large viewing angles vertically but not horizontally.) A great number of issues must be addressed in producing a classical mosaic. The mosaic tiles must be pieced together; they can simply be abutted together, or they can be blended together. However the tiles are pieced together, correspondence must be established between neighboring tiles before the piecing process begins. Establishing correspondence can be difficult if images are not clearly in focus. The difficulties encountered with getting images in focus can include adverse atmospheric conditions, not being able to accurately determine the depths of objects being photographed, and differing depths used in taking contiguous images. (On the early surveyor missions, depths were determined by trial and error experimentation with images taken at different depths; on later missions, depths were determined by using stereo techniques.) One major issue in producing classical mosaics is compilation time — on the surveyor missions, for example, compilation time was so long that compilation was normally done after images were recorded.

Classical mosaics are planar; spherical images are spherical, not planar. Indeed, because of the (extrinsic) curvature of a spherical image, some distortion must occur whenever any spherical image is flattened into a planar image. Thus spherical images are ideally suited to computer analysis: on one hand, they cannot exist as analog planar images, and on the other hand there is nothing in the architecture of computers that destines computers to create or work with only planar images. Indeed, a spherical image can exist in (and only in) computer memory (either as a bit map or as an object map), with only a small part of the image displayed at any given time: that part of a spherical image to be displayed at a given time is projected onto the tangent plane to S_f at a point of contact. (We return to the implementation of these ideas in Sects. 5 and 6.) Spherical images thus avoid a serious problem that is encountered in creating classical mosaics — namely compromising the local distortion that occurs at the juncture of two mosaic tiles, and the global distortion that occurs since a true panoramic image cannot be flat.

We close this section with a brief discussion of planar perspective projection and spherical perspective projection that is related to the analysis of motion (see Chen and Penna[17] and Penna and Chen[7]). If we study the relationship between motions of a surface and changes in images of the surface using the planar perspective model, then there are three maps that must be considered (see Fig. 16(a)): the motion $F : S \rightarrow S'$ of the surface, the change $f_I : I \rightarrow I'$ in the images of the surface, and the motion $f_U : U \rightarrow U'$ of the domains of the parametrized surfaces that describe S and S'. Using the orthographic and spherical perspective models, there are only two maps to be considered (see Figs. 16(b) and (c)): the motion $F : S \rightarrow S'$ of the surface, and the motion $f_I : I \rightarrow I'$ in the images of the surface (which is now the same as the motion $f_U : U \rightarrow U'$ of the domains of the parametrized surfaces that describe S and S'). Our problem is simplified by using the orthographic and spherical perspective models since there is a natural inverse relationship between Monge surfaces and orthographic projection, and between spherical coordinate surfaces and spherical perspective projection.

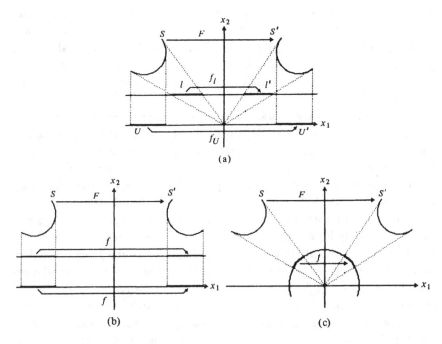

Fig. 16. The analysis of motion.

4. THE FUNDAMENTALS OF SPHERICAL GEOMETRY

In this section, we briefly discuss some of the fundamental results of spherical geometry, and how spherical geometry relates to projective geometry. Although practically we are often interested in the sphere S_f, in this section we restrict our attention, for simplicity, to the unit sphere

$$S^2 = \{P(p_1, p_2, p_3)|p_1^2 + p_2^2 + p_3^2 = 1\} \ .$$

The points of spherical geometry are the elements $P(p_1, p_2, p_3)$ of S^2. We also write $P(\mathbf{p})$ where the components of the (unit) vector $\mathbf{p}$ are the coordinates of P : $\mathbf{p} = \langle p_1, p_2, p_3 \rangle$. Associated to each point $P(\mathbf{p})$ in spherical geometry is the antipodal point $P^*(-\mathbf{p})$.

There are two types of lines in spherical geometry: lines (great circles on S^2) and directed lines (directed great circles on S^2).

Everyline l in S^2 is of the form

$$\{P(p_1, p_2, p_3) \in S^2|p_1l_1 + p_2l_2 + p_3l_3 = 0\}$$

where l_1, l_2 and l_3 are variables. The equation $p_1l_1 + p_2l_2 + p_3l_3 = 0$ is the equation of l. The components of the vector $\mathbf{l} = \langle l_1, l_2, l_3 \rangle$ are the coordinates of l. We write $l(\mathbf{l})$, and think of the vectors $\mathbf{l}$ as column vectors. (Indeed, l is the intersection of S^2 and the plane passing through the origin whose normal vector is $\mathbf{l}$.) By normalizing each $\mathbf{l}$ so that $|\mathbf{l}| = 1$, we may think of $l(\mathbf{l})$ as an element of S^2. Observe that $l(\mathbf{l}) = l(-\mathbf{l})$.

A directed line in S^2 is a line l in S^2 together with a preferred orientation of l. A directed line l can be specified by specifying a preferred choice $\mathbf{l}$ for the coordinates of l. (If we use the right-hand rule, this is equivalent to specifying a preferred choice for a unit normal vector to the plane in which l lies.) From this point of view, the directed lines $l(\mathbf{l})$ and $l^*(-\mathbf{l})$ are antipodal lines.

Every point $P(p_1, p_2, p_3)$ in S^2 is the intersection of all lines passing through it, and hence may be written in the form

$$\{l = \langle l_1, l_2, l_3 \rangle \in S^2|p_1l_1 + p_2l_2 + p_3l_3 = 0\}$$

where l_1, l_2 and l_3 are variables. The equation $p_1l_1 + p_2l_2 + p_3l_3 = 0$ is the equation of P. We think of vectors $\mathbf{p} = \langle p_1, p_2, p_3 \rangle$ representing the coordinates of a point as row vectors.

There are two types of duality between points and lines in spherical geometry. If we restrict our attention to undirected lines, then associated to each point $p(\mathbf{p})$ — and the antipodal point $P^*(-\mathbf{p})$ of P — is the line $l(\mathbf{p})$, and associated to each line $l(\mathbf{l})$ are the two antipodal points $P(\mathbf{l})$ and $P^*(-\mathbf{l})$. If we consider directed lines, then associated to each point $P(\mathbf{p})$ is the line $l(\mathbf{p})$, and associated to each line $l(\mathbf{l})$ is the point $P(\mathbf{l})$.

If $P(\mathbf{p})$ and $Q(\mathbf{q})$ are two non-antipodal points of S^2 then there is a unique undirected line l determined by P and Q, and $l = l(\mathbf{p} \times \mathbf{q})$. (This is because the vector $\mathbf{p} \times \mathbf{q}$ is normal to the plane determined by the origin, P, and Q.) The directed line from P to Q is $l(\mathbf{p} \times \mathbf{q})$, and the directed line from Q to P is $l^*(-\mathbf{p} \times \mathbf{q}) = l^*(\mathbf{q} \times \mathbf{p})$.

There are no parallel lines in spherical geometry: every line meets every other line. The intersection of the lines $l(\mathbf{l})$ and $m(\mathbf{m})$ consists of the two antipodal points $P(\mathbf{l} \times \mathbf{m})$ and $P^*(-\mathbf{l} \times \mathbf{m})$. (This is because the vector $\mathbf{l} \times \mathbf{m}$ is normal to the planes of both l and m.) The directed intersection of $l(\mathbf{l})$ and $m(\mathbf{m})$ is $P(\mathbf{l} \times \mathbf{m})$.

The three points $P(\mathbf{p}), Q(\mathbf{q})$, and $R(\mathbf{r})$ are collinear if and only if the three vectors $\mathbf{p}, \mathbf{q}$, and $\mathbf{r}$ are collinear, or, equivalently, if and only if the triple scalar product $[\mathbf{p}, \mathbf{q}, \mathbf{r}] = 0$. The three lines $l(\mathbf{l}), m(\mathbf{m})$, and $n(\mathbf{n})$ meet in a single pair of antipodal points if and only if the three vectors $\mathbf{l}, \mathbf{m}$ and $\mathbf{n}$ are collinear, or, equivalently, if and only if the triple scalar product $[\mathbf{l}, \mathbf{m}, \mathbf{n}] = 0$.

To see how spherical geometry is related to projective geometry, first recall (see Penna and Patterson[16] that the projective plane RP^2 is the set of all points $P[\mathbf{p}] = P[p_1, p_2, p_3]$ where $\mathbf{p} = \langle p_1, p_2, p_3 \rangle$ is a nonzero vector in R^3, two triplets $[\mathbf{p}]$ and $[\mathbf{q}]$ being considered equal if and only if there is a nonzero constant c for which $\mathbf{p} = c\mathbf{q}$. In a similar manner, we can think of S^2 as the set of all points $P[\mathbf{p}] = P[p_1, p_2, p_3]$ where $\mathbf{p} = \langle p_1, p_2, p_3 \rangle$ is a nonzero vector in R^3, two triples $[\mathbf{p}]$ and $[\mathbf{q}]$ being considered equal if and only if $\mathbf{p}/|\mathbf{p}| = \mathbf{q}/|\mathbf{q}|$ or $\mathbf{p} = (|\mathbf{p}|/|\mathbf{q}|)\mathbf{q}$. Thus, the definition of RP^2 and S^2 are similar in that in the definition of RP^2 the constant c is arbitrary, while in the definition of S^2 the specific constant $c = |\mathbf{p}/|\mathbf{q}|$ is used. The definitions of RP^2 and S^2 differ in that in RP^2, $[\mathbf{p}]$ and $[-\mathbf{p}]$ are equal since $\mathbf{p} = (-1)*(-\mathbf{p})$, but in S^2, $[\mathbf{p}]$ and $[-\mathbf{p}]$ are equal since $\mathbf{p}/|\mathbf{p}| \neq -\mathbf{p}/|\mathbf{p}|$. (In fact the vectors $\mathbf{p}/|\mathbf{p}|$ and $-\mathbf{p}/|\mathbf{p}|$ have opposite directions.) In summary, we can think of RP^2 as being obtained by identifying antipodal points $P[\mathbf{p}]$ and $P^*[-\mathbf{p}]$ in S^2.

This framework for thinking about spherical geometry explains the similarity between the incidence results of spherical and projective geometry. Furthermore, it can be extended to accommodate results that are of interest in computer vision and image understanding.

For example, spherical perspective projection π_s onto S^2 is given (using Cartesian coordinates in 3-dimensional world space) by

$$\pi_s(x, y, z) = [x, y, z] = \left[\frac{x}{\rho}, \frac{y}{\rho}, \frac{z}{\rho} \right]$$

where $\rho = \sqrt{x^2 + y^2 + z^2}$, or (using spherical coordinates in 3-dimensional world space) by

$$\pi_s(\rho, \theta, \phi) = [\sin \phi \cos \theta, \sin \phi \sin \theta, \cos \phi] \ .$$

The component functions x/ρ, y/ρ, and z/ρ of π_s are, in fact, the first order spherical harmonics defined in Ref. 6.

Further, if we project the line

$$x_1 = a_1 t + b_1, \quad x_2 = a_2 t + b_2, \quad x_3 = a_3 t + b_3$$

in 3-dimensional world space to S^2, we obtain half of the line $l(\mathbf{a} \times \mathbf{b})$ where $\mathbf{a} = \langle a_1, a_2, a_3 \rangle$ and $\mathbf{b} = \langle b_1, b_2, b_3 \rangle$, and the vanishing points of this half-line are $A[\mathbf{a}]$ and $A^*[-\mathbf{a}]$. (See Magee and Aggarwal[3].) Not only are vanishing points easy to compute, but, as opposed to projective geometry in which only one vanishing point is associated to each line, in spherical geometry two vanishing points are associated to each half-line: in many applications having two vanishing points is intuitively more natural than having just one.

In addition to the existence of concepts and formulas in spherical geometry similar to the concepts and formulas of projective geometry, there are also a number of other concepts and formulas that apply in spherical geometry that do not easily extend to projective geometry.

The concept of directed lines allows discussion of betweenness — as in "B is between A and C" — and consequently discussion of (line or great circle) segments. With projective geometry, the corresponding concept is separation — separation with respect to an ideal point is equivalent to betweenness. The concept of directed lines also allows discussion of the sides of a line (see Chazelle et al.[9]).

In spherical geometry, there are also simple metric concepts (concepts of measurement). (The techniques of spherical trigonometry are presented in Ayres[15].) For points, the distance d between $P[\mathbf{p}]$ and $Q[\mathbf{q}]$ is the length of the minimal geodesic joining P and Q. Hence d is always between 0 and π. If P and Q are not antipodal points, $\cos d = \langle \mathbf{p}, \mathbf{q} \rangle / |\mathbf{p}| |\mathbf{q}|$; if P and Q

are antipodal, then $d = \pi$. For lines, the angle θ between $l[\mathbf{l}]$ and $m[\mathbf{m}]$ is the angle between the planes that determine l and m. Hence θ is also always between 0 and π, and, in fact, $\cos\theta = \langle \mathbf{l}, \mathbf{m}\rangle/|\mathbf{l}||\mathbf{m}|$. The projective analogs for these concepts is based on the cross ratio — a nonlinear scaling of the projective plane. (The nonlinearity of the cross ratio reflects the distortion that occurs in the projected image of an object as the object is moved relative to a fixed observer and image plane as illustrated in Figs. 11 and 12.)

The transformations of the sphere that preserve spherical concepts are more restrictive than the transformations of the projective plane that preserve projective concepts, and hence they are also much simpler. The transformations of the sphere that preserve spherical concepts are generated by rotations and the antipodal map. Rotations are maps $T : S^2 \rightarrow S^2$ of the form $T(\mathbf{p}) = \mathbf{p} * R$ where R is a 3×3 rotation matrix — a matrix for which $R * R^T = I^{3\times3}, T$ denoting transpose and $I^{3\times3}$ denoting 3×3 identity matrix. The dimension of the space of rotations is 3-generators for the rotations of S^2 are rotations through the Euler angles θ (pan), ϕ (tilt), and ψ (swing): rotation through θ radians about the x_3-axis followed by rotation through ϕ radians about the resulting x_2-axis followed by rotation through ψ radians about the resulting x_1-axis (see Fig. 17). The rotation matrix representing an arbitrary such rotation written in Cartesian coordinates is

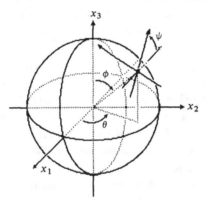

Fig. 17. The Euler angles, θ, ϕ, and ψ.

$$R =$$
$$\begin{pmatrix} \cos\theta\cos\phi & \sin\theta\cos\phi & -\sin\phi \\ \cos\theta\sin\phi\sin\psi - \sin\theta\cos\psi & \sin\theta\sin\phi\sin\psi + \cos\theta\cos\psi & \cos\phi\sin\psi \\ \cos\theta\sin\phi\cos\psi + \sin\theta\sin\psi & \sin\theta\sin\phi\cos\psi - \cos\theta\sin\psi & \cos\phi\cos\psi \end{pmatrix} .$$

Rotations preserve orientation. The antipodal map is given by $T(\mathbf{p}) = -\mathbf{p}$; the antipodal map reverses orientation.

5. CREATING AND DISPLAYING BIT ORIENTED SPHERICAL IMAGES—THEORETICAL IMAGES

A *bit oriented image* (whether it is planar or spherical) is an image that is defined by an image intensity function: a function that associates to each picture element — or pixel — a number representing a level of color, brightness, and/or tint. An *object oriented image* (whether it is planar or spherical) is an image that is defined by geometric figures such as curves and surfaces. In this section and in Sect. 6 we discuss the process of creating and displaying bit oriented spherical images; in Sect. 7 we discuss the process of creating and displaying object oriented spherical images.

Two different types of bit oriented spherical images can arise in the study of computer vision and image understanding: theoretically defined images and real images. In this section we discuss theoretically defined images; in Sect. 6 we discuss real images.

The basic components in the process of creating and displaying theoretically defined bit oriented spherical images are illustrated in Fig. 18. The first component is a parametrization of S_f; throughout this paper we primarily use the parametrization $\mathbf{s}: (0, 2\pi) \times (0, \pi) \to S_f$ given by

$$\mathbf{s}(\theta, \phi) = (\sin\phi\cos\theta, \sin\phi\sin\theta, \cos\phi)/f .$$

The second component is an intensity function $i = i(\theta, \phi)$ that associates an image intensity to each point in the space parametrizing S_f. The third component is a parametrization $\mathbf{y}$ of the tangent plane to S_f at each point P_0 that allows an image to be mapped to a display device. To display a spherical image, a point P_0 on S_f is specified, as well as parameters ψ_0, and $d\theta$ and $d\phi$ that determine the orientation (or swing) and extent of the image to be displayed, respectively. To determine the image intensity of a pixel on the display device, the pixel is mapped to the tangent plane to S_f at P_0, projected onto S_f, and then traced back through the parameterization $\mathbf{s}$ to a pair (θ, ϕ) in the space $(0, 2\pi) \times (0, \pi)$ parametrizing S_f; the image intensity at the original point is the intensity value associated to (θ, ϕ).

This mechanism is important for two reasons. On one hand, as we see in Sect. 6, real image intensity is determined from a flat recording; that is, from an image obtained by projecting an object onto a flat recording surface such as the film of a camera. Thus, to create a real spherical image

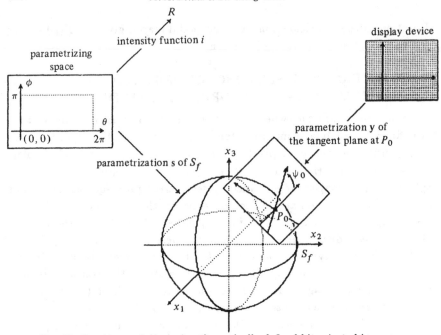

Fig. 18. Creating and displaying theoretically defined bit oriented images.

in computer memory, it is necessary to relate planar and spherical images. On the other hand, display devices (currently, at least) display only planar images. Thus, even though a spherical image can be saved in computer memory, only part of a spherical image can be displayed at any given time; and to display part of a spherical image, we approximate it by a planar image. (From the point of view of computer graphics, a spherical image can only be viewed in an interactive environment in which the user can vary that part of a spherical image which is to be displayed at any given time.)

To illustrate this procedure, we first discuss computation of image intensity. Suppose $i : I \to R$ denotes the *Lambertian intensity function*, which is defined for each point $Q = \pi(P)$ in the image I of a spherically parametrized surface S by

$$f(Q) = \begin{cases} r(P)\langle \mathbf{n}_p, \boldsymbol{\sigma} \rangle & \text{if} \quad \mathbf{n}_p, \boldsymbol{\sigma} \geq 0 \\ 0 & \text{if} \quad \langle \mathbf{n}_p, \boldsymbol{\sigma} \rangle < 0 \end{cases}$$

where $r(P)$ is the albedo of S, at p, $<\!\!-\!\!, -\!\!>$ is the Euclidean product, $\mathbf{n}_p$ is the unit normal vector to S at P, and $\boldsymbol{\sigma} = \langle \sigma_1, \sigma_2, \sigma_3 \rangle$ is a unit vector in the direction of a light source, which we assume is at infinity. For simplicity, we assume that r is constant; in fact, we assume $r = 1$.

Now

$$s_1 = (-\sin\phi\sin\theta, \sin\phi\cos\theta, 0)/f$$
$$\text{and} \quad s_2 = (\cos\phi\cos\theta, \cos\phi\sin\theta, -\sin\phi)/f$$

so

$$\langle s, s \rangle = 1/f^2 \qquad \langle s_1, s_1 \rangle = \sin^2\phi/f^2 \qquad \langle s_2, s_2 \rangle = 1/f^2$$
$$\langle s, s_1 \rangle = 0 \qquad \langle s, s_2 \rangle = 0 \qquad \langle s_1, s_2 \rangle = 0$$
$$s \times s_1 = -\sin\phi/f s_2 \quad s_1 \times s_2 = -\sin\phi/f s \quad s \times s_2 = \csc\phi/f s_1 \ .$$

Thus if $S = x(U)$ where $U \subseteq (0, 2\pi) \times (0, \pi)$ and $x = \rho s$ then

$$x_1 = \rho_1 s + \rho s_1, \quad x_2 = \rho_2 s + \rho s_2$$

$$\langle x_1, x_1 \rangle = \langle \rho_1 s + \rho s_1, \rho_1 s + \rho s_1 \rangle = (\rho_1^2 + \rho^2 \sin^2\phi)/f^2$$
$$\langle x_1, x_2 \rangle = \langle \rho_1 s + \rho s_1, \rho_2 s + \rho s_2 \rangle = \rho_1\rho_2/f^2$$
$$\langle x_2, x_2 \rangle = \langle \rho_2 s + \rho s_2, \rho_2 s + \rho s_2 \rangle = (\rho_2^2 + \rho^2)/f^2$$

and

$$x_1 \times x_2 = \rho\rho_1 \csc\phi/f s_1 + \rho\rho_2 \sin\phi/f s_2 - \rho^2 \sin\phi/f s \ .$$

If follows that

$$n = \frac{x_1 \times x_2}{|x_1 \times x_2|} = \frac{\rho_1 \csc\phi s_1 + \rho_2 \sin\phi s_2 - \rho\sin\phi s}{(\rho_1^2 + \rho_2^2 \sin^2\phi + \rho^2 \sin^2\phi)^{1/2}} \ .$$

Thus

$$i(Q) = \frac{\rho_1 \csc\phi \langle s_1, \sigma \rangle + \rho_2 \sin\phi \langle s_2, \sigma \rangle - \rho\sin\phi, \langle s, \sigma \rangle}{(\rho_1^2 + \rho_2^2 \sin^2\phi + \rho^2 \sin^2\phi)^{1/2}} \ .$$

Next we determine the parametrization $y : R^2 \to \Pi$ of the tangent plane Π to S_f at P_0. To do this (see Fig. 19), we must know the spherical coordinates $(1/f, \theta_0, \phi_0)$ of P_0 and the swing angle ψ_0 of the coordinate system of Π at P_0 relative to the (standard) coordinate system whose x_1-direction is

$$v_1 = \langle p_2/\sqrt{p_1^2 + p_2^2}, -p_1/\sqrt{p_1^2 + p_2^2}, 0 \rangle$$

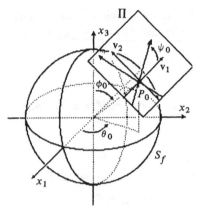

Fig. 19. Parametrizing Π.

and whose x_2-direction is

$$\mathbf{v}_2 = \langle -f p_1 p_3/\sqrt{p_1^2 + p_2^2}, -f p_2 p_3/\sqrt{p_1^2 + p_2^2}, f\sqrt{p_1^2 + p_2^2} \rangle$$

where, for simplicity, we denote the Cartesian coordinates of P_0 by (p_1, p_2, p_3). (The vector $\mathbf{v}_1$ is parallel to the $x_1 x_2$-coordinate plane, and the position vector $\mathbf{O}P_0 = \langle p_1, p_2, p_3 \rangle$, $\mathbf{v}_1$, and $\mathbf{v}_2$ are mutually perpendicular; thus the vector $\mathbf{v}_2$ points north on S_f to the north pole $NP(0, 0, 1/f)$ of S_f.) We must also know the parameters $d\theta$ and $d\phi$ determine the horizontal and vertical size of the window to be displayed in radians.

The equation of Π is

$$p_1 x_1 + p_2 x_2 + p_3 x_3 = 1/f^2$$

so the map $\mathbf{z} : R^2 \to \Pi$ given, in affine coordinates, by

$$\mathbf{z}(u_1, u_2) = \mathbf{O}P_o + u_1 \mathbf{v}_1 + u_2 \mathbf{v}_2 = M^* \begin{pmatrix} u_1 \\ u_2 \\ 1 \end{pmatrix}$$

where

$$M = \begin{pmatrix} \dfrac{p_2}{\sqrt{p_1^2+p_2^2}} & \dfrac{-fp_1p_3}{\sqrt{p_1^2+p_2^2}} & p_1 \\[2mm] \dfrac{-p_1}{\sqrt{p_1^2+p_2^2}} & \dfrac{-fp_2p_3}{\sqrt{p_1^2+p_2^2}} & p_2 \\[2mm] 0 & f\sqrt{p_1^2+p_2^2} & p_3 \end{pmatrix}$$

parametrizes Π. This parametrization takes the origin $O(0, 0)$ to P_o. The Jacobian matrix $d\mathbf{z}$ of $\mathbf{z}$ is

$$d\mathbf{z} = \begin{pmatrix} \dfrac{p_2}{\sqrt{p_1^2+p_2^2}} & \dfrac{-fp_1p_3}{\sqrt{p_1^2+p_2^2}} \\[2mm] \dfrac{-p_1}{\sqrt{p_1^2+p_2^2}} & \dfrac{-fp_2p_3}{\sqrt{p_1^2+p_2^2}} \\[2mm] 0 & f\sqrt{p_1^2+p_2^2} \end{pmatrix}$$

so multiplication by $d\mathbf{z}$ takes the vector $\langle 1, 0\rangle$ to $\mathbf{v}_1$, and the vector $\langle 0, 1\rangle$ to $\mathbf{v}_2$. Thus $\mathbf{z}$ represents the (standard) parametrization of Π. Consequently $\mathbf{y} = \mathbf{z} \circ R : R^2 \to \Pi$, where R represents rotation through the swing angle ψ_0

$$\mathbf{y}(u_1, u_2) = (\mathbf{z} \circ R)(u_1, u_2) = M * \begin{pmatrix} \cos\psi_0 & \sin\psi_0 & 0 \\ -\sin\psi_0 & \cos\psi_0 & 0 \\ 0 & 0 & 1 \end{pmatrix} * \begin{pmatrix} u_1 \\ u_2 \\ 1 \end{pmatrix}$$

is the desired parametrization of Π.

(The parametrization $\mathbf{z}$ of Π is related to the standard parametrization

$$\mathbf{z}_0(u_1, u_2) = (u_1, u_2, 1/f)$$

of the usual viewplane $x_3 = 1/f$ as follows (see Fig. 20): Let M_1 represent counterclockwise rotation of the viewplane $x_3 = 1/f$ through $\pi/2 + \tan^{-1}(p_2/p_1)$ radians about the origin — or, equivalently, counterclockwise rotation

$$\begin{pmatrix} x_1 \\ x_2 \\ x_3 \end{pmatrix} \to M_1 * \begin{pmatrix} x_1 \\ x_2 \\ x_3 \end{pmatrix}$$

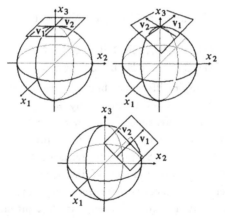

Fig. 20. Obtaining the coordinate system on Π through rotations.

of Euclidean three-space through $\pi/2 + \tan^{-1}(p_2/p_1)$ radians about the x_3-axis — and let M_2 represent counterclockwise rotation

$$\begin{pmatrix} x_1 \\ x_2 \\ x_3 \end{pmatrix} \to M_2 * \begin{pmatrix} x_1 \\ x_2 \\ x_3 \end{pmatrix}$$

of Euclidean three-space about the axis determined by the vector

$$\langle 0, 0, 1 \rangle \times \langle p_1, p_2, p_3 \rangle = \langle p_2, -p_1, 0 \rangle$$

through $\cos^{-1}(p_3/\sqrt{p_1^2 + p_2^2 + p_3^2})$ radians. Then $M = M_2 * M_1$.)

Assuming the spherical coordinates $(1/f, \theta_0, \phi_0)$ of P_0, as well as the swing angle ψ_0, and the horizontal and vertical extents $d\theta$ and $d\phi$ of the image are specified, the image intensity of the pixel whose coordinates are (X_1, X_2) is determined as follows: Let (q_1, q_2, q_3) denote the Cartesian coordinates of $Q = \mathbf{y}(X_1, X_2)$. The Cartesian coordinates of the projection of Q onto S_f are

$$\left(q_1/\sqrt{q_1^2 + q_2^2 + q_3^2}, q_2/\sqrt{q_1^2 + q_2^2 + q_3^2}, q_3/\sqrt{q_1^2 + q_2^2 + q_3^2} \right) .$$

Thus $Q = \mathbf{s}(\theta, \phi)$ where

$$\theta = \begin{cases} \tan^{-1}(q_2/q_1) & \text{if} \quad q_1 > 0 \\ \pi + \tan^{-1}(q_2/q_1) & \text{if} \quad q_1 < 0 \end{cases}$$

$$\phi = \cos^{-1}(q_3/\sqrt{q_1^2 + q_2^2 + q_3^2})$$

and the image intensity associated to (X_1, X_2) is $i(\theta, \phi)$.

6.   CREATING AND DISPLAYING BIT ORIENTED SPHERICAL IMAGES — REAL IMAGES

There are several major differences between creating and displaying real bit oriented spherical images and theoretically defined bit oriented spherical images. The first major difference is that with real bit oriented spherical images, the parametrizing space of S_f and the intensity function defined on the parametrizing space of S_f must be replaced by a block of computer memory and storage in that memory of intensity values. In particular, instead of being defined on a continuum, intensity functions are defined on a discrete set. The second major difference is that intensity functions are defined by a sampling procedure that essentially reverses the process used to display a theoretically defined bit oriented spherical image.

The basic components in the process of creating and displaying real bit oriented spherical images are illustrated in Fig. 21. The first component is a block of memory in which a virtual spherical image is stored. The second component is a subdivision of S_f into picture elements, or pixels. The third component is a parametrization of S_f by the block of memory,

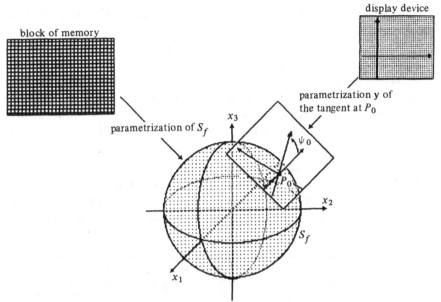

Fig. 21. Creating and displaying real bit oriented images.

which associates a pixel to each location in the block of memory, and hence the image intensity associated to each location to the corresponding pixel.

To create a spherical image, we assume that fiducial readings obtained when an image is taken (as might be obtained in the process of taking an aerial photograph) or other photogrammetric techniques (see Wolf[18]), are used to determine the spherical coordinates $(1/f, \theta_0, \phi_0)$ of the point P_0 of contact of the plane Π of the image and S_f, the swing angle ψ_0 of the coordinate system of Π relative to the (standard) coordinate system of P_0 whose x_1-direction is $\mathbf{v}_1$ and whose x_2-direction is $\mathbf{v}_2$, and the parameters $d\theta$ and $d\phi$ that determine the horizontal and vertical size of the window to be displayed. The image intensity for a position in memory corresponding — under parametrization of S_f and radial projection from S_f to Π — to a point in the real image is obtained by sampling the real image at that (real image) point. By repeating this procedure with multiple images, a spherical mosaic is created. To display a spherical image, as before, a point (P_0 on S_f is specified, as well as parameters ψ_0, and $d\theta$ and $d\phi$ that determine the orientation (or swing) and extent of the image to be displayed. To determine the image intensity of a pixel on the display device, the pixel is mapped to the tangent plane to S_f at P_0, projected to a pixel on S_f, and traced back through the parametrization $\mathbf{s}$ to a position (θ, ϕ) in memory;

the image intensity at the original pixel is the intensity value associated to
(θ, ϕ).

This procedure for creating and displaying spherical images is similar to
the procedure used for creating and displaying real orthographic and planar
perspective images. When creating and displaying real orthographic and
planar perspective images, however, memory may be viewed as a planar
array of images intensities — equally spaced both horizontally and vertically
— and that part of the image to be displayed at a given time is viewed as
a subset of this array (see Fig. 22). Since a sphere cannot be flattened into
a planar region, creating and displaying real spherical images cannot be
viewed in the same way. If memory is to be viewed as a planar array of
image intensities, creating and displaying real bit oriented spherical images
requires using a nonlinear map (or parametrization) of S_f by a block of
memory.

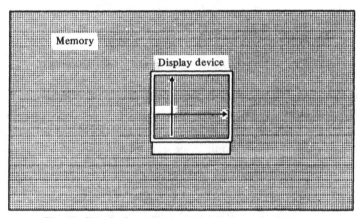

Fig. 22. Standard memory and display organization.

An important issue consequently arises in creating and displaying spherical images, that does not arise in creating and displaying orthographic or
planar perspective images. The issue is how to make efficient use of memory
while maintaining an easy scheme for addressing pixels on S_f. Throughout this paper, for example, we think of memory as a $\theta\phi$-coordinate plane,
where $(\theta, \phi) \in (0, 2\pi) \times (0, \pi)$, and we parametrized S_f by

$$s(\theta, \phi) = (\sin\phi\cos\theta, \sin\phi\sin\theta, \cos\phi)/f \ .$$

Although this parametrization has the virtue of simplicity in addressing
pixels on S_f, it has the drawback of not always being an efficient use of

memory. The reason for this (see Fig. 23) is that the pixels that cover S_f are denser near the north and south poles than they are near the equator; thus if a subdivision of S_f is chosen that yields sufficient resolution near the equator, memory is wasted in excessive resolution near the poles. For an image that does not contain the north and south poles, however, this may not necessarily be a significant issue. (Nor, for that matter, is it necessarily a significant issue for any image that does not contain a single pair of antipodal points P and P^*: if $P = \mathbf{s}(\theta_0, \phi_0)$, then the poles of the parametrization

$$\mathbf{s}_{\theta_0, \phi_0}(\theta, \phi) = \left(\sin(\phi - \phi_0)\cos(\theta - \theta_0), \sin(\phi - \phi_0)\sin(\theta - \theta_0), \cos(\phi - \phi_0)\right)/f$$

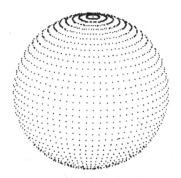

Fig. 23. Pixels are denser near the poles.

are P and P^*.) For other images, however, this may be a significant issue. In this case, and in general, there are several techniques that may be applied to make a more efficient use of memory.

One technique is to interpolate intensity values where the density of pixels is low. Although this technique is simple, it can produce fuzzy images. A better technique is to view memory as a planar array of image intensities — unequally spaced horizontally, vertically, or both horizontally and vertically — and to view that part of the image to be displayed at a given time as a subset of this array (see Fig. 24).

Another technique is to use a subdivision and parametrization of S_f (other than $\mathbf{s}$) that complement the image (better than $\mathbf{s}$). One such choice, for example, might be the polar parametrization

$$\mathbf{s}(\alpha, \beta) = \left(\frac{\alpha \sin\sqrt{\alpha^2 + \beta^2}}{\sqrt{\alpha^2 + \beta^2}}, \frac{\beta \sin\sqrt{\alpha^2 + \beta^2}}{\sqrt{\alpha^2 + \beta^2}}, \cos\sqrt{\alpha^2 + \beta^2}\right) \Big/ f$$

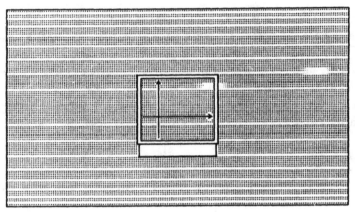

Fig. 24. A nonuniform memory map.

where $\sqrt{\alpha^2 + \beta^2} \leq \pi$. (This parametrization — see Fig. 25 — maps circles centered at the origin to circles of latitude, and radial lines through the origin to circles of longitude.) Another choice might be the stereographic parametrization

$$s(u_1, u_2) = \left(\frac{4u_1}{u_1^2 + u_2^2 + 4}, \; \frac{4u_2}{u_1^2 + u_2^2 + 4}, \; \frac{u_1^2 + u_2^2 - 4}{u_1^2 + u_2^2 + 4} \right) \Big/ f$$

where $(u_1, u_2) \in R^2$. (This parametrization — see Fig. 26 — maps a point P in the tangent plane S_f at the south pole to the point Q of intersection of S_f and the line joining P and the north pole.) In both cases, for the sake of efficiency, we may again choose to view memory as a planar array of image intensities — unequally spaced both horizontally and vertically — and that part of the image to be displayed at a given time as a subset of this array. (Stereographic parametrization has the advantage of being a conformal map from R^2 to S_f. An isometry between two surfaces is a map from one surface to the other which preserves dot products of tangent vectors, and hence lengths of curves and angles between curves. A conformal mapping is a mapping from one surface to another surface for which the lengths of tangents vectors need not be preserved, but for which the tangent vectors at each point are all stretched by the same factor, the specific factor possibly varying from point to point. Thus a conformal map preserves angles between curves.)

Another technique is to view memory as being arranged in a nonrectangular fashion and to use a standard parametrization. For example, with the polar parametrization an annular configuration (see Fig. 27) similar

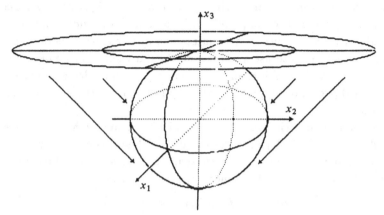

Fig. 25. The polar parametrization.

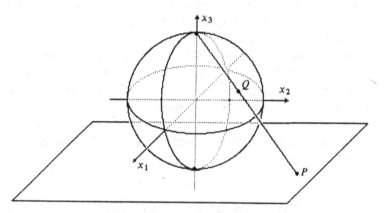

Fig. 26. Stereographic projection.

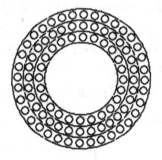

Fig. 27. An annular memory configuration.

to the configuration used in storing data on a disk, might be appropriate. The (virtual) distribution of points in the annuli — the width and number of points in each annulus — determines the distribution of points on S_f. Another technique is to use a nonstandard subdivision and a nonstandard parametrization of S_f. For example, S_f might be subdivided and addressed by equiareal pixels, or by pixels located by projecting integer lattice points R^3 down to S_f.

The analytic description of how a real bit oriented spherical image is created and displayed depends the specific combination of memory configuration and parametrization of S_f chosen. To illustrate general techniques, however, let us return to the standard parametrization

$$\mathbf{s}(\theta, \phi) = (\sin \phi \cos \theta, \sin \phi \sin \theta, \cos \phi)/f$$

of S_f. The formulas for displaying a real bit oriented spherical image are the same as those for displaying theoretically defined spherical bit oriented images presented in Sect. 5. It remains, therefore, to discuss how to create a real bit oriented spherical image.

To do this, assume we are given a real image and that from fiducial readings obtained when the image is taken (as might be obtained in the process of taking an aerial photograph) or from other photogrammetric techniques (see Wolf[18]) we can determine the Cartesian coordinates (p_1, p_2, p_3) of the point P_0 of contact of the image plane Π and S_f, as well as the swing angle ψ_0, and the horizontal and vertical extents $d\theta$ and $d\phi$ of the image.

The equation of Π is

$$p_1 x_1 + p_2 x_2 + p_3 x_3 = 1/f^2 \ .$$

If Q' is the point on S_f whose spherical coordinates are $(1/f, \theta, \phi)$, the Cartesian coordinates of Q' are

$$(\sin \phi \cos \theta, \sin \phi \sin \theta, \cos \phi)/f$$

and the coordinates of the perspective projection Q of Q' onto Π can be obtained by intersecting the line passing through Q' and the origin with Π; the coordinates of Q are

$$(\sin \phi \cos \theta, \sin \phi \sin \theta, \cos \phi)/f^2(p_1 \sin \phi \cos \theta + p_2 \sin \phi \sin \theta + p_3 \cos \phi) \ .$$

The Cartesian $X_1 X_2$-coordinates of $Q(q_1, q_2, q_3)$ are given by $\mathbf{z}^{-1}(q_1, q_2, q_3)$. Since

$$M^T M = \begin{pmatrix} 1 & 0 & 0 \\ 0 & 1 & 0 \\ 0 & 0 & 1/f^2 \end{pmatrix}$$

where M is the 3×3 matrix defining the parametrization $\mathbf{z}$ (see Sect. 5), it follows that

$$\mathbf{z}^{-1}(q_1, q_2, q_3) = (q_1 q_2 q_3) \begin{bmatrix} \frac{p_2}{\sqrt{p_1^2+p_2^2}} & \frac{-fp_1p_3}{\sqrt{p_1^2+p_2^2}} \\ \frac{-p_1}{\sqrt{p_1^2+p_2^2}} & \frac{-fp_2p_3}{\sqrt{p_1^2+p_2^2}} \\ 0 & f\sqrt{p_1^2+p_2^2} \end{bmatrix} .$$

Thus the image intensity associated to the memory location (θ, ϕ) is the image intensity associated to the point whose image coordinates are

$$X_1 = k(p_2 \sin\phi \cos\theta - p_1 \sin\phi \sin\theta)$$

$$X_2 = kf\left(-p_1 p_3 \sin\phi \cos\theta - p_2 p_3 \sin\phi \sin\theta + \sqrt{p_1^2 + p_2^2} \cos\phi\right)$$

where

$$k = 1/f^2 \left(p_1 \sin\phi \cos\theta + p_2 \sin\phi \sin\theta + p_3 \cos\phi\right) .$$

7. CREATING AND DISPLAYING OBJECT ORIENTED SPHERICAL IMAGES

One important aspect of object oriented images that distinguishes object oriented spherical images from bit oriented images is that figures which define object oriented images can be described in terms of equations. Such images can thus be characterized by the parameters that determine the set of equations describing them. In this section we discuss some standard spherical curves and their equations. The study of these curves and their equators is important since, for example, they are level curves of spherical harmonics, and hence understanding them contributes to understanding the complete set of geometric features defined by the expansion of an intensity function in terms of spherical harmonics (see Chen[6]). As in Sect. 4, we restrict our attention in this section to the unit sphere S^2 for simplicity.

In Sect. 4, we saw that the equation of a line on the sphere (a great circle) may be written in the form $\langle \mathbf{p}, \mathbf{l} \rangle = 0$ for some (unit) vector $\mathbf{l}$ in S^2. More generally, the equation of a circle on S^2 whose 3-dimensional world center is $(1 - r^2)^{1/2} \mathbf{l}_0$, where $\mathbf{l}_0$ is in S^2, and whose radius is r, where r is in the interval $[0,1]$, is $\langle \mathbf{p}, \mathbf{l} \rangle = (1 - r^2)^{1/2}$. This is because the graph of the equation $\langle \mathbf{p}, \mathbf{l} \rangle = (1 - r^2)^{1/2}$ on S^2 is the intersection of S^2 and the plane in R^3 whose equation is $\langle \mathbf{p}, \mathbf{l} \rangle = (1 - r^2)^{1/2}$:

$$\{P(\mathbf{p}) \in S^2 | \langle \mathbf{p}, \mathbf{l} \rangle = (1 - r^2)^{1/2}\} = S^2 \cap \{P(\mathbf{p}) \in R^3 | \langle \mathbf{p}, \mathbf{l} \rangle = (1 - r^2)^{1/2}\} .$$

From the point of view of an observer positioned at the origin, the equation of the circle whose spherical center is l_0 and whose radius is subtended by an arch of ϕ radians is $\langle \mathbf{p}, \mathbf{1} \rangle = \sin \phi$.

In spherical geometry, the equations of curves are not unique. For example, the circle whose equation is $p_3 = \sqrt{2}/2$ also has the equation $p_1^2 + p_2^2 = 1/2$. The equations in p_1, p_2, and p_3 of any curve are related by the universal relation $p_1^2 + p_2^2 + p_3^2 = 1$. For example, if $p_3 = \sqrt{2}/2$ then $p_3^2 = 1/2$; thus if $p_1^2 + p_2^2 + p_3^2 = 1$ then $p_1^2 + p_2^2 + 1/2 = 1$ so $p_1^2 + p_2^2 = 1/2$. (Another way to think of this is that the intersection of S^2 with the plane in R^3 whose equation is $p_3 = \sqrt{2}/2$ is the same as the intersection of S^2 with the right circular cylinder in R^3 whose equation is $p_1^2 + p_2^2 = 1/2$.) It does not, therefore, make sense to classify spherical curves by the order of their equation(s) in p_1, p_2, and p_3. Observe, in passing, that the equation of the circle discussed above can also be written $\phi = \pi/4$ since $p_3 = \cos \phi = \cos \pi/4 = \sqrt{2}/2$.

Circles are spherical curves determined by the intersection of S^2 and planes in R^3. Circles are, from this point of view, only one type of a broad class of spherical curves. In general, this class of quadric curves consists of the set of all intersections of S^2 with arbitrary quadric surfaces whose equations are of the form

$$ap_1^2 + bp_2^2 + cp_3^2 + dp_1p_2 + ep_1p_3 + fp_2p_3 + gp_1 + hp_2 + ip_3 + j = 0 \ ,$$

$a, b, c, d, e, f, g, h, i$, and j being real constants.

While circles are planar curves, quadric curves are, in general, not planar. Thus quadric curves are not simply the familiar quadric sections. Quadric curves are, however, closed.

In addition to the curves obtained by the intersecting S^2 with other surfaces in R^3, another important class of spherical curves are those curves obtained by projecting curves in R^3 down to curves on S^2 by π_s. In Sect. 4, for example, we discussed the projection of lines in R^3 to circles on S^2. As that example illustrates, the most efficient way to handle such curves is parametrically: if $\boldsymbol{\alpha}(t) = (\alpha_1(t), \alpha_2(t), \alpha_3(t))$, then $(\pi_s \circ \boldsymbol{\alpha})(t) = [\alpha_1(t), \alpha_2(t), \alpha_3(t)]$.

There are a great number of general results that relate to spherical curves. We simply cite some of these results here; see Millman and Parker[19] for more results and further details. For example, there is a special Frenet-Serret apparatus and Frenet-Serret Theorem for spherical curves that involves the First and Second Fundamental Forms on a sphere (see also Sect 9). The normal curvature κ_n of a spherical curve is constant; on

S^2, that constant is 1, and the square κ^2 of the Gaussian curvature of any spherical curve on S^2 is $1 + \kappa_g^2$ where κ_g is the geodesic curvature of the curve. The total torsion of any spherical curve is 0. Finally, spherical curves can be completely classified by their curvature and torsion (see Bishop[20]], Wong[21], and Breuer and Gottlieb[22]).

PART II — APPLICATIONS

8. PHOTOMETRIC STEREO AND VARIATIONS IN DEPTH

In Sects. 5 and 6 we determined the image intensity i as a function of θ and ϕ for bit oriented spherical images. In this section we use photometric stereo (also known as the method of multiple light sources) to determine the variations $\rho_1 = \partial\rho/\partial\theta$ and $\rho_2 = \partial\rho/\partial\phi$ of ρ with respect to θ and ϕ for a spherical surface $\mathbf{x} = \rho\mathbf{s}$. (See Penna and Chen[7].) Since $\mathbf{x}$ is completely determined by ρ, knowing the depth value ρ of one point is theoretically enough to completely determine $\mathbf{x}$ locally since we can use finite difference methods to numerically solve a corresponding system of partial differential equations.

For simplicity, we assume that $r = 1$ throughout this section. We rewrite the image intensity equation

$$i(Q) = \frac{\rho_1 \csc\phi\langle\mathbf{s}_1,\boldsymbol{\sigma}\rangle + \rho_2 \sin\phi\langle\mathbf{s}_2,\boldsymbol{\sigma}\rangle - \rho\sin\phi\langle\mathbf{s},\boldsymbol{\sigma}\rangle}{(\rho_1^2 + \rho_2^2\sin^2\phi + \rho^2\sin^2\phi)^{1/2}}$$

(see Sect. 5) as

$$\left(\csc\phi\langle\mathbf{s}_1,\boldsymbol{\sigma}\rangle \sin\phi\langle\mathbf{s}_2,\boldsymbol{\sigma}\rangle - \sin\phi\langle\mathbf{s},\boldsymbol{\sigma}\rangle\right)\begin{bmatrix}\frac{\rho_1}{(\rho_1^2+\rho_2^2\sin^2\phi+\rho^2\sin^2\phi)^{1/2}}\\[2mm]\frac{\rho_2}{(\rho_1^2+\rho_2^2\sin^2\phi+\rho^2\sin^2\phi)^{1/2}}\\[2mm]\frac{\rho}{(\rho_1^2+\rho_2^2\sin^2\phi+\rho^2\sin^2\phi)^{1/2}}\end{bmatrix} = i(Q) .$$

If the direction $\mathbf{s}$ of the light source is known, then at any point P on S_f whose spherical coordinates are $(1/f, \theta, \phi)$ are known, we can treat this as a single linear equation in the three unknowns

$$\rho_1/(\rho_1^2 + \rho_2^2\sin^2\phi + \rho^2\sin^2\phi)^{1/2}$$
$$\rho_2/(\rho_1^2 + \rho_2^2\sin^2\phi + \rho^2\sin^2\phi)^{1/2}$$
$$\rho/(\rho_1^2 + \rho_2^2\sin^2\phi + \rho^2\sin^2\phi)^{1/2} .$$

Photometric stereo is the process of recording multiple images in rapid succession using a fixed camera and multiple light sources (see Figs. 28). If three images of S are recorded in rapid succession using three light sources whose directions σ_1, σ_2, and σ_3 are linearly independent, then at P we obtain three equations

$$
\begin{bmatrix}
\csc\phi\langle s_1,\sigma_1\rangle & \sin\phi\langle s_2,\sigma_1\rangle & -\sin\phi\langle s,\sigma_1\rangle \\
\csc\phi\langle s_1,\sigma_2\rangle & \sin\phi\langle s_2,\sigma_2\rangle & -\sin\phi\langle s,\sigma_2\rangle \\
\csc\phi\langle s_1,\sigma_3\rangle & \sin\phi\langle s_2,\sigma_3\rangle & -\sin\phi\langle s,\sigma_3\rangle
\end{bmatrix}
\begin{bmatrix}
\dfrac{\rho_1}{(\rho_1^2+\rho_2^2\sin^2\phi+\rho^2\sin^2\phi)^{1/2}} \\[4mm]
\dfrac{\rho_2}{(\rho_1^2+\rho_2^2\sin^2\phi+\rho^2\sin^2\phi)^{1/2}} \\[4mm]
\dfrac{\rho}{(\rho_1^2+\rho_2^2\sin^2\phi+\rho^2\sin^2\phi)^{1/2}}
\end{bmatrix}
$$

$$
=\begin{bmatrix} i_1(Q) \\ i_2(Q) \\ i_3(Q) \end{bmatrix}
$$

which can be solved for

$$
\rho_1/(\rho_1^2+\rho_2^2\sin^2\phi+\rho^2\sin^2\phi)^{1/2}
$$
$$
\rho_2/(\rho_1^2+\rho_2^2\sin^2\phi+\rho^2\sin^2\phi)^{1/2}
$$
$$
\rho/(\rho_1^2+\rho_2^2\sin^2\phi+\phi^2\sin^2\phi)^{1/2}
$$

since $i_1(Q), i_2(Q)$, and $i_3(Q)$ can be determined from the three images, and since the coefficient matrix

$$
\begin{bmatrix}
\csc\phi\langle s_1,\sigma_1\rangle & \sin\phi\langle s_2,\sigma_1\rangle & -\sin\phi\langle s,\sigma\rangle \\
\csc\phi\langle s_1,\sigma_2\rangle & \sin\phi\langle s_2,\sigma_2\rangle & -\sin\phi\langle s,\sigma_2\rangle \\
\csc\phi\langle s_1,\sigma_3\rangle & \sin\phi\langle s_2,\sigma_3\rangle & -\sin\phi\langle s,\sigma_3\rangle
\end{bmatrix}
$$

is nonsingular:

$$
\begin{bmatrix}
\dfrac{\rho_1}{(\rho_1^2+\rho_2^2\sin^2\phi+\rho^2\sin^2\phi)^{1/2}} \\[4mm]
\dfrac{\rho^2}{(\rho_1^2+\rho_2^2\sin^2\phi+\rho^2\sin^2\phi)^{1/2}} \\[4mm]
\dfrac{\rho}{\rho_1^2+\rho_2^2\sin^2\phi+\rho^2\sin^2\phi)^{1/2}}
\end{bmatrix}
=
\begin{bmatrix}
\csc\phi\langle s_1,\sigma_1\rangle & \sin\phi\langle s_2,\sigma_1\rangle & -\sin\phi\langle s,\sigma_1\rangle \\
\csc\phi\langle s_1,\sigma_2\rangle & \sin\phi\langle s_2,\sigma_2\rangle & -\sin\phi\langle s,\sigma_2\rangle \\
\csc\phi\langle s_1,\sigma_3\rangle & \sin\phi\langle s_2,\sigma_3\rangle & -\sin\phi\langle s,\sigma_3\rangle
\end{bmatrix}^{-1}
$$

$$
\begin{bmatrix} i_1(Q) \\ i_2(Q) \\ i_3(Q) \end{bmatrix}.
$$

Since the normal vector

$$
\mathbf{n}=\frac{\mathbf{x}_1\times\mathbf{x}_2}{|\mathbf{x}_1\times\mathbf{x}_2|}=\frac{\rho_1\csc\phi\, s_1+\rho_2\sin\phi\, s_2-\rho\sin\phi\, s}{(\rho_1^2+\rho_2^2\sin^2\phi+\rho^2\sin^2\phi)^{1/2}}
$$

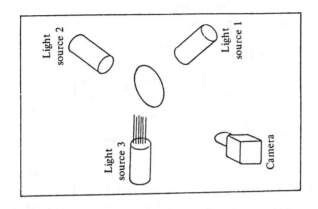

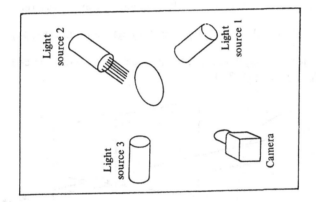

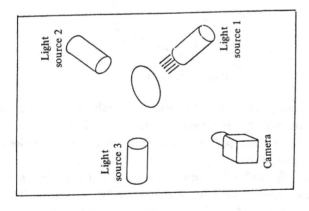

Fig. 28. Photometric stereo.

it can thus be determined immediately. Furthermore, we can compute ρ_1 and ρ_2 in terms of ρ: If, for example,

$$\begin{bmatrix} \frac{\rho_1}{(\rho_1^2+\rho_2^2\sin^2\phi+\rho^2\sin^2\phi)^{1/2}} \\ \frac{\rho_2}{(\rho_1^2+\rho_2^2\sin^2\phi+\rho^2\sin^2\phi)^{1/2}} \\ \frac{\rho}{(\rho_1^2+\rho_2^2\sin^2\phi+\rho^2\sin^2\phi)^{1/2}} \end{bmatrix} = \begin{bmatrix} k_1 \\ k_2 \\ k_3 \end{bmatrix}$$

then $\rho_1/\rho = k_1/k_3$, so that $\rho_1 = \rho k_1/k_3$, and $\rho_2/p = k_2/k_3$, so that $p_2 = \rho k_2/k_3$.

Thus to find ρ_1 and ρ_2, it suffices to know the depth value ρ. Indeed, if we know the depth value $\rho = \rho_0$ at just one point (θ_0, ϕ_0), the system $\rho_1 = \rho k_1/k_3, \rho_2 = \rho k_2/k_3$ becomes a system of first order partial differential equations that can be solved for ρ: these equations are rewritten

$$\partial(\ln\rho)/\partial\theta = \ln(k_1/k_3), \partial(\ln\rho)/\partial\phi = \text{lin}(k_2/k_3), \text{ and } \ln\rho(\theta_0,\phi_0) = \ln\rho_0$$

and solve for $\ln\rho$—or, equivalently, for ρ — using finite difference methods. (See Mitchell and Griffiths[28].)

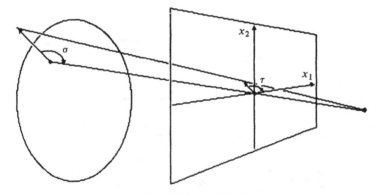

Fig. 29. Tilt and slant.

The quantities ρ_1/ρ and ρ_2/ρ arise frequently in spherical analysis. They can be interpreted (see Clocksin[12] and Ballard and Brown[21]) as the tangents $\rho_1/p = \tan\tau$ and $\rho_2/\rho = \tan\sigma$ of the tilt and slant angles τ and σ (see Fig. 29) which determine the normal vector at a point on the surface. Since ρ_1/ρ and p_2/p can be determined from visual observations made using the photometric stereo method, they are observable quantities. The spherical coordinates θ and ϕ of a point in Euclidean 3-space are also observable quantities since they, too, can be determined from visual observations.

In practice, we should, for great accuracy, use more than three light sources whose directions are in general position, and least squares to find ρ_1/ρ and ρ_2/ρ. Using more than three light sources and a small modification of the technique presented above, we can also determine the albedo r at each point, whether or not as a function it is constant.

9. RECOVERY OF SURFACE GEOMETRY

Associated to each parametrized surface $\mathbf{x} : U \rightarrow R^3$ are two important matrices: these are the matrices $(g_{ij}) = (\langle \mathbf{x}_i, \mathbf{x}_j \rangle)$ and $(L_i^j) = (L_{ij})(g_{ij})^{-1}$, where $(L_{ij}) = -d\mathbf{n}^T * d\mathbf{x})$, that represent the first and second fundamental forms of $S = \mathbf{x}(U)$. The first fundamental form contains information about lengths and angles on S, and the second fundamental form contains information about the curvature of S. In particular, although the specific form of the matrix (L_i^j) of the second fundamental form depends on the specific parametrization $\mathbf{x}$ of S, the invariants of (L_i^j) — the eigenvalues and eigenvectors of (L_i^j), and the determinant and the trace of (L_i^j) — are geometric features that are independent of the specific way in which S is parametrized. At each point of S, the eigenvalues of (L_i^j) are the principal curvatures of S, the image of the eigenvectors of (L_i^j) under multiplication by $d\mathbf{x}$ are the principle directions of S, the determinant of (L_i^j) is the Gaussian curvature of S, and half the trace of (L_i^j) is the mean curvature of S. These features are important since knowing them at each point of a surface is equivalent to knowing the surface, up to a rigid motion. (See Millman and Parker[19], Chen and Penna[17], and Penna and Chen[7].) In this section we discuss the extent to which the geometric features of a surface can be recovered from information — or observations — provided by photometric stereo and a given depth without numerically solving the system of partial differential equations with initial condition presented in Sect. 8.

The fact that the geometric features of a surface completely determine the surface locally up to a rigid motion, is proved using the theory of partial differential equations. The common bond between the numerical implementation of this proof and the numerical solution of the system of partial differential equations presented in the last section underscores the close theoretical relationship between the results of this section and those presented in the last section.

The first fundamental form of a spherically parametrized surface $\mathbf{x} = \rho \mathbf{s}$ is represented by the matrix

$$(g_{ij}) = d\mathbf{x}^T * d\mathbf{x} = \begin{pmatrix} \rho_1^2 + \rho^2 \sin^2 \phi & \rho_1 \rho_2 \\ \rho_1 \rho_2 & \rho_2^2 + \rho^2 \end{pmatrix} .$$

To compute the second fundamental form, we first address computation of the matrix $(L_{ij}) = \mathrm{dn}^T*\mathrm{dx}$. Observe that once we have determined $\mathbf{n}$ using photometric stereo, we can theoretically compute dn. Practically, however, computing dn in this manner involves the numerical differentiation of ρ, ρ_1, and ρ_2. Since this type of computation may not be stable in the presence of noise, we use the following technique instead: If the albedo r and S is constant in a neighborhood of a point P, then for a single light source

$$i(Q) = r\langle \mathbf{n}_p, \sigma \rangle \ .$$

where $Q = \pi_s(P)$, so that

$$\mathrm{d}i = r\langle \mathrm{dn}, \sigma \rangle$$

or

$$(\partial i/\partial\theta \ \ \partial i/\partial\phi) = r(\sigma_1 \ \sigma_2 \ \sigma_3) * \mathrm{dn} \ .$$

(One of the big reasons spherical coordinate surfaces and spherical perspective projection are simpler to use than Monge surfaces and planar perspective projection is that $\mathrm{d}\pi_s * \mathrm{dx}$ is the identity in the former case. Thus the equation $\mathrm{d}i * \mathrm{d}\pi_p * \mathrm{dx} = r\langle \mathrm{dn}, \sigma \rangle$ that arises when using Monge surfaces and planar perspective projection reduces to the equation $\mathrm{d}i = r\langle \mathrm{dn}, \sigma \rangle$ when using spherical coordinate surfaces and spherical perspective projection.) Since the intensities i_1, i_2, and i_3 are known for the three light sources σ_1, σ_2, and σ_3, we obtain three such equations

$$\begin{bmatrix} \partial i_1/\partial\theta & \partial i_1/\partial\phi \\ \partial i_2/\partial\theta & \partial i_2/\partial\phi \\ \partial i_3/\partial\theta & \partial i_3/\partial\phi \end{bmatrix} = r \begin{bmatrix} \sigma_1^1 & \sigma_2^1 & \sigma_3^1 \\ \sigma_1^2 & \sigma_2^2 & \sigma_3^2 \\ \sigma_1^3 & \sigma_2^3 & \sigma_3^3 \end{bmatrix} \mathrm{dn}$$

that can be solved for dn, since σ_1, σ_2, and σ_3 are assumed to be linearly independent (and hence $\det(\sigma_1, \sigma_2, \sigma_3) \neq 0$) :

$$\mathrm{dn} = \frac{1}{r} \begin{bmatrix} \sigma_1^1 & \sigma_2^1 & \sigma_3^1 \\ \sigma_1^2 & \sigma_2^2 & \sigma_3^2 \\ \sigma_1^3 & \sigma_2^3 & \sigma_3^3 \end{bmatrix}^{-1} \begin{bmatrix} \partial i_i/\partial\theta & \partial i_1/\partial\phi \\ \partial i_2/\partial\theta & \partial i_2/\partial\phi \\ \partial i_3/\partial\theta & \partial i_3/\partial\phi \end{bmatrix} \ .$$

Now

$$\mathrm{dx} = (\rho_1 \mathbf{s} + \rho \mathbf{s}_1 \rho_2 \mathbf{s} + \rho \mathbf{s}_2) \ .$$

Thus if we know the depth value ρ of P, we can compute $dx, (L_{ij}) = -dn^T * dx, (L_i^j) = (L_{ij})(g_{ij})^{-1}$, the principal directions and principal curvatures, and the Gaussian and mean curvatures of S at P. Consequently, the osculating quadric surface to S at P (the second order approximation to S at P) can be determined. In other words, in the same way depth information acts as an initial condition that specifies a surface as a solution of a system of partial differential equations (as discussed in Sect. 8), depth information acts as an initial condition that specifies the geometry of the surface.

10. MOTION ANALYSIS

The goal of this section is to determine a generalized motion of a known nonrigid elastic body given images of the body before and after the generalized motion. In the case of static elasticity generalized motions are diffeomorphisms (one-to-one differentiable transformations of R^3 whose inverses are differentiable), and in the case of dynamic elasticity generalized motions (including deformations) are 1-parameter families of diffeomorphisms. (In the case of static elasticity, Hooke's Law and the Fundamental Theorem of Statics can be used to show that deformations of such bodies are diffeomorphisms. In the case of dynamic elasticity, Hooke's Law and Newton's Law can be used to show that generalized motions — including deformations — of such bodies are 1-parameter families of diffeomorphisms. See Chen and Penna[17]. For simplicity, we consider a single diffeomorphism of bodies; a 1-parameter family of diffeomorphisms of bodies can be viewed as a sequence of single diffeomorphisms of intermediate bodies.) The analysis presented in this section applies to smooth bodies; for an analysis that applies to polyhedral bodies see Yen and Huang[4]. For a planar perspective analysis that applies to smooth bodies, see Chen and Penna[17].

We recover the image transformation between two spherical images by using point correspondences and least squares. Although there is no unique way to determine an arbitrary generalized motion from a single pair of spherical images, we obtain an essentially unique generalized motion in closed form by restricting attention to a class of isometric generalized motions (diffeomorphisms of R^3 which are isometric on the body surface). This class includes rigid motions and bendings, but not shearing. We recover the Jacobian of a generalized motion and the ratio depth values for a given point and its image by coupling the Jacobian of the image transformation (its linear approximation) with the Jacobian of spherical perspective projection; having recovered the Jacobian of a generalized motion and the ratio of depth values, the first-order Taylor series approximation of the generalized motion can be obtained if the initial depth value is known.

We assume that the surface S of a body is the graph of a spherically parametrized surface $\mathbf{x} = \rho\mathbf{s}$. A generalized motion $F = (F_1, F_2, F_3)$: $R^3 \rightarrow R^3$ transforms the graph S of a spherically parametrized surface $\mathbf{x} = \rho\mathbf{s}$ into the graph S' of the spherically parametrized surface $\mathbf{x}' = \rho'\mathbf{s}$ where $\mathbf{x}' = F \circ \mathbf{x}$. If F is a generalized motion from S to S', and $f = (f_1, f_2) : (\theta, \phi) \rightarrow (\theta', \phi')$ is the corresponding image transformation, then as long as P and the image $P' = F(P)$ are visible, $\pi'_S \circ F = f \circ \pi_S$ (we use π_S to denote spherical projection at P, and π'_S to denote spherical projection at P').

Spherical perspective projection may be written

$$\pi_S(x_1, x_2, x_3) = (\theta, \phi)$$

where

$$\theta = \begin{cases} \tan^{-1}(x_2/x_1) & \text{if} \quad x_1 > 0 \\ \pi + \tan^{-1}(x_2/x_1) & \text{if} \quad x_1 < 0 \end{cases}$$

$$\phi = \cos^{-1}\left(x_3/\sqrt{x_1^2 + x_2^2 + x_3^3}\right) .$$

Restricted to the visible part of S, spherical perspective projection is a one-to-one differentiable transformation whose Jacobian matrix

$$d\pi_3 = \begin{bmatrix} -\dfrac{\sin\theta}{\rho\sin\phi} & \dfrac{\cos\theta}{\rho\sin\phi} & 0 \\ \dfrac{\cos\theta\cos\phi}{\rho} & \dfrac{\sin\theta\cos\phi}{\rho} & -\dfrac{\sin\phi}{\rho} \end{bmatrix} .$$

If dF and df denote the Jacobian matrices of F and f, respectively,

$$dF = \begin{bmatrix} \partial F_1/\partial x_1 & \partial F_1/\partial x_2 & \partial F_1/\partial x_3 \\ \partial F_2/\partial x_1 & \partial F_2/\partial x_2 & \partial F_2/\partial x_3 \\ \partial F_3/\partial x_1 & \partial F_3/\partial x_2 & \partial F_3/\partial x_3 \end{bmatrix} = \begin{bmatrix} F_{11} & F_{12} & F_{13} \\ F_{21} & F_{22} & F_{23} \\ F_{31} & F_{32} & F_{33} \end{bmatrix}$$

and

$$df = \begin{bmatrix} \partial f_1/\partial\theta & \partial f_1/\partial\phi \\ \partial f_2/\partial\theta & \partial f_2/\partial\phi \end{bmatrix} = \begin{bmatrix} f_{11} & f_{12} \\ f_{21} & f_{22} \end{bmatrix}$$

then since $\pi'_S \circ F = f \circ \pi_S$, $(d\pi'_S * dF)\mathbf{v} = (df * d\pi_S)\mathbf{v}$ for all tangent vectors $\mathbf{v}$ to S at P.

An *isometric generalized motion* is a generalized motion of Euclidean 3-space that preserves the length of curves on S, and the angles between

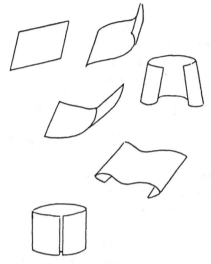

Fig. 30. Isometric generalized motions.

the intersections of curves in S. Such motions are more general than rigid motions; in fact the set of isometric generalized motions contains the set of rigid motions as a proper subset. A rigid motion is a combination of a rotation and translation of S through Euclidean 3-space. Under an isometric generalized motion, S may be bent like a piece of paper (see Fig. 30). Such motions do not, however, include shearings.

In this section, we consider isometric generalized motions that preserve normal vectors: if u and v are tangent vectors to S and P, then at P' we require that

$$dF(u) \times dF(v) = dF(u \times v) \ .$$

For example, the 1-parameter family of isometric generalized motions (see Fig. 31) taking the helicoid

$$\mathbf{x}(u_1, u_2) = (\sinh u_1 \cos u_2, \sinh u_1 \sin u_2, u_2)$$

where $-\sinh^{-1}(1) < u_1 < \sinh^{-1}(1)$ and $0 < u_2 < 2\pi$, to the catenoid

$$\mathbf{y}(u_1, u_2) = (\cosh u_1 \cos u_2, \cosh u_1 \sin u_2, u_1)$$

where $-\sinh^{-1}(1) < u_1 < \sinh^{-1}(1)$ and $0 < u_2 < 2\pi$, given by

$$F_t(u_1, u_2) = (\cos \pi t/2)\mathbf{x}(u_1, u_2) + (\sin \pi t/2)\mathbf{y}(u_1, u_2), t \in [0, 1]$$

is a 1-parameter family of isometric generalized motions to which our technique applies. For an isometric generalized motion of the surface S that preserves normal vectors, it follows that dF is an orthogonal matrix when restricted to S. (See Chen and Penna[17].) Since dF^T is then also an orthogonal matrix when restricted to S, it follows that both

$$(dF*\mathbf{u}) \times (dF*\mathbf{v}) = dF*(\mathbf{u} \times \mathbf{v}) \quad \text{and} \quad (\mathbf{u}'*dF) \times (\mathbf{v}'*dF) = (\mathbf{u}' \times \mathbf{v}')*dF$$

for all tangent vectors $\mathbf{u}$ and $\mathbf{v}$ to S at P, and for all tangent vectors $\mathbf{u}'$ and $\mathbf{v}'$ to S' at P'.

Given n points Q_i in I and n points Q_i' in I', $n \geq 6$, for which $f(Q_i) = Q_i'$, we can determine the coefficients of the second-order Taylor series approximations for f_1 and f_2 about Q

$$f_1(\theta, \phi) \approx q_1' + a_{11}\theta + a_{12}\phi + b_1\theta^2 + c_1\theta\phi + d_1\phi^2$$
$$f_2(\theta, \phi) \approx q_2' + a_{21}\theta + a_{22}\phi + b_2\theta^2 + c_2\theta\phi + d_2\phi^2$$

and thus the Jacobian df of f at Q, by applying least squares to the system of $2n$ linear equations in 12 unknowns that arises when we evaluate the second-order Taylor series approximation to f at Q_j. We use a second-order approximation instead of a first-order approximation since f is nonlinear. To obtain a better approximation, we could use higher-order Taylor series approximation to f; but to account for the nonlinearity of f, we must use at least a second-order approximation.

We now assume that we are given points $Q_0(\theta, \phi)$ in l and $Q_0'(\theta', \phi')$ in l' and $Q_0' = f(Q_0)$; Q_0 is the projection of a point $P_0(p_1, p_2, p_3)$ of S, and Q_0' is the projection a point $P_0'(p_1', p_2', p_3')$ of S'. Typically, we would know S, and hence also P_0, but S', and also P_0' would be unknown. We assume that we know the Jacobian $df = (f_{ij})$ of f at Q_0, and we compute the Jacobian dF of F at P_0 in terms of ρ/ρ', which we also compute.

Even though we do not know p_1', p_2', or p_3', we do not know θ' and ϕ'. Since

$$p_1' = p' \sin \phi' \cos \phi', \quad p_2' = \rho' \sin \phi', \quad p_3' = \rho' \cos \phi'$$

we can couple knowing ρ and $\rho\rho'$ with knowing θ' and ϕ' to find p_1', p_2', and p_3'. This allows us to recover the first-order Taylor series approximation for F about P_0:

$$F(x_1, x_2, x_3) \approx F(p_1, p_2, p_3) + (x_1 - p_1, x_2 - p_2, x_3 - p_3)dF^T$$
$$= (p_1', p_2', p_3') + (x_1 - p_1, x_2 - p_2, x_3 - p_3)dF^T .$$

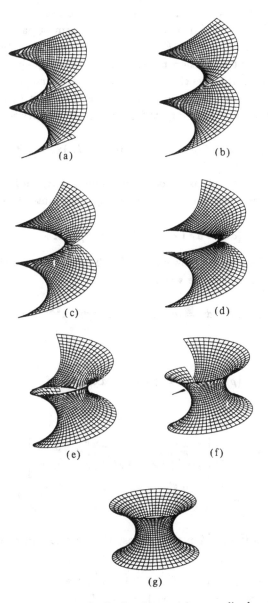

Fig. 31. A 1-parameter family of isometric generalized motions.

From the point of view of dynamic elasticity, we are assuming we know the original surface — initial conditions for a system of partial differential equations governing the motion F — and incrementally solving the system. That is, we represent a solution to this system as a sequence of solutions: we know the first solution — the initial conditions — and we compute each successive solution from the previous one. (See Chen and Penna[17].)

Since $(d\pi'_S * dF)\mathbf{v} = (df * d\pi_S)\mathbf{v}$ for all tangent vectors $\mathbf{v}$ to S at P,

$$(d\pi'_S * dF)\mathbf{x}_1 = (df * d\pi_S)\mathbf{x}_1 \quad \text{and} \quad (d\pi'_S * dF)\mathbf{x}_2 = (df * d\pi_S)\mathbf{x}_2 .$$

Since $d\mathbf{x}$ in the 2×2 matrix whose first column is $\mathbf{x}_1$ and whose second column is $\mathbf{x}_2$, we may combine both of these equations into the single matrix equation

$$(d\pi'_S * dF) * d\mathbf{x} = (df * d\pi_S) * d\mathbf{x} .$$

Since $\pi_S \circ \mathbf{x}$ is the identity, however, $d\pi_S * d\mathbf{x}$ is the 2×2 identity matrix $1^{2 \times 2}$, so this equation may be written

$$d\pi'_S * dF * d\mathbf{x} = df * d\pi_S * d\mathbf{x} = df * 1^{2 \times 2} = df$$

or, equivalently,

$$(\rho/\rho') * (\rho' d\pi'_S) * dF * (d\mathbf{x}/\rho) = df$$

where

$$\rho' d\pi'_S = \rho' \begin{bmatrix} -\dfrac{\sin \theta'}{\rho' \sin \phi'} & \dfrac{\cos \theta'}{\rho' \sin \phi'} & 0 \\ \dfrac{\cos \theta' \cos \phi'}{\rho'} & \dfrac{\sin \theta' \cos \phi'}{\rho'} & -\dfrac{\sin \phi'}{\rho'} \end{bmatrix}$$

$$= \begin{bmatrix} -\dfrac{\sin \theta'}{\sin \phi'} & \dfrac{\cos \theta'}{\sin \phi'} & 0 \\ \cos \theta' \cos \phi' & \sin \phi' \cos \phi' & -\sin \phi' \end{bmatrix}$$

and where $d\mathbf{x}/\rho$ is the 3×2 matrix whose first and second columns are

$$\mathbf{x}_1/\rho = (\rho_1 \mathbf{s} + \rho \mathbf{s}_1)/\rho = (\rho_1/\rho)\mathbf{s} + \mathbf{s}_1 \quad \text{and}$$
$$\mathbf{x}_2/p = (\rho_2 \mathbf{s} + \rho \mathbf{s}_2)/p = (\rho_2/\rho)\mathbf{s} + \mathbf{s}_2 ,$$

respectively. The reason for writing this equation in this manner is that doing so emphasizes the fact that $\rho' d\pi'_S, d\mathbf{x}/\rho$ and df are all observable quantities.

Now if the ratio ρ/ρ' of depth values is known, then since $\rho' d\pi'_S$ and the normal vector $\mathbf{n}_{P'}$ to S' at $P' = F(P)$ are observable,

$$\begin{pmatrix} a_{13} \\ a_{23} \end{pmatrix} = (\rho/\rho')(\rho' d\pi'_S)(\mathbf{n}_{P'}) = (\rho/\rho')(\rho' d\pi'_S * dF)(\mathbf{n}_P)$$

is observable, and

$$(\rho/\rho') * (\rho' d\pi'_S) * dF * (x_1/\rho,\, x_2\rho,\, \mathbf{n}_P) = \begin{bmatrix} f_{12} & f_{12} & a_{13} \\ f_{21} & f_{22} & a_{23} \end{bmatrix}$$

where $(\mathbf{x}_1/\rho, \mathbf{x}_2/\rho, \mathbf{n})$ denotes the 3×3 matrix whose column vectors are $\mathbf{x}_1/\rho, \mathbf{x}_2/\rho$, and $\mathbf{n}$, respectively. Since the columns of $(\mathbf{x}_1/\rho, \mathbf{x}_2/\rho, \mathbf{n})$ are linearly independent, $(\mathbf{x}_1/\rho, \mathbf{x}_2/\rho, \mathbf{n})$ is nonsingular, so that

$$(\rho/\rho') * (\rho' d\pi'_S) * dF = \begin{bmatrix} f_{11} & f_{12} & a_{13} \\ f_{21} & f_{22} & a_{23} \end{bmatrix} * (\mathbf{x}_1/\rho, \mathbf{x}_2/\rho, \mathbf{n}_P)^{-1} .$$

Now let the vector $\langle b_{13}, b_{23}, b_{33} \rangle$ be defined by requiring that $\langle b_{13}, b_{23}, b_{33} \rangle * (\mathbf{x}_1/\rho, \mathbf{x}_2/\rho, \mathbf{n})^{-1}$ is the cross product of the first and second row vectors on the right-hand side of this equation:

$$\langle b_{13}, b_{23}, b_{33} \rangle * (\mathbf{x}_1/\rho, \mathbf{x}_2/\rho, \mathbf{n})^{-1} =$$
$$(\langle f_{11}, f_{12}, a_{13} \rangle * (\mathbf{x}_1/\rho, \mathbf{x}_2/\rho, \mathbf{n})^{-1}) \mathrm{x} (\langle f_{21}, f_{22}, a_{23} \rangle * (\mathbf{x}_1/\rho, \mathbf{x}_2/\rho, \mathbf{n})^{-1})$$

Then $\langle b_{13}, b_{23}, b_{33} \rangle * (\mathbf{x}_1/\rho, \mathbf{x}_2/\rho, \mathbf{n})^{-1}$ is also the cross product $(\rho/\rho')^2 \langle -\cos\theta', -\sin\theta', -\cot\phi' \rangle * dF$ of the first and second row vectors on the left-hand side. (The cross product of the first and second row vectors on the left hand side can be computed by using the fact that the first and second rows of $(\rho/\rho') * (\rho' d\pi'_S)$ are tangent vectors to S' at P', the fact that $(\mathbf{u}' * dF) \times (\mathbf{v}' * dF) = (\mathbf{u}' \times \mathbf{v}') * dF$ for any tangent vectors $\mathbf{u}'$ and $\mathbf{v}'$ to S' at P', and the fact that the cross product of the first two row vectors of $\rho' d\pi'_S$ is $\langle -\cos\theta', -\cot\phi' \rangle$.) Thus

$$\begin{bmatrix} \rho/\rho' & 0 & 0 \\ 0 & \rho/\rho' & 0 \\ 0 & 0 & (\rho/\rho')^2 \end{bmatrix} * \begin{bmatrix} -\sin\theta' \csc\phi' & \cos\theta' \csc\phi' & 0 \\ \cos\theta' \cos\phi' & \sin\theta' \cos\phi' & \sin\phi' \\ -\cos\theta' & -\sin\theta' & -\cot\phi' \end{bmatrix}$$
$$* dF = \begin{bmatrix} f_{11} & f_{12} & a_{13} \\ f_{21} & f_{22} & a_{23} \\ b_{31} & b_{32} & b_{33} \end{bmatrix} * (\mathbf{x}_1/\rho, \mathbf{x}_2/\rho, \mathbf{n})^{-1} .$$

On one hand, we can use this equation to compute ρ/ρ' up to sign: Since dF is orthogonal, the determinant $\det(dF)$ of dF is 1. By equating the determinants of both sides of this equation, we find that

$$(\rho/\rho')^4 = \sin^2 \phi' * \begin{bmatrix} f_{11} & f_{12} & a_{13} \\ f_{21} & f_{22} & a_{23} \\ b_{31} & b_{32} & b_{33} \end{bmatrix} * \det(\mathbf{x}_1/\rho, \mathbf{x}_2/\rho, \mathbf{n})^{-1} \ .$$

On the other hand, this equation can be solved for dF:

$$dF = \begin{bmatrix} \rho'/\rho & 0 & 0 \\ 0 & \rho'/\rho & 0 \\ 0 & 0 & (\rho'/\rho)^2 \end{bmatrix} * \begin{bmatrix} -\sin\theta'\csc\phi' & \cos\theta'\csc\phi' & 0 \\ \cos\theta'\cos\phi' & \sin\theta'\cos\phi' & -\sin\phi' \\ -\cos\theta' & -\sin\theta' & -\cot\phi' \end{bmatrix}^{-1}$$

$$* \begin{bmatrix} f_{11} & f_{12} & a_{13} \\ f_{21} & f_{22} & a_{23} \\ b_{31} & b_{32} & b_{33} \end{bmatrix} * (\mathbf{x}_1/\rho, \mathbf{x}_2/\rho, \mathbf{n})^{-1}$$

$$= \begin{bmatrix} \rho'/\rho & 0 & 0 \\ 0 & \rho'/\rho & 0 \\ 0 & 0 & (\rho'/\rho)^2 \end{bmatrix} * \begin{bmatrix} -\sin\theta'\sin\phi' & \cos\theta'\cos\phi' & -\cos\theta'\sin^2\phi' \\ \cos\theta'\sin\phi' & \sin\theta'\cos\phi' & -\sin\theta'\sin^2\phi' \\ 0 & -\sin\phi' & -\sin\phi'\cos\phi' \end{bmatrix}$$

$$* \begin{bmatrix} f_{11} & f_{12} & a_{13} \\ f_{21} & f_{22} & a_{23} \\ b_{31} & b_{32} & b_{33} \end{bmatrix} * (\mathbf{x}_1/\rho, \mathbf{x}_2/\rho, \mathbf{n})^{-1} \ .$$

Computation of these expressions is facilitated by the fact that the 3×3 inverse $(\mathbf{x}_1/\rho, \mathbf{x}_2/\rho, \mathbf{n})^{-1}$ can be computed in closed form: Since

$$(\mathbf{x}_1/\rho, \mathbf{x}_2/\rho, \mathbf{n}) * (\mathbf{x}_1/\rho, \mathbf{x}_2/\rho, \mathbf{n})^T = \begin{bmatrix} \langle \mathbf{x}_1/\rho, \mathbf{x}_1/\rho \rangle & \langle \mathbf{x}_1/\rho, \mathbf{x}_2/\rho \rangle & 0 \\ \langle \mathbf{x}_2/\rho, \mathbf{x}_1/\rho \rangle & \langle \mathbf{x}_2/\rho \rangle & 0 \\ 0 & 0 & 1 \end{bmatrix}$$

it follows that

$$(\mathbf{x}_1/\rho, \mathbf{x}_2/\rho, \mathbf{n})^{-1} = (\mathbf{x}_1/\rho, \mathbf{x}_2/\rho, \mathbf{n})^T * \begin{pmatrix} \langle \mathbf{x}_1/\rho, \mathbf{x}_1/\rho \rangle & \langle \mathbf{x}_1/\rho, \mathbf{x}_2/\rho \rangle & 0 \\ \langle \mathbf{x}_2/\rho, \mathbf{x}_1/\rho \rangle & \langle \mathbf{x}_2/\rho, \mathbf{x}_2/\rho \rangle & 0 \\ 0 & 0 & 1 \end{pmatrix}^{-1}$$

$$= (\mathbf{x}_1/\rho, \mathbf{x}_2/\rho, \mathbf{n})^T * \begin{pmatrix} \langle \mathbf{x}_1/\rho, \mathbf{x}_1/\rho \rangle & \langle \mathbf{x}_1/\rho, \mathbf{x}_2/\rho \rangle^{-1} & 0 \\ \langle \mathbf{x}_2/\rho, \mathbf{x}_1/\rho \rangle & \langle \mathbf{x}_1/\rho, \mathbf{x}_2/\rho \rangle & 0 \\ 0 & 0 & 1 \end{pmatrix}$$

reducing the computation of a 3×3 inverse to the computation of a 2×2 inverse.

11. OPTICAL FLOW

An *optical flow field* is a function that associates to each point in a 2-dimensional image and to each time t, a velocity vector (see Fig. 32); this velocity vector arises as result of the motion of an object or scene relative to an observer (see Ballard and Brown[21].) The problem we address in this section is how to retrieve — from observable quantities — the motion that creates an optical flow field. (See Chen and Penna[8].)

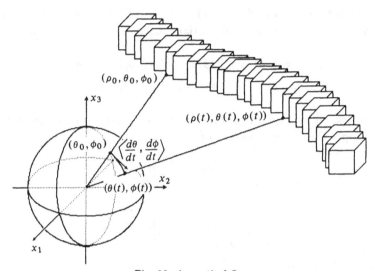

Fig. 32. An optical flow.

More specifically, we assume, for convenience, that an observer is fixed at the origin, and that an object or scene moves relative to the observer. An optical flow field on S_f associates to each point on S_f whose spherical coordinates are $(1/f, \theta, \phi)$ a vector

$$\langle d\theta/dt, d\phi/dt \rangle = \langle d\theta(\theta, \phi, t)/dt, d\phi(\theta, \phi, t)/dt \rangle$$

in the $\theta - \phi$-coordinate plane, at time t. Our goal is to retrieve — from a time dependent family $i = i(\theta, \phi, t)$ of image intensities — the path $(\rho, \theta, \phi) = (\rho(t), \theta(t), \phi(t))$ followed by an object point whose image at time t_0 has spherical coordinates $(\rho_0, \theta_0, \phi_0)$.

Before proceeding, observe that this problem does not have a unique solution: any strictly radial motion of the form

$$(\rho, \theta, \phi) = (\rho(t), \theta_0, \phi_0)$$

produces the zero optical flow field

$$\langle d\phi/dt, d\phi/dt\rangle = \langle d\theta_0/dt, d\phi_0/dt\rangle = \langle 0, 0\rangle .$$

As with the previous problems we have examined, the problem of retrieving the motion that creates an optical flow field has a unique solution when $\theta = \theta_0$ and $\phi = \phi_0$ up to initial depth value ρ_0 specified at time t_0.

To begin our analysis, observe that given initial conditions $\theta = \theta_0$, $\phi = \phi_0$ when $t = t_0$, we can find $\theta = \theta(t)$ and $\phi = \phi(t)$ by solving the coupled first order system of ordinary differential equations (with initial conditions)

$$d\theta/dt = d\theta(\theta, \phi, t), d\phi/dt = d\phi(\theta, \phi, t) \quad \text{where}$$
$$\theta = \theta_0 \quad \text{and} \quad \phi = \phi_0 \quad \text{when} \quad t = t_0 .$$

Thus the crucial part of our problem is to determine $\rho = \rho(t)$. To do this, we first apply the Chain Rule to find that

$$\frac{d\rho}{dt} = \frac{\partial\rho}{\partial\theta}\frac{d\theta}{dt} + \frac{\partial\rho}{\partial\phi}\frac{d\phi}{dt} .$$

Thus

$$\frac{1}{\rho}\frac{d\rho}{dt} = \frac{1}{\rho}\frac{\partial\rho}{\partial\theta}\frac{d\theta}{dt} + \frac{1}{\rho}\frac{\partial\rho}{\partial\phi}\frac{d\phi}{dt} .$$

We rewrite this equation

$$\frac{d(\ln\rho)}{dt} = \frac{\rho_1}{\rho}\frac{d\theta}{dt} + \frac{\rho_2}{\rho}\frac{d\phi}{dt}$$

and integrate with respect to t to find that

$$\ln\rho = \int_{t_0}^{t}\left(\frac{\rho_1}{\rho}\frac{d\theta}{dt} + \frac{\rho_2}{\rho}\frac{d\phi}{dt}\right) dt + \ln\rho_0$$

or

$$\rho = \rho_0 \exp\left(\int_{t_0}^{t}\left(\frac{\rho_1}{\rho}\frac{d\theta}{dt} + \frac{\rho_2}{\rho}\frac{d\phi}{dt}\right) dt\right) .$$

In this expression, $d\theta/dt$ and $d\phi/dt$ are given, and ρ_1/ρ and ρ_2/ρ are observables (see Sect. 8). Thus, as with the previous problems we have examined, the optical flow problem has a unique solution when $\theta = \theta_0$ and $\phi = \phi_0$ up to initial depth value ρ_0 specified at time t_0.

12. CONCLUSION

Spherical methods have great potential in the study of computer vision and image understanding. In this paper we have discussed spherical geometry, creating and displaying spherical images, and applications of spherical methods to problems in surface recovery, motion analysis, and optical flow. As we have illustrated, spherical techniques are particularly applicable in problems that involve images which subtend a wide viewing angle. Spherical methods are quite useful since much is known about spherical analysis exists and since spherical geometry is, in many ways, much more natural geometry than projective geometry. In general, however, while spherical techniques are superior to planar techniques in some applications, and planar techniques are superior to spherical techniques in others, where spherical and planar techniques both apply, they tend to complement, rather than oppose, each other.

References

1. R. Batson and K. Larson, "Compilation of surveyor television mosaics," *Photogrammetric Engineering* **33** (1967) 163-173.
2. W. Clocksin, "Computer prediction of visual thresholds for surface slant and edge detection from optical flow fields," Ph.D. Dissertation, Univ. of Edinburgh, 1980.
3. M. J. Magee and J. K. Aggarwal, "Determining vanishing points from perspective images," *Computer Vision, Graphics, and Image Processing* **26** (1984) 256-267.
4. B. Yen and T. Huang, "Determining 3-D motion and structure of a rigid body using the spherical projection," *Computer Vision, Graphics, and Image Processing* **21** (1983) 21-32.
5. J. Roach, J. Wright, and V. Ramesh, "Spherical dual images: a 3D representation method for solid objects that combines dual space and Gaussian spheres," *Proc. of IEEE Computer Society Conference on Computer Vision and Pattern Recognition*, FL, Jun. 1986, pp. 236-241.
6. S. Chen, "An intelligent computer vision system," *Int'l J. Intelligent Systems* **1** (1986) 15-28.
7. M. Penna and S. Chen, "Shape from shading using multiple light sources," *Int'l J. Intelligent Systems* **1** (1986) 263-292.
8. S. Chen and M. Penn, "A spherical perspective approach to optical flow," *Proc. SPIE Cambridge Symposium on Optical and Optoelectronic Eng., Advances in Intelligent Robotics Systems*, Cambridge, MA, 1987.
9. B. Chazelle, L. Guibas, and D. Lee, "The power of geometric duality," *BIT* **25** (1985) 76-90.
10. S. Coren and J. Girgus, *Seeing is Deceiving: The Psychology of Visual Illusions*, Lawrence Erlbaum Associates, (distributed by Halsted Press, a division of John Wiley & Sons), 1978.
11. J. Gibson, *The Perception of the Visual World*, Houghton Mifflin Company, MA, 1950.

12. M. Luckiesch, *Visual Illusions: Their Causes, Characteristics, and Applications*, Dover, NY, 1965.
13. G. Murch, *Visual and Auditory Perception*, Bobbs-Merrill, 1973.
14. A. Synder, T. Bossomaier, and A. Hughes, "Optical image quality and the cone mosaic," *Science* **231** (1986) 499-500.
15. F. Ayres, Jr., *Theory and Problems of Plane and Spherical Trigonometry*, Schaum, 1954.
16. M. Penna and R. Patterson, *Projective Geometry and its Applications to Computer Graphics*, Prentice-Hall, 1986.
17. S. Chen and M. Penna, "Shape and motion of nonrigid bodies," *Computer Vision, Graphics, and Image Processing* **36** (1986) 175-207.
18. P. R. Wolf, *Elements of Photogrammetry*, McGraw-Hill, 1974.
19. R. Millman and G. Parker, *Elements of Differential Geometry*, Prentice-Hall, 1977.
20. R. Bishop, "There is more than one way to frame a curve," *Amer. Math. Monthly*, **82** (1975) 246-251.
21. Y. Wong, "A global formulation of the condition for a curve to lie on a sphere," *Monatschefte für Mathematik* **67** (1963) 363-365.
22. S. Breuer and D. Gottlieb, "Explicit characterizations of spherical curves," *Proc. of the Amer. Math. Society*, **28** (1971) 126-127.
23. A. Mitchell and D. Griffiths, *The Finite Difference Method in Partial Differential Equations*, Wiley Interscience, 1980.
24. D. Ballard and C. Brown, *Computer Vision*, Prentice-Hall, 1982.
25. S. T. Barnard, "Methods for interpreting perspective images," *Proc. of the Image Understanding Workshop*, Stanford University, CA, Sept. 1982, pp. 193-203.
26. A. Bruss, "Shape from Shading and Boundary Contour," Ph.D. Dissertation, Department of Electrical Engineering and Computer Science, MIT, 1981.
27. S. Chen, "A new vision system and the Fourier descriptor method by group representation theory," *Proc. of IEEE Computer Society Conference on Computer Vision and Pattern Recognition*, CA, Jun 9-13, 1985, pp. 106-110.
28. S. Chen and M. Penna, "A geometric approach to motion analysis," *Proc. of the Conf. on Intelligent Systems and Machines*, Oakland University, MI, 1986.
29. S. Chen and M. Penna, "Recognizing deformations of nonrigid bodies," *Proc. of IEEE Computer Society Conference on Computer Vision and Pattern Recognition* FL, 1986, pp. 452-455.
30. S. Chen and M. Penna, "Shape and correspondence," *Proc. of Advances in Intelligent Robotics Systems*, SPIE's Cambridge Symp. on Optical and Optoelectronic Engineering, MA, Oct. 26-31, 1986.
31. R. Duda and P. Hart, *Pattern Classification and Scene Analysis*, John Wiley, 1973.
32. R. M. Haralick, *Using perspective transformations in scene analysis*, Computer Vision Graphics and Image Processing **13** (1980) 191-221.
33. B. Horn, "Understanding image intensities," *Artificial Intelligence* **8** (1977) 202-231.
34. B. Horn and B. Schunck, "Determining optical flow," *Artificial Intelligence* **17** (1981) 185-204.
35. T. S. Huang, "Determining three-dimensional motion/structure from two perspective views," *Pattern Recognition and Image Processing Handbook*, eds. T. Y. Young and K. S. Fu, 1986.

36. T. Kanade and J. Kender, "Mapping Image Properties into shape constraints: skewed symmetry and affine-transformable patterns," *IEEE Workshop on Picture Data Description and Management*, NY, Aug. 1980, pp. 130-135.

37. K. Kanatani, "Camera rotation invariance of image characteristics," *Proc. of IEEE Computer Society Conference on Computer Vision and Pattern Recognition*, FL, Jun. 1986, pp. 266-271.

38. H. Malde, "Panoramic photographs," *American Scientist* (Mar-Apr 1983), pp. 132-140.

39. D. Marr, *Vision: A Computation Investigation into Human Representation and Processing of Visual Information*, W. H. Freeman, 1982.

40. A. Pentland, "Local shading analysis," *IEEE Trans. Pattern Analysis and Machine Intelligence* 6 (1984) 170-187.

41. A. Rosenfeld and A. Kak, *Digital Image Processing*, Academic Press, 1986.

42. R. Y. Tsai and T. S. Huang, "Analysis of Three-Dimensional Time Varying Scenes," *Proc. of SPIE — The International Society for Optical Engineering*, Aug. 1982, pp. 309-320.

43. S. Ullman, *The Interpretation of Visual Motion*, MIT Press, 1979.

44. J. A. Webb and J. K Aggarwal, "Shape and correspondence," *Computer Vision, Graphics, and Image Processing* 21 (1983) 145-160.

45. R. J. Woodham, *Photometric Stereo*, Al Memo 479, MIT, 1978.

5

SPATIAL INFORMATION PROCESSING: UNDERSTANDING REMOTE SENSING IMAGERY

Mingchuan Zhang and Su-shing Chen

Department of Computer Science
University of North Carolina at Charlotte
Charlotte, NC 28223, USA

A spatial reasoning and decision support system for remote sensing is being developed. An image processing and understanding module is employed to process input sensory data and to extract features so that its classification results can be used in other spatial information processing modules, such as reasoning and decision support. In this paper, three Bayesian decision theoretic approaches to contextual classification are developed in the image processing and understanding module which make use of spatial information. These approaches are then applied to understanding of remote sensing imagery.

1. INTRODUCTION

A spatial information system with reasoning and decision support capabilities are useful to military, industrial and environmental applications. There have been a large number of expert and decision support systems concerning nonspatial information and knowledge. On the contrary, systems which are concerned with additional spatial information are only in the research stage. In dealing with spatial (2-D and 3-D) data and knowledge, new techniques are often required. The complexity of spatial information systems is also much greater than ordinary expert and decision support systems. A spatial reasoning and decision support (SRDS) system is being developed. This system consists of several components: (1) a human-machine interface module, (2) a 2-D and 3-D spatial database management system, (3) an image processing and understanding module, (4) a spatial and application domain knowledge base, and (5) a LISP-based approximate reasoning and decision support system. There are two system characteristics: (1) The image processing and understanding module interacts with the spatial database management system and the spatial application domain knowledge base during the image preprocessing and spatial reasoning stages, and (2) Probabilistic image models are used to represent uncertain information; partial evidences are combined into more complete information by the Dempster-Shafer combination rule.

In this paper, three methods supporting the second system characteristic will be discussed. First, a multispectral image contextual classification technique, based on a recursive algorithm for optimal state estimation of a two-dimensional discrete Markov random field, is developed. This recursive algorithm is implemented by a dynamic programming formulation. The second is based on a stochastic relaxation algorithm of Markov-Gibbs random fields. This relaxation algorithm is a simulated annealing optimization method[1,2]. These two contextual classification schemes provide quite significant results in comparison with other Bayesian classification methods[3-5]. The third uses high-level or object-based spatial information so that contextual classification is further improved by the Dempster-Shafer combination rule which reduces uncertainty and resolves contradictions that arise from input sensory data[6,7].

Remote sensing MSS (multispectral scanner) data represent an important class of image understanding problems in unstructured environment. Multispectral scanner data are spectral data in quantitative format over a broad range of wavelengths. When spectral information from more than one observation time for the same object area are stacked in the same measurement pattern vector, we have a multispectral and multitemporal pattern vector. For any treatment of such kind of data, random field models are still the most powerful and natural approach. There is very little structural knowledge as in a structured environment.

2. SYSTEM DESCRIPTION

A spatial reasoning and decision support (SRDS) system[8] is developed for military battlefield management and target tracking, environmental planning, land development decision support, and industrial robotics and automation. A basic system characteristic is uncertainty and approximate reasoning. In computer vision and spatial reasoning, sensory data are usually partial and uncertain. Some requirements of these areas are beyond the scope of the current state-of-the-art of uncertainty and approximate reasoning. In this system, spatial features are extracted and sent, together with linguistic and numerical features, to an uncertainty and approximate reasoning scheme which provides decision support outputs. Another characteristic is the capability of fuzzy linguistic variables for human-machine interface[9-11]. For instance, we may reason with ratings of { not important, important, very important, extremely important}.

The SRDS system has several components: (1) a human-machine interface module, (2) a 2-D or 3-D spatial semantic database management system, (3) an image processing module, (4) a spatial and application knowledge base, and (5) a reasoning and decision support system. A decision maker has a visual/literal interface with the main system. The visual interface deals with 2-D or 3-D images and data. Preprocessed or on-line sensed data and images may be input into the main system. The output of the system is displayed to the decision maker. The literal interface is an OPS5 and LISP based system with natural language capability. The spatial semantic database is composed of (1) spatial data, such as geographical data and maps, (2) binary preprocessed data, such as freeways, rivers and specific area boundaries, (3) semantic information of spatial data, such as population, weather, and description of a scenic site. The image processing module operates on the spatial database under the OPS5 control system. Some common operations of the image processing module are intersection, union, thinning, complementation, and display commands, although sophisticated models are needed for image understanding.

The knowledge base encodes spatial knowledge and application for reasoning and decision support. Adopted in this system is a structured combination of two main knowledge representation schemes—production rules and fuzzy relations. In addition, semantics of linguistic terms are represented by fuzzy sets in the three categories: rating, weighting and certainty[11]. The advantage of this system is a combination of numerical computation and linguistic representation. The reasoning system employs both exact and approximate reasoning.

Spatial data types of the database is quite complex. Moreover, spatial data constraints are different from ordinary data constraints. Geometric and topological relations among spatial data entities are considered. Database query is involved with pictorial display of spatial information. This is the visual interface mentioned in the introduction. Associated with each spatial data entity, there are several numerical and linguistic attributes. In the reasoning and decision support system, additional attributes and features may be derived and used for reaching decisions. In order to aid extraction of additional attributes and features, an image processing module is used to manipulate geographical data and preprocessed binary data.

3. PROBABILISTIC IMAGE MODELS

For our multispectral image processing applications, we consider 2-D discrete Markov random image fields. Each component of a random observation vector $\{d_{ij}\}$ assumes one gray tone value from the set $\{0, 1, \dots, N\}$ of integer values. The pixel position (i, j) is defined on the 2-D finite set $I \times J$, where I designates the row index set, and J designates the column index set. The Markov random field model characterizes the statistical dependency among pixels by requiring that

$$P\big(d_{lk}\big| \quad \text{all} \quad (i, j) \neq (l, k)\big) = P\big(d_{lk}\big| \quad (l, k) \in (i, j) + \mathbf{N}\big) \,,$$

where $\mathbf{N}$ is a symmetric neighborhood. For instance, $\mathbf{N} = \{(0, 1), (0, -1), (-1, 0), (1, 0)\}$ corresponds to the simplest Markov model whose statistical dependency is only the nearest neighbors. By including more neighbors, we can construct more complicated Markov models. Since the model is defined only for symmetric neighborhoods, often $\mathbf{N}$ is equivalently described by means of an asymmetrical neighborhoods $\mathbf{N}_s$. In this paper, we shall use only the nearest neighbors. Let the observation vector d_{ij} at pixel (i, j) have fixed but unknown classification C_{ij} as shown in Fig. 1. The assignment of the best category label C_{ij} to the pixel is based on the conditional probability $P(C_{ij}|d_{ij})$ for pixel independent processing.

Before presenting our algorithms, we first give the notation and assumptions for the 2-D Markov random image field under which these algorithms will be derived:

(1) R: the set of possible measurement vectors.

(2) Ω: the set of possible categories.

(3) d_{ij}: an observed measurement vector on pixel (i, j); $d_{ij} \in R$.

(4) C_{ij}: an assigned category label C to pixel (i, j); $C_{ij} \in \Omega$.

(5) D_{IJ}: the collection of all observed measurements on the set of $I \times J$ pixels.

(6) D_{IJ}^{ij}: the set of all observed data values d_{lk} for (l, k) to the left or above (i, j) including (i, j).

(7) E_{IJ}^{ij}: the set of all observed data values d_{lk} for (l, k) to the right or below (i, j) including (i, j).

(8) DD_{IJ}^{ij}: the set of all observed data value d_{lk} for (l, k) to the left or above (i, j) excluding (i, j).

(9) EE_{IJ}^{ij}: the set of all observed data values d_{lk} for (l, k) to the right or below (i, j) excluding (i, j).

See Figs. 1 and 2 for the geometric pictures of the above sets.

4. A DYNAMIC PROGRAMMING APPROACH

4.1. Three Recursive Algorithms

The first contextual classification algorithm uses only past context with no look-ahead context (Fig. 3). The assignment of the best category label for pixel (i, j) depends only on the set of all observed data values d_{lk} in D_{IJ}^{ij}. The decision rule is:

$$\text{assign pixel } (i, j) \quad \text{to category} \quad C_{ij} \quad \text{if}$$
$$P(C_{ij} | D_{IJ}^{ij}) \geq P(Z_{ij} | D_{IJ}^{ij}) \text{ for all } Z_{ij} \in \Omega .$$

The second algorithm uses some fixed look-ahead context. With n-step look-ahead, the context dependent processing makes the assignment of the best category label using D_{IJ}^{ij} and the $(n + 1) \times (n + 1)$ neighborhood whose center pixel is (i, j). Figure 4 shows the one-step look-ahead algorithm whose decision rule is:

$$\text{assign pixel } (i, j) \text{ to category } C_{ij} \text{ if}$$
$$P(C_{ij} | D_{IJ}^{ij}, d_{ij+1}, d_{i+1j}, d_{i+1j+1})$$
$$\geq P(Z_{ij} | D_{IJ}^{ij}, d_{ij+1}, d_{i+1j}, d_{i+1j+1}) \text{ for all } Z_{ij} \in \Omega .$$

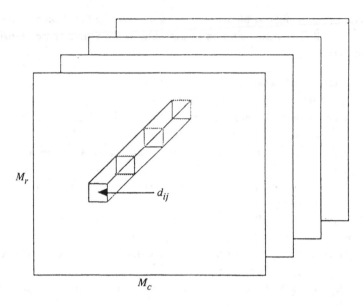

Fig. 1. Two-dimensional discrete Markov Random Field for multispectral image processing application. M_r: row size of image, M_c: column size of image; I: row index set of image, J: column index set of image d_{ij}: random observation vector, each of whose components takes one gray tone value from the pixel position (i, j) which is an element of the 2-D finite set $I \times J$. The Markov Random Field is characterized by $P(d_{ij} |$ all $(l, k); (i, j) \neq (l,k)) = P(d_{ij} |$ all $d_{lk}, l, k \in N)$; where N is a symmetric neighbor set.

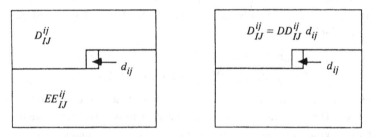

Fig. 2. Notation for a two pass recursive algorithm. d_{ij}: an observed measurement vector from pixel (i,j); D_{IJ}^{ij}: set of all observed data values d_{lk} for (l,k) to the left or above (i,j), including (i,j). E_{IJ}^{ij}: set of all observed data values d_{lk} for (l,k) to the right or below (i, j) including (i,j). DD_{IJ}^{ij}: set of all observed data values d_{lk} for (l,k) to the left or above (i,j), excluding (i,j). EE_{IJ}^{ij}: set of all observed data values d_{lk} for (l,k) to the right or below (i,j) excluding (i,j).

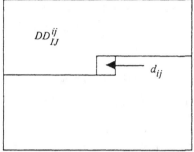

Fig. 3. Notation for no look-ahead recursive context classification algorithm. DD_{IJ}^{ij}: set of all observed data values d_{lk} for (l,k) to the left or above (i,j), excluding (i,j)). d_{ij}: an observed measurement vector from pixel (i,j).

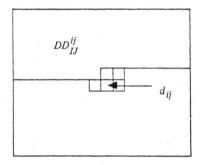

Fig. 4. Notation for fixed step look-ahead recursive context classification algorithm. DD_{IJ}^{ij}: set of all observed data values d_{lk} for (l,k) to the left or above (i,j), excluding (i,j). d_{ij}: an observed measurement vector from pixel (i,j).

This algorithm is sometimes referred to as the "forward backward look-ahead algorithm".

In summary, the above context dependent algorithm make the assignment of the best category label based on the conditional probabilities $P(C_{ij}|D_{IJ}^{ij})$, $P(C_{ij}|D_{IJ}^{ij}, d_{lk}; (l,k) \in \mathbf{N})$, and $P(C_{ij}|D_{IJ})$ respectively.

4.2. Independency Assumptions

We assume that an n-tuple of measurements is determined by some local measurement process. The full dependency of a process is quite difficult to capture and will be studied using constraint satisfaction techniques. In the following, we exhibit some independency assumptions.

(1) Given the true category of a pixel, all measurements of all pixels are

independent of each other. That is, given the true state of affairs, the observed measurement variations are independent.

$$P(D_{IJ}|C_{ij}) = P(DD_{IJ}^{ij}|C_{ij})P(EE_{IJ}^{ij}|C_{ij})P(d_{ij}|C_{ij})$$
$$P(D_{IJ}^{ij}|C_{ij}) = P(DD_{IJ}^{ij}|C_{ij})P(d_{ij}|C_{ij})$$
$$P(E_{IJ}^{ij}|C_{ij}) = P(EE_{IJ}^{ij}|C_{ij})P(d_{ij}|C_{ij}) \ .$$

(2) The n-tuple measurement of pixel (i,j) depends only on the true interpretation associated with pixel (i,j) and does not depend on any relation that pixel (i,j) may have with other units or on the interpretation associated with any other unit.

$$P(d_{ij}|C_{ij}, D_{IJ}^{ij-1}) = P(d_{ij}|C_{ij})$$
$$P(d_{ij-1}|C_{ij-1}, C_{i-1j}, D_{IJ}^{ij-1}) = P(d_{ij-1}|C_{ij-1})$$
$$P(d_{ij}|C_{ij}, E_{IJ}^{ij+1}) = P(d_{ij}|C_{ij})$$
$$P(d_{ij+1}|C_{ij+1}, C_{i+1j}, E_{IJ}^{ij+1}) = P(d_{ij+1}|C_{ij+1}) \ .$$

(3) Given the true categories of some neighboring pixels, the observed measurement data for all pixels before the current pixel, in raster scan order, gives nothing more about the current pixel's category.

$$P(C_{ij}|C_{ij-1}, C_{i-1j}, D_{IJ}^{ij-1}) = P(C_{ij}|C_{ij-1}, C_{i-1j})$$
$$P(C_{ij}|C_{ij+1}, C_{i+1j}, E_{IJ}^{ij+1}) = P(C_{ij}|C_{ij+1}, C_{i+1j}) \ .$$

(4) Given the measurements of all pixels up to and including the current pixel, the true category of its diagonally adjacent neighbor gives nothing more.

$$P(C_{ij-1}|C_{i-1j}, D_{IJ}^{ij-1}) = P(C_{ij-1}|D_{IJ}^{ij-1})$$
$$P(C_{ij+1}|C_{i+1j}, E_{IJ}^{ij+1}) = P(C_{ij+1}|D_{IJ}^{ij+1}) \ .$$

(5) Approximation (conditioning on a set so that omission of a row of data values should not make much of a difference)

$$P(C_{i-1j}|D_{IJ}^{ij-1}) = P(C_{i-1j}|D_{IJ}^{i-1j})$$
$$P(C_{i+1j}|E_{IJ}^{ij+1}) = P(C_{i+1j}|E_{IJ}^{i+1j}) \ .$$

(6) A weaker assumption than the independency of neighboring categories is the Markov random field assumption, which is used when the true interpretation of any unit given the true interpretation of all the surrounding

depends only on the interpretation of the nearest neighboring pixel. In the four neighbor system, given the true interpretation of pixel (i, j), the categories of diagonal pixels are independent of each other.

$$P(C_{ij-1}, C_{i-1j}|C_{ij}|C_{ij}) = P(C_{ij-1}|C_{ij})P(C_{i-1j}|C_{ij})$$
$$P(C_{ij+1}, C_{i+1j}|C_{ij}) = P(C_{ij+1}|C_{ij})P(C_{i+1j}|C_{ij}) .$$

4.3. Implementation of the Recursive Algorithms

The recursive algorithms determine the Bayesian labeling under the Markov random field assumption. We determine the labeling $\{C_{ij}|i = 1, 2, \ldots, I; j = 1, 2, \ldots, J\}$ by maximizing $P(C_{ij}|D_{IJ}^{ij})$ (past context, no look-ahead), $P(C_{ij}|D_{IJ}^{ij}, d_{lk}; (l, k) \in \mathbf{N})$ (fixed n-step look-ahead), and $P(C_{ij}|D_{IJ})$ (forward-backward look-ahead). The first two algorithms can be regarded as special cases of the last forward-backward look-ahead algorithm. Here, we shall only derive the two pass forward-backward algorithm.

From the definition of conditional probability,

$$P(C_{ij}|D_{IJ}) = P(D_{IJ}|C_{ij})P(C_{ij})/P(D_{IJ}) .$$

Then,

$$P(C_{ij}|D_{IJ}) = P(C_{ij}|D_{IJ}^{ij})P(C_{ij}|E_{IJ}^{ij})P(D_{IJ}^{ij})P(E_{IJ}^{ij})/$$
$$P(C_{ij})P(d_{ij}|C_{ij})P(D_{IJ}) .$$

In the above equation, probability distributions $P(C_{ij})$ and $P(d_{ij}|C_{ij})$ are either known or estimated in the supervised remote sensing classification situation. $P(D_{IJ}), P(D_{IJ}^{ij})$ and $P(E_{IJ}^{ij})$ do not depend on the true category. The maximization problem of C_{ij} is reduced to the calculation of $P(C_{ij}|D_{IJ}^{ij})$ and $P(C_{ij}|E_{IJ}^{ij})$. Using independency assumptions (1)–(5), we have

$$P(C_{ij}|D_{IJ}^{ij}) = (P(d_{ij}|C_{ij})/\Delta_D)$$
$$\times \sum_{C_{ij-1}} \sum_{C_{i-1j}} P(C_{ij}|C_{i-1j}, C_{ij-1})P(C_{ij-1}|D_{IJ}^{ij-1})P(C_{i-1j}|D_{IJ}^{i-1j}) ,$$

where

$$\Delta_D = \sum_{k_{ij}} P(d_{ij}|k_{ij}) \sum_{k_{ij-1}} \sum_{k_{i-1j}} P(k_{ij}|k_{i-1j}, k_{ij-1}) .$$
$$P(k_{ij-1}|D_{IJ}^{ij-1}) \cdot P(k_{i-1j}|D_{IJ}^{i-1j}) ,$$

a normalizing constant, not dependent on the optimizing category label. This recursive formula requires a left-right top to bottom recursive scan of the image. Similarly, $P(C_{ij}|E_{IJ}^{ij})$ requires a right-left bottom to top recursive scan as shown in the following:

$$P(C_{ij}|E_{IJ}^{ij}) = (P(d_{ij}|C_{ij})/\Delta_E)$$

$$\times \sum_{Cij+1} \sum_{Ci+1j} P(C_{ij}|C_{i+1j}, C_{ij+1})P(C_{ij+1}|E_{IJ}^{ij+1})P(C_{i+1j}|E_{IJ}^{i+1j}) \,,$$

where

$$\Delta_E = \sum_{kij} P(d_{ij}|k_{ij}) \sum_{kij+1} \sum_{ki+1j} P(k_{ij}|k_{i+1j}, k_{ij+1})$$

$$\cdot P(k_{ij+1}|E_{IJ}^{ij+1})P(k_{i+1j}|E_{IJ}^{i+1j}) \,,$$

a normalizing constant. In the above equations, $P(d_{ij}|C_{ij})$ is either known or estimated in the supervised remote sensing classification situation. The transition probabilities $P(C_{ij}|C_{ij-1}, C_{i-1j})$ and $P(C_{ij}|C_{i+1j}, C_{ij+1})$ are estimated from the conventional noncontextual preclassification results.

When $i = 1$ or $j = 1$, D_{IJ}^{ij} and E_{IJ}^{ij} are out of the image. For these cases, we assume that the triple sums are constants which do not depend on the true category. So the initial values are evaluated from $P(d_{ij}|C_{ij})$.

4.4. Summary of the Recursive Contextual Classification Procedure

(1) Evaluate training statistics. This includes the mean vector and covariance matrices of the Gaussian conditional distributions.

(2) Preclassify the image using a pixel independent or context free Bayesian classification technique.

(3) Estimate the transition probabilities $P(C_{ij}|C_{ij-1}, C_{i-1j})$ from the preclassification results.

(4) For the full look-ahead, two pass algorithm, we use the recursive formulas to compute $P(C_{ij}|D_{IJ}^{ij})$ and $P(C_{ij}|E_{IJ}^{ij})$, and then evaluate $P(C_{ij}|D_{IJ})$ for each category.

(5) Use the classification rule to select that label C_{ij} which produces the maximum posterior probability of the category label, given the context.

5. CONTEXTUAL CLASSIFICATION BY STOCHASTIC RELAXATION

5.1. Bayesian Contextual Decision Rule

The contextual information is a form of correlation among successive pattern classes in a 2-D image. Every pixel in the image can be considered as having a random variable associated with a 2-D Markov random field. Two pixels in spatial proximity to one another are unconditionally correlated, with the degree of correlation decreasing as the distance between them increased. All spatial correlations among site variables on an image lattice can be extracted by specified spatial processes. The most important quantity in the contextual Bayesian decision problem is the joint density function of all the site variables within the specified contextual neighborhood. So the best way to incorporate these correlations statistically is to estimate the joint probability density function of all site variables.

The Markov random field and its Gibbs equivalence constitute a promising and natural technique for the contextual classification. Consider a random observation vector $d_{ij}, (i,j) \in I \times J$. The Markov random field is characterized by the condition:

$$(^*)P(d_{ij}|d_{mn}, (m,n) \in I \times J, \ (m,n) \neq (i,j))$$
$$= P(d_{ij}|d_{mn}, \ (m,n) \in \mathbf{N}_{ij}) \ .$$

An alternative approach to Markov random field is the Gibbs distribution. A random field is said to have a Gibbs distribution if its density function is given by

$$P(D_{ij}) = (1/Z) \exp(-U(D_{ij})/KT) \ ,$$

where K is the Boltzmann constant, T is the temperature, D_{ij} is the collection of all measurement vectors in $\mathbf{N}_{ij}$, and $U(D_{ij})$ is the energy associated with the Gibbs distribution. The normalizing constant Z is given by

$$Z = \sum_{D_{ij}} \exp(-U(D_{ij})/KT) \ .$$

The energy $U(D_{ij})$ is the sum of local potentials $V_L(D_{ij})$ such that

$$U(D_{ij}) = - \sum_{L \in W} V_L(D_{ij}) \ ,$$

where L is a clique in $\mathbf{N}_{ij}$, and W is the family of cliques in $\mathbf{N}_{ij}$. A clique is a subset such that each pixel is a neighbor of all pixels in the subset. The local potentials $V_L(D_{ij})$ are evaluated over cliques L.

A neighborhood system $\mathbb{N}$ is defined as a collection of subsets $\mathbf{N}_{ij}$ of $I \times J$ such that $(1)\,\mathbf{N}_{ij}$ is a neighborhood of (i,j) which is not in $\mathbf{N}_{ij}$, and (2) if $(k,l) \in \mathbf{N}_{ij}$, then $(i,j) \in \mathbf{N}_{kl}$, for any $(i,j) \in I \times J$. A random field $\{d_{ij} : (i,j) \in I \times J\}$ is a Markov random field with respect to a neighborhood system if the Markov property $(*)$ is satisfied for $\mathbb{N}$.

5.2. The Factorization Property

Suppose that the rectangular lattice $G = I \times J$ has several rectangular sublattices (connected components) $G_m, m = 1, 2, \ldots$. If $D = \{d_{ij} : (i,j) \in G\}$ is a Markov random field, and each $D_m = \{d_{ij} : (i,j) \in G_m\}$ is also a Markov random field, then the probability measure P over G is the product probability measure

$$P = \Pi_m P_m ,$$

where P_m is the probability measure of G_m. The factorization property guarantees the decomposition of the complex potential function into a set of simple potential functions of each clique of the neighborhood.

5.3. The Markov and Gibbs Equivalence

In Ref. 12, Preston proved the equivalence for a state π of a 2-D discrete random field to be an equilibrium state, a state of Markov random field, and a Gibbs state with nearest neighbor potential. The Markov-Gibbs equivalence implies that a pure probabilistic concept—Markov random field, is equivalent to a physical notion—Gibbs distribution. The Gibbs model describes the interaction of a macroscopic system in thermal equilibrium, similar to the local spatial dependence given by the Markov model. For a Markov random field, the conditional probabilities are expressed in terms of nearest neighborhoods, while the energy E of a Gibbs distribution is the sum of potentials V measured over the same neighborhood.

Thus, the Markov-Gibbs equivalence provides an explicit formula for the joint probability distribution in terms of an energy function and supplies a powerful mechanism for modeling spatial features.

5.4. Maximizing Entropy

We note that the Gibbs distribution can be derived also by maximizing entropy. For any probability measure $P(\omega)$ on $I \times J$, the entropy $S(P)$ is defined by

$$S(P) = - \sum_{\theta_{ij} \in Q} P(\theta_{ij}) \log P(\theta_{ij}) ,$$

where Q is the set of all possible pattern configurations of assigned labels in the neighborhood, and θ_{ij} is a certain pattern configuration. The entropy of a probability measure is the amount of uncertainty in the outcome. The maximal entropy is attained when all outcomes are assigned with equal probability. In the well-known Ising model, one attempts to assign a probability measure to a sample space of outcomes which are not observable. In fact, only macroscopic properties are observable in statistical mechanics. Assume that we can estimate at least the expected value of energy $U(D_{ij})$. Then, among all probability measures having the expected energy value, the Gibbs measure

$$P(D_{ij}) = (1/Z)\exp(-U(D_{ij})/KT)$$

is the measure which maximizes the entropy among all probability measures with the expected energy.

5.5. The Markov-Gibbs Model for Bayesian Contextual Classification

We now incorporate the Markov-Gibbs model into the Bayesian contextual classification problem, and define an optimal decision rule of an interpretation C for the pixels in $\mathbf{N}_{ij}$ which satisfies a maximality condition. The maximality condition for interpretation C is the following

$$\prod_{(l,k)\in\mathbf{N}_{ij}} P(d_{lk}|C_{lk})P(C) \geq \prod_{(l,k)\in\mathbf{N}_{ij}} P(d_{lk}|C'_{lk})P(C') \,,$$

for all $C' \in \Omega$.

The probability distribution

$$P(D_{ij}, C) = \Pi_{(l,k)\in\mathbf{N}_{ij}} P(d_{lk}|C_{lk})P(C)$$

is a Gibbs distribution. We have

$$P(D_{ij}, C) = (1/Z)\exp(-U(D_{ij}, C)/KT) \,,$$

where $U(D_{ij}, C)$ is the energy function associated with the Gibbs distribution $P(D_{ij}, C)$, which has the form:

$$U(D_{ij}, C) = -\sum \log P(d_{lk}|C_{lk}) + U(C) \,,$$
$$P(C) = (1/Z)\exp(-U(C)/KT) \,,$$

where Z and K are constants, and $U(C)$ is the energy function associated with $P(C)$, which has the following form:

$$U(C) = \sum_{L \in W_{ij}} V_L(C) ,$$

where W_{ij} is the family of cliques in the neighborhood $\mathbf{N}_{ij}$ of (i,j). The local potential functions V_L represent contributions to the energy function $U(C)$ from external fields (singleton cliques), pair interactions (doubletons), and etc.

The temperature T controls the degree of "peak" in the "density". Choosing T small, it is easier to find the minimal energy configurations by sampling — the principle of annealing. The assigned category, in the sense of Bayesian inference, is determined by maximizing $P(D_{ij}, C)$ — maximum posterior estimate. The probability is maximized, when the energy is minimized. For the case of Bayesian contextual classification, the most probable labeling occurs, when the negative exponent is minimized. Using conventional gradient techniques, maximizing posterior probability is virtually impossible for all but the first order Markov random field models, because of the existence of many local minima. The stochastic relaxation method developed by Kirkpatrick et al.[2], offers a practical approach for multivariate combinatorial optimization problems.

According to the Gibbs model for Bayesian contextual classification, the problem is reduced to compute $U(D_{ij}, C)$. A general formula of $U(D_{ij}, C)$ is the following:

(I) $U(D_{ij}, C) = \sum_{l,k} \log P(d_{lk}|C_{lk}) + U(C)$

$$U(C) = \sum_{(l,k) \in \mathbf{N}_{ij}} V_{(l,k)}(C_{lk}) + \sum_{(l,k) \in \mathbf{N}_{ij}} V_{(l,k)(l+1,k)}(C_{lk}, C_{l+1k})$$
$$\sum_{(l,k) \in \mathbf{N}_{ij}} V_{(l,k)(l,k+1)}(C_{lk}, C_{lk+1}).$$

A useful theorem of potential function is given as follows. If the random field $D = \{d_{ij} : (i,j) \in I \times J\}$ is Markov, then its potential function is given by

$$V_L(D) = \sum_{L_i \in W} (-1)^{|W - L_i|} \log P(D_{L_i}) ,$$

where the summation is over all cliques in W, D_{L_i} is the configuration which agrees with D on L_i, but assigns value 0 at all sites outside of L_i, and $(-1)^{|W - L_i|}$ is the Moebius function of $W - L_i$. Thus the local characteristics uniquely determine this canonical potential function of a Markov random field.

Based on the factorization property and neighboring cliques (of size two only) assumption, we define

(II)
$$\sum_{(l,k)\in \mathbf{N}_{ij}} V_{(l,k)}(C_{lk}) = \sum_{(l,k)\in \mathbf{N}_{ij}} \log P(C_{lk}) \,,$$

$$\sum_{(l,k)\in \mathbf{N}_{ij}} V_{(l,k)(l+1,k)}(C_{lk}, C_{l+1k}) = 2 \sum_{(l,k)\in \mathbf{N}_{ij}} \log P(C_{lk}|C_{l+1k}) \,,$$

$$\sum_{(l,k)\in \mathbf{N}_{ij}} V_{(l,k)(l,k+1)}(C_{lk}, C_{lk+1}) = 2 \sum_{(l,k)\in \mathbf{N}_{ij}} \log P(C_{lk}|C_{lk+1}) \,.$$

Thus, the assigned category is determined by minimizing $U(D_{ij}, C)$. Because of the existence of many local minima, the computation cost of maximizing the posterior probability for Bayesian classification is computationally high. For example, if an MSS image has N class categories on an $M \times M$ lattice, the number of configurations is at least N^{M*M}.

5.6. Implementation of the Stochastic Relaxation Contextual Classification

The method used in this stochastic relaxation scheme for Bayesian contextual classification is essentially a variant of the algorithm of Metropolis et al.[13] In this procedure, samples are randomly generated from a Gibbs distribution at constant temperature. This simulates the behavior of a physical system in thermal equilibrium. The algorithm is briefly described as follows. For each state D_{ij} of a model D, a random perturbation is made. The change ΔU in energy is computed. If $\Delta U \leq 0$, the perturbation is accepted. That is, the new pattern configuration, which corresponds to the new energy $U' = U + \Delta U$, replaces the original one. If ΔU is positive, then the perturbation is accepted with probability

(III) $P(\Delta U) = \exp(-\Delta U/T) \,.$

This conditional acceptance is easily implemented by choosing a random number R uniformly distributed between 0 and 1. If $R \leq P(\Delta U)$, then the perturbation is accepted; otherwise the existing model is retained. Random perturbation according to this rule eventually causes the system to reach equilibrium (or the configuration θ corresponds to the maximum probability). Slowly, the technique is to lower the temperature T during this iterative procedure. If the system is cooled in a sufficiently slow manner and equilibrium condition is maintained, the model converges to a state of minimum energy or maximum *a posterior* probability[1]. An important aspect of the cooling is the slowness, especially near the critical temperature where the convergence is rapid. The successful choice of an annealing schedule requires experience. Ideally, the procedure should be interactive. As T decreases, samples from the distribution are forced towards the minimum energy configurations. The temperature $T(k)$ used in Ref. 1 satisfies the bound.

(IV) $T(k) \geq G/\log(1+k)$,

where $T(k)$ is the temperature of the kth iteration and G is a constant independent of k. When k approaches infinity, the configurations converge to those of minimum energy.

5.7. The Stochastic Relaxation Contextual Classification Procedure

(1) Evaluate training statistics. This includes the mean vector and the covariance matrix required for the Gaussian distribution.

(2) Preclassify the image using a pixel independent or contextual free Bayesian classification technique.

(3) Evaluate the transition probabilities $P(C_{ij}|C_{ij+1})$ and $P(C_{ij}|C_{i+1j})$ from preclassified results.

(4) Use (I) – (IV) to perform stochastic relaxation contextual classification.

5.8. An Improved Scheme

The stochastic relaxation method, for an MSS image which has N class categories and the image size of $M \times M$, the number of configurations is at least N^{M*M}. In the scheme of Ref. 1, pattern samples are randomly collected from a large pattern configuration space. In contrast to our approach, Geman and Geman did nothing to reduce the pattern configuration space. Experimental results showed that for a significant improvement in classification accuracy, the number of iterations is sizable. In order to reduce further the computational complexity, it is essential to reduce the large pattern configuration space size or to place some configurations on the pattern generation procedure. In this paper, we use homogeneous assumption to control the pattern configuration sampling procedure. Most Landsat and aerial photograph images are divided into a number of elementary regions at the classification stage. Each region is finite, fairly homogeneous, and has similar spectral properties over its entire ground surface. These homogeneous regions correspond to uniform categories on the earth surface.

We believe that smooth and homogeneous pattern configurations are more probable, while irregular patterns have very low probabilities.

Our strategy for the iterative procedure is to use most probable homogeneous patterns at the first stage. At the second stage, we randomly generate pattern configurations and omit irregular patterns with low probability. Although we select a limited number of special pattern configurations in the beginning stage, the overall procedure is still random. A Markov random process is generated by the annealing procedure. Thus, this is a refined stochastic relaxation technique.

6. EVIDENTIAL REASONING

In this section, we present some results of evidential reasoning in understanding multispectral images of remote sensing systems. The Dempster-Shafer approach of combination of evidences is pursued to yield contextual classification results, which are compared with previous results of the Bayesian context free classification, contextual classifications of dynamic programming and stochastic relaxation approaches.

There has been a significant amount of research of evidential reasoning in symbolic and linguistic information processing. However, evidential reasoning in spatial information processing is only emerging to be a subject of interest recently. In addition to the usual uncertainty in AI, uncertainty that arises from spatial information requires somewhat different consideration. Some experimental results of alternate approaches — the Bayesian context free classification, contextual classification using a dynamic programming approach, contextual classification using the stochastic relaxation approach, and the contextual classification using the Dempster-Shafer approach will be given. It turns out that the percentage of multispectral image classification accuracy is increasing in the above order.

There are two types of context information in real world images. One is local or pixel-based context information; the other is global or object-based context information. Most of the existing contextual classification methods have been developed using local context information on small neighborhoods. One of the most difficult problems in remote sensing as yet unsolved is how to deal with "mixed pixels" effectively. In order to solve this problem and to meet increasing demand of classification accuracy, further research should focus on both local and global context information. General context information processing is potentially a powerful tool in spatial reasoning, for it is concerned with all kinds of information — local or global; certain or uncertain; complete or incomplete. Such a process may also incorporate relatively high-level intelligence in decision-making operations. Here, a new contextual reasoning method using Dempster-Shafer theory for multispectral image classification is proposed.

6.1. Uncertain and Incomplete Knowledge in MSS

A multispectral scanner system (MSS) provides spectral data in quantitative format over a broad range of wavelengths. Spatial features, such as size, shape, texture or linear feature, are extracted from pixel data which are the lowest level of image data. Classification methods are used to analyse these quantitative feature data. Data sets of this kind are often uncertain and incomplete, both in evidence and in world knowledge. For illustration, let us consider information of multispectral terrain reflectance. It is only a single parameter that is useful as an indicator of terrain classes. If the terrain within a pixel of the multispectral image is composed of a single feature, such as deep clear water, then the reflectance can be correlated in a high degree of confidence with a particular parameter of interest. However, the radiance received from the ground in a pixel of multispectral image is usually originated from a combination of soil, rock, vegetation, water, and man-made features within the pixel. Thus a pixel encompasses a variety of terrain features and the received radiance is the integration of the reflectance of all features. In this case, the Bayesian probabilistic model of random fields has some limitation and is not able to capture the full information due to incomplete evidences.

6.2. Dempster-Shafer Theory

As mentioned above, multispectral scanner system probing an environment deals often with incomplete and uncertain information. We shall use the Dempster-Shafer theory to represent uncertainty and to use the combination rule to reduce uncertainty and resolve contradictions.

Spatial information and knowledge are represented by propositions. These propositions may range from simple ones, such as "A certain region belongs to a particular terrain class", to high-level decision making ones, such as "Robot X should perform a particular task". For each proposition P, its belief is represented by an evidential interval $[\text{Spt}(P), \text{Pls}(P)]$, where $\text{Spt}(P)$ is the degree to which the evidence supports P and $\text{Pls}(P)$ is the degree to which the evidence fails to refute P (the degree to which it remains plausible). A frame of discernment Q is a set of propositions of mutually exclusive possibilities in a specific domain of a spatial reasoning system. The belief function Bel over Q is defined by a probability distribution function m which is called the mass distribution in Ref. 6.

For the subsystem of contextual classification, regions of multispectral images are classified into a set of possible categories. First, a collection of spatial features are extracted from the scene. For each feature, there is a set of propositions to which it can directly contribute beliefs. Thus, a mass distribution $m(f)$ is associated with each feature f over the frame Q of discernment which is determined from ground truth or preclassified results. Furthermore, simple belief function is used for each feature f. That is, the belief function $\text{Bel}(f)$ is the same as the mass distribution $m(f)$ for each feature f.

If each extracted feature is considered as a piece of evidence, evidences of several features can be combined to be an accumulated evidence. The Dempster's combination rule is used to form an orthogonal sum of several belief functions. Since this rule is associative and commutative, features can be combined in any order.

In our problem domain, bodies of evidence may point to different subsets of Q. This situation is called heterogeneous evidence in Ref. 6. In the case of $A \cap B$ being not empty, the combination of two simple support functions S_1 and S_2, focussed on A and B respectively, is carried out as follows. If $S_1(A) = s_1$ and $S_2(B) = s_2$, the Dempster's combination rule implies that $m(A \cap B) = s_1 s_2, m(A) = s_1(1 - s_2), m(B) = s_2(1 - s_1)$, and $m(Q) = (1 - s_1)(1 - s_2)$. Recursively, this combination rule is extended to any number of features. In the case of $A \cap B$ being empty, the situation is called conflicting evidence in Ref. 6. We refer to this for details of the rule.

The procedure of this evidential approach to contextual classification is as follows:

1. Partition ground truth or preclassification results into multiple bands. Each band corresponds to one labeling of the preclassification process.
2. Use the maximal connected component operation to label maximal connected components of each image band.
3. Extract all features and form a feature vector of each maximal connected component of an image band.
4. Select some regions as ground truth data. Determine mass distributions of all features of the ground truth data set for each image band.
5. For each region in an image band, generate hypothesis of classification.
6. Determine simple belief functions of all features of the given region.
7. Use the combination rule to compute the belief function of multi-features of the given region.

8. If the hypothesis is rejected, the region is merged to a neighboring region. The new region is tested. If the hypothesis is accepted, the remaining regions are tested.

6.3. Spatial Features

The following spatial features are used in our classification system.

(1) Region Size. In MSS images, one pixel corresponds to 57 by 79 M^2 ground area. For instance, an image of one-crop farming fields (Fig. 1) should have a finite number of fairly homogeneous regions. In view of the classification results of the Bayesian context free classification method and contextual classification methods in previous sections, there are misclassified isolated pixels or small regions, because they are assigned to different classes from neighboring homogeneous regions. This evidential reasoning scheme will enable us to verify the hypothesis of these misclassified pixels or regions. The mass distribution associated to the size feature of each image band is determined as follows. Using a ground truth data set, we obtain a histogram of region size measurement. The normalized frequency values of the histogram are used to determine the mass distribution.

(2) Texture. Texture refers to a description of the spatial variation within a contiguous group of pixels. There are small objects in forest and residential areas, such as trees, houses, roads and shadows. As a result, these regions show a great variety of color and brightness. They indicate a "high-contrast texture" area. On the other hand, crop fields, land, lakes and sea indicate a "fine texture" area. To determine the mass distribution of the texture feature, we measure the amount of edges per unit image area. The Roberts gradient is computed over image windows.

(3) Region Shapes. The region shape can be characterized by three features — FIT, ELONG and DIREC of the region. The minimum bounding rectangle (MBR) of a region is computed. The MBR is defined as the rectangle such that the ratio of the area of the region and the area of the enclosing rectangle with sides parallel to the coordinate axes is maximum, under rotations of 0 to 80 degrees. FIT is this maximum which measures the degree of matching of the region with rectangles. The elongatedness ELONG of a region is defined by ELONG = L/W, where L and W denote the lengths of the long and short sides of the MBR respectively. DIREC denotes the direction of the long side of the MBR. The mass distributions of these features are computed also by histograms of related measurements.

(4) Compactness. Another global shape feature is compactness of a region, which is defined by 4π area/perimeter^2. Normally, objects with high

compactness feature are candidates of man-made structures. The mass distribution is determined by histogram of feature measurements.

(5) Spectral Information. The spectral feature of a region is defined by the intensity mean vector. The mass distribution is similarly computed.

(6) Spatial Relationships. The adjacency graph describes the interrelationships of regions. A probability transition matrix is defined to provide feature measurements.

6.4. Experimental Results

We have investigated multispectral images of crop fields at Clarke, Oregon and aerial mountain region photographs of Roanoke, Virginia. In the Oregon images (Figs. 5-8), eight classes of wheat, alfalfa, potatoes, corn, beans, apple, pasture and rangeland are selected from multispectral scanner data. In the Virginia images (Figs. 9-12), urban, agricultural, range and forest lands are classified. Part of the selected data is used for training and a much larger part is used for testing. The accuracy of maximum likelihood classification performed by Thomas in 1982 is about 75%. The contextual classification using a dynamic programming approach raised the classification accuracy to 80.5%. The contextual classification using the stochastic relaxation approach raised the classification accuracy to 80.8% The contingency tables in Tables 1 and 2 give comparisons of these methods with the evidential reasoning approach which has a more than 2.5% accuracy improvement.

7. CONCLUSION

In multispectral image understanding, it is very difficult to build an exact world model for the analysis of complex aerial photographs. There are uncertainty and incompleteness in information and knowledge. The evidential reasoning approach using the Dempster-Shafer theory is a powerful tool that proves to be useful in this application. Information from multiple sources are combined to reduce uncertainty and to obtain real world information.

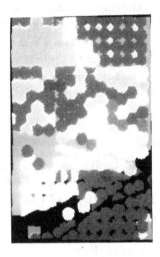

Fig. 5. Ground truth image of crop field at Clarke, Oregon: 1982, image size 150×150.

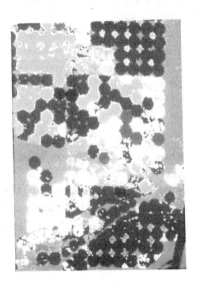

Fig. 6. Bayes preclassification result of MSS, Clarke, Oregon.

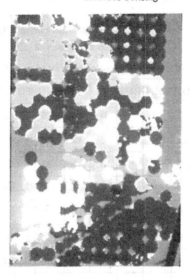

Fig. 7. Markov contextual classification result of MSS, Clarke, Oregon.

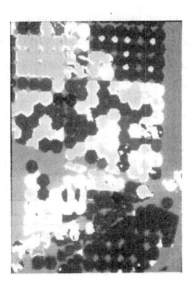

Fig. 8. Contextual classification result by stochastic relaxation, Clarke, Oregon.

Table 1. Contingency tables for classification results of test image "Clark". Scale factor of the number of pixel 10**. 1. COL = assigned categories, 2. ROW = true categories.

(A) Pixel independent Bayes classification result

CLASS	WHT	ALF	POT	CRN	BNS	APL	PAS	RNG	TOTAL	ACC(%)*
WHT	1017	47	30	5	4	0	10	75	1188	85.5%
ALF	17	382	135	10	13	6	12	39	668	57.1%
POT	40	32	522	5	19	0	2	32	652	84.6%
CRN	1	5	1	65	2	0	0	4	78	83.3%
BNS	0	1	0	1	1	0	0	0	3	0%
PAS	0	0	0	0	0	0	9	2	11	81.1%
RNG	15	12	14	2	4	1	9	335	392	85.4%
TOTAL	1146	483	704	89	78	7	42	490	3040	77.5%**

(B) Context classification result using a dynamic programming approach

CLASS	WHT	ALF	POT	CRN	BNS	APL	PAS	RNG	TOTAL	ACC(%)*
WHT	1073	26	26	1	11	0	10	601	1248	90.9%
ALF	89	390	150	3	1	0	1	34	668	58.4%
POT	58	29	534	2	6	0	0	23	652	81.9%
CRN	1	5	1	68	0	0	0	4	79	86.1%
BNS	1	6	2	1	36	0	0	3	49	73.5%
APL	0	2	0	0	0	0	0	0	2	0%
PAS	0	1	0	0	0	0	8	3	11	72.7%
RNG	19	16	15	1	3	0	1	339	394	86.1%
TOTAL	1681	605	777	82	58	0	23	1064	3040	80.5%**

Table 1. Cont'd

(C) Stochastic relaxation context classification result

CLASS	WHT	ALF	POT	CRN	BNS	APL	PAS	RNG	TOTAL	ACC(%)*
WHT	1080	23	25	1	1	0	0	58	1118	90.9%
ALF	91	378	155	1	0	0	0	41	666	56.8%
POT	54	23	544	1	3	0	0	29	654	83.2%
CRN	1	5	1	65	0	0	0	6	78	83.3%
BNS	2	5	2	0	35	0	0	4	48	73.9%
APL	1	2	0	0	0	0	0	0	3	0%
PAS	0	1	0	0	0	0	7	3	11	63.7%
RNG	17	11	14	1	0	0	1	349	392	89.1%
TOTAL	1643	573	787	72	47	0	10	1158	3040	80.8%**

*Classification accuracy.

**Overall classification accuracy: ratio of the number of correctly classified pixels to the number of total classified pixels.

WHT — Wheat
ALF — Alfalfa
POT — Potatoes
CRN — Corn
BNS — Beans
APL — Apples
PAS — Pasture (irrigated)
RNG — Rangeland

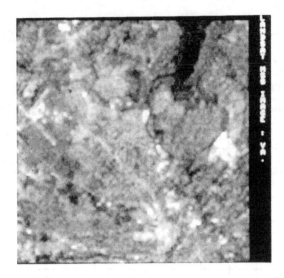

Fig. 9. First band of MSS scene of Roanoke, VA. 13 April 1976, image size 151×151.

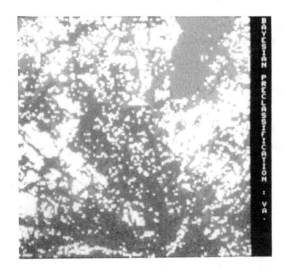

Fig. 10. Bayes preclassication result of MSS, Roanoke, VA. Blue (class 1) — urban or built-up land, white (class 2) — agriculture land, green (class 4) — forest land.

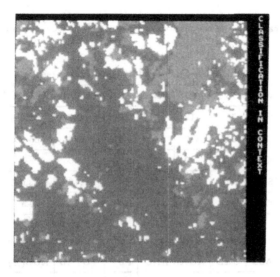

Fig. 11. Markov contextual classification result of MSS, Roanoke, VA. Blue (class 1) — urban or built-up land, white (class 2) — agricultural land, green (class 4) — forest land.

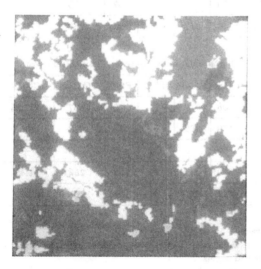

Fig. 12. Context classification result by stochastic relaxation of MSS, Roanoke, VA. Blue (class 1) — urban or built-up land, white (class 2) — agriculture land, green (class 4) — forest land.

Table 2. Contingency tables for classification results of 13 April 1976 MSS scene of Roanoke, VA. Scale factor of the number of pixels 10^{**}. 1. COL = assigned categories, 2. ROW = true categories.

(A) Bayes pixel independent classification result

CLASS	URB	AGR	RNG	FST	TOTAL	ACC(%)*
URB	760	512	0	162	1437	52.8%
AGR	116	379	0	83	578	65.6%
RNG	0	0	0	0	0	–
FSN	15	28	0	210	253	83.0%
TOTA	894	919	0	455	2268	59.5**

(B) Context classification result using a dynamic programming approach

CLASS	URB	AGR	RNG	FST	TOTAL	ACC(%)*
URB	999	418	0	20	1437	69.5%
AGR	183	371	0	24	578	64.2%
RNG	0	0	0	0	0	–
FSN	58	28	0	167	253	66.0%
TOTA	1240	817	0	211	2268	67.8**

(C) Stochastic relaxation context classificationc result

CLASS	URB	AGR	RNG	FST	TOTAL	ACC(%)*
URB	1108	317	0	12	1437	77.1%
AGR	179	385	0	14	578	66.6%
RNG	0	0	0	0	0	–
FSN	50	35	0	168	253	64.4%
TOTA	1337	737	0	194	2268	73.3**

*Classification accuracy.

**Overall classification accuracy: ratio of the number correctly classified pixels to the number of total classified pixels.

URB — Urban or built-up Land

AGR — Agricultural Land

RNG — Rangeland

FST — Forest Land

References

1. S. Geman and D. Geman, "Stochastic relaxation, Gibbs distribution, and the Bayesian restoration of images," *IEEE Trans. PAMI* 6 (1984) 721-741.

2. S. Kirkpatrick, C. D. Gelatt, Jr., and M. P. Vecchi, "Optimization by simulated annealing," *Science* 220 (1983) 671-680.

3. T. S. Yu and K. S. Fu, "Recursive contextual classification using a spatial stochastic model," *Pattern Recognition* 16 (1983) 89-106.

4. J. C. Tilton, S. B. Vardeman and P. H. Swain, "Estimation of context for statistical classification of multispectral image data," *IEEE Trans. Geoscience and Remote Sensing*, 20 (1982) 428-441.

5. P. Swain and S. M. Davis, *Remote Sensing: The Quantitative Approach*, McGraw-Hill, 1978.

6. G. Shafer, *A Mathematical Theory of Evidence*, Princeton University Press, 1976.

7. Z. Li and L. Uhr, "Evidential reasoning in parallel hierarchical vision programs," *Proc. AAAI Workshop, Uncertainty in AI*, University of Pennsylvania, Aug. 1986.

8. S. Chen, M. Zhang, and W. Zhang, "A spatial reasoning and decision support system, Methodologies for Intelligent Systems," Proc. of the 2nd Int'l Symposium, Elsevier, North-Holland, 1987.

9. L. A. Zadeh, "Fuzzy sets," *Information and Control* 8 (1965) 338-353.

10. L. A. Zadeh, "Similarity relations and fuzzy ordering," *Information Sciences* 3 (1971) 177-200.

11. J. C. Bezdek, R. O. Pettus, L. M. Stephens and W. R. Zhang, "Knowledge representation using linguistic fuzzy similarity relations," *Int'l J. Man-Machine Studies*, 1986.

12. C. J. Preston, *Gibbs States on Countable Sets*, Cambridge University Press, 1974.

13. N. Metropolis, A. W. Rosenbluth, M. N. Rosenbluth, A. H. Teller, and E. Teller, "Equations of state of calculations by fast computing machines," *J. Chem. Phys.* 21 (1953) 1087-1091.

14. R. M. Haralick, M. C. Zhang and J. B. Campbell, "Multispectral image contextual classification using the Markov random field," *PECORA Proceedings*, Oct. 1984.

15. M. C. Zhang, R. M. Haralick and J. B. Campbell, "Context classification by stochastic relaxation," *Proc. IEEE Computer Society Workshop on Computer Architecture for Pattern Analysis and Image Database Management*, Nov. 1985.

16. T. Pavilidis, *Structural Pattern Recognition*, Springer-Verlag, 1977.

17. F. Hayes-Roth, D. A. Waterman and D. B. Lenat, *Building Expert Systems*, Addison-Wesley, 1983.

18. E. H. Shortliffe and B. G. Buchanan, "A model of inexact reasoning in medicine," *Math. Biosciences* 23 (1975) 351-379.

19. A. P. Dempster, "Upper and lower probabilities induced by multivalued mappings," *Ann. Math. Statistics* 38 (1967) 325-339.

20. P. P. Bonissone and K. S. Decker, "Selecting uncertainty calculi and granularity: An experiment in trading-off precision and complexity," GE Technical Report, 1985.

21. S. Chen, "A data flow computer architecture for Markov image models," *IEEE Computer Society Workshop on Computer Architecture for Pattern Analysis and Image Database Management*, 1985, pp. 75-79.

22. R. O. Duda and P. E. Hart, *Pattern Classification and Scene Analysis*, John Wiley & Sons, 1973, pp. 405-424.

23. K. S. Fu and A. Rosenfeld, "Pattern recognition and image processing," *IEEE Trans. Computers* 25 (1976) 1336-1346.

24. M. Zhang and S. Chen, "Evidential reasoning in image understanding," *AAAI Workshop on Uncertainty in AI*, Seattle, WA, Jul. 1987.

25. M. Zhang and J. B. Campbell, "Automatic delineation of drainage basins within digital elevation data using the topographic primal sketch and facet model," *J. Int'l Asso. for Math. Geology*, 1987.

26. M. Zhang and J. B. Campbell, "A geographical information system within the GYPSY environment, " *American Congress on Surveying and Mapping and American Society for Photogrammetry and Remote Sensing Convention*, Washington, DC, Mar. 1986.